Class Structure
in
Contemporary Japan

JAPANESE SOCIETY SERIES

General Editor: Yoshio Sugimoto

Lives of Young Koreans in Japan
Yasunori Fukuoka

Globalization and Social Change in Contemporary Japan
J.S. Eades Tom Gill Harumi Befu

Coming Out in Japan: The Story of Satoru and Ryuta
Satoru Ito and Ryuta Yanase

Japan and Its Others:
Globalization, Difference and the Critique of Modernity
John Clammer

Hegemony of Homogeneity:
An Anthropological Analysis of *Nihonjinron*
Harumi Befu

Foreign Migrants in Contemporary Japan
Hiroshi Komai

A Social History of Science and Technology in
Contempory Japan, Volume 1
Shigeru Nakayama

Farewell to Nippon: Japanese Lifestyle Migrants in Australia
Machiko Sato

The Peripheral Centre:
Essays on Japanese History and Civilization
Johann P. Arnason

A Genealogy of 'Japanese' Self-images
Eiji Oguma

Class Structure in Contemporary Japan
Kenji Hashimoto

Class Structure in Contemporary Japan

Kenji Hashimoto

Trans Pacific Press
Melbourne

First published in Japanese in 2001 by Aoki Shoten (Tokyo) as *Kaikyū shakai Nippon*.

This English edition first published in 2003 by
Trans Pacific Press, PO Box 120, Rosanna, Melbourne, Victoria 3084, Australia
Telephone: +61 3 9459 3021 Fax: +61 3 9457 5923
Email: info@transpacificpress.com
Web: http://www.transpacificpress.com

Published as no.108 of the Musashi University Research Series

Copyright © Trans Pacific Press 2003

Designed and set by digital environs, Melbourne
enquiries@digitalenvirons.com

Printed by BPA Print Group, Burwood, Victoria, Australia

Distributors

Australia
Bushbooks
PO Box 1958, Gosford, NSW 2250
Telephone: (02) 4323-3274
Fax: (02) 9212-2468
Email: bushbook@ozemail.com.au

USA and Canada
International Specialized Book Services (ISBS)
5824 N. E. Hassalo Street
Portland, Oregon 97213-3644
USA
Telephone: (800) 944-6190
Fax: (503) 280-8832
Email: orders@isbs.com
Web: http://www.isbs.com

Japan
Kyoto University Press
Kyodai Kaikan
15-9 Yoshida Kawara-cho
Sakyo-ku, Kyoto 606-8305
Telephone: (075) 761-6182
Fax: (075) 761-6190
Email: sales@kyoto-up.gr.jp
Web: http://www.kyoto-up.gr.jp

UK and Europe
Asian Studies Book Services
3554 TT Utrecht
The Netherlands
Telephone: +31 30 289 1240
Fax: +31 30 289 1249
Email: marie.lenstrup@planet.nl
Web: http://www.asianstudiesbooks.com

All rights reserved. No production of any part of this book may take place without the written permission of Trans Pacific Press.

ISSN 1443–9670 (Japanese Society Series)
ISBN 1–8768–4365–9 (Hardback)
ISBN 1–8768–4371–3 (Paperback)

National Library of Australia Cataloging in Publication Data

Hashimoto, Kenji, 1959– .
Class structure in contemporary Japan.
Bibliography.
Includes index.
ISBN 1 876843 71 3 (pbk.).
ISBN 1 876843 65 9.

1. Social classes - Japan. I. Title. (Series : Japanese society series).

305.50952

Contents

Figures	vi
Tables	viii
Preface to the English Edition	ix
1 Class Studies: Self-images of Modern Society	1
2 When Class 'Disappeared' from Japan	16
3 Class Structure in Contemporary Society: From Marxist to Marxian Theory	40
Promenade: Transgression of Class Borders – Two Versions of 'Tsurumoku Bachelor Dormitory'	62
4 Four Classes: Four Life-worlds	86
5 Can Class Borders Be Crossed? The Structure of Cross-class Mobility	112
6 Differentiation of the Farming Class in Postwar Japan	135
7 Women in Class Structure	157
8 Closed-up Political Space	186
9 Towards a New Egalitarian Society	205
Notes	225
References	235
Index	247

Figures

2.1	Comparison of Ōhasi's two class schemes	22
3.1	The relationship of contradictory class positions to class forces in capitalist society	52
3.2	Typology of class locations in capitalist society	54
3.3	Class structure in contemporary capitalist society	57
3.4	Class composition by firm size	61
4.1	Class structure of contemporary Japan and average annual individual income by class	96
4.2	Transition of income differentials between classes	99
4.3	Extent of work authority by class	101
4.4	Network of personal relationships of each class	104
4.5	Class difference in leisure activities (males, 20% or greater participation)	106
4.6	Participation in 'high culture' activities by members of capitalist and new middle classes by class of origin	109
5.1	Change in pure mobility rate and unrealized mobility rate (male)	119
5.2	Odds ratio and coefficient of openness of the respondent's class at age 40 by class of origin and birth cohort (male)	123
5.3	Odds ratio of the respondent's occupation at age 40 and his father's main occupation by birth cohort (male)	124
5.4	Odds ratio of the respondent's present class and class of origin by birth cohort (male)	126
5.5	Class location at different ages (sample of 40 years old or older)	128
5.6	Amount of assets owned by class origin	130
5.7	Rate of advancing to higher education by class of origin and birth cohort (male and female)	132
6.1	Trends of farming households, the farming population and agricultural workers	137
6.2	In-flow and out-flow of the farming labor force	140
7.1	Coefficient of openness of the couple at marriage by times of marriage	164

8.1	Changes in political party support of working class by the scale of enterprise (male)	192
8.2	Class affiliation, occupation and ideology	199
9.1	Rate of personal computer consumption ownership	207

Tables

2.1	International comparison of 'middle consciousness'	31
3.1	Class composition on five-class categories (%)	59
4.1	Structure of SSM Surveys from 1955 to 1995	88
4.2	Characteristics of four classes as indicated by the 1995 SSM Survey	89
5.1	Intergenerational mobility and mobility index	115
5.2	Class location during career for respondents at age 50 (male)	129
5.3	Ratio of students advancing to higher education by class origin and school record at the 9th grade (male & female cohort born in the 1960s)	133
6.1	Intergenerational mobility table by class categories (male)	142
6.2	Intergenerational mobility based on the five-class schema (female)	144
6.3	Class locations of persons of farm origin at various time points by cohort	145
6.4	Non-mobility rates of persons of farming class origin by various attributes	148
7.1	Intergenerational mobility in 1995 (female)	160
7.2	A comparison of male & female odds ratios of intergenerational mobility (father × respondent)	161
7.3	Class location of married couples (couples married during 1981–1995)	162
7.4	Husband's class location by wife's class location	165
7.5	Profiles of 13 groups of women	166
8.1	Relationship between class/strata location and political party support (in 1991)	189
8.2	Changes in the relationship between class affiliation and political party support (male) (%)	191
8.3	Views about relaxation of economic restrictions and distribution principles (%)	198
8.4	Political consciousness and class affiliation	202
9.1	Information media usage rates by literacy group	208

Preface to the English Edition

Contemporary Japan, a highly advanced capitalist society, is a class society. This does not appear to be widely recognized though, either by the Japanese themselves, or by international observers. The argument of this book is that a four-class model – capitalist, working, new and old middle classes – applies squarely to Japanese society today and provides the best framework for its interpretation.

Readers in English-speaking societies may find it strange that there have been relatively few class studies in contemporary Japanese sociology, which has instead focused on social stratification studies. There are several reasons for this situation: for starters, it is widely believed that social stratification and social class are totally separate. Many analysts interpret social stratification as a social scientific concept that points to the unequal distribution of social resources in a population while regarding class as a political notion used by conventional and dogmatic Marxism. The Japanese term *kaikyū*, which corresponds to the English word *class*, did not originally have political connotations. Combining two ideographic characters, *kai* (steps or ranks) and *kyū* (grades), it was already in circulation in eighth-century Japan as an expression indicating different status positions between people. There is no other Japanese term that might serve as a better translation of the English term/concept. In chapter 2 we will explore the political background that led to the distortion of this concept, reducing its use to the particular jargon of a particular political ideology.

Another reason can be found in the widespread belief among the Japanese that Japan is an egalitarian society with little disparity. Since the 1970s several analysts have maintained that Japan enjoys a high standard of living and low income differentials, drawing on various income distribution studies, as well as opinion surveys that found that some 90% of Japanese identify themselves as being in the middle stratum of society. The Japanese appear to have found some consistency between these ideas and the widely held 'myth of a homogenous nation' (Oguma 2002) that perpetuates the popular concept that Japan is ethnically and culturally uniform. In this intellectual climate, sociologists, economists and political scientists found the notion of class unsuitable to the analysis of such a uniquely egalitarian society. Thus, the concept of class, fundamental to the modern social sciences, became an obsolete and unfashionable word in Japanese sociology.

More recently these claims have undergone great revision. It has become apparent that the level of income disparity in Japan was at its lowest around 1970 and has been increasing ever since, now resembling the levels of inequity common to Western societies. The methodology of the opinion surveys that found that 90% of Japanese identified themselves in the middle stratum have been brought into question by the fact that virtually identical results are found in every nation where the survey is conducted, regardless of objective differences in the material standard of living in different societies. The social and economic disparities in Japan will most likely continue to expand in the future as a consequence of economic globalization, the IT revolution and the changes in Japanese employment practices. Thus it seems likely that, in spite of the so-called 'death of class', a concept popularly propagated in some quarters, the 'existence of class' will gradually become more clear and visible.

The present volume is an endeavor to demonstrate the existence of a variety of classes in contemporary Japanese society, drawing on the massive data collected by the Social Stratification and Mobility (SSM) Survey project conducted every ten years since 1955. Whilst numerous studies have been published on class structure and various social classes in Europe and North America, the number of specialists in class analysis is limited. The few English language publications on this topic have remained relatively unnoticed for a long time. It is my hope that the present volume will both fill a gap and provide a stepping stone for further research, stimulating an international exchange of studies on this issue of interest and concern that cuts across countries and cultures.

At the same time, I have made an attempt to not only explore the variety of analyses that have been produced about Japan's class structure, but also more generally to raise some fundamental issues about class theories and analytic methodologies. I have used, with some modifications, both the structuralist and analytical Marxisms that have developed in Europe and the United States as the theoretical and methodological bases for framing my analysis. I consider structuralist Marxism and analytical Marxism as the most effective and empirically applicable mode of analysis for contemporary capitalist societies; hence, they are central to the construction of my four-class scheme. While simple, this scheme proves to be highly valid, taking into account the coexistence of two different modes of production. Furthermore, my theoretical examination of female class structure led to an empirically oriented joint-classification scheme which might provide a basis for similar investigations in other countries for comparative analysis. Finally, I have argued that it is unlikely that the working class will be the agent of social change in advanced capitalism, proposing instead that a new society can be developed through the formation of a social imagery based on the consensus of a majority of the population after some ethical and normative scrutiny into what and how an egalitarian society should be. Investigations into this approach have only just begun; hopefully they will be carried out in depth in the future.

This book was initially published in Japanese by Aoki Shoten under the title *Kaikyū shakai Nippon* (Japan as a class society). This English edition includes a new chapter on the differentiation of the farming class. I am grateful to Professor Yoshio Sugimoto, sociologist at La Trobe University and director of Trans Pacific Press, for his advice and encouragement. Thanks are also due to the team who translated the Japanese text into English, and to Mr Karl Smith for his competent and detailed copyediting throughout the preparation of this volume. Finally, I must thank Musashi University for their generous grant towards this project, which appears both as a volume in TPP's Japanese Society Series and as Musashi University Research Publication Series No.108.

Kenji Hashimoto
November 2002

1 Class Studies: Self-images of Modern Society

Self-images of modern society

'Class studies' comprise first, those theories that focus on the distribution of social resources, classifying individuals into a few groupings according to their location in an unequal distribution schema, thereby providing a basis for clarifying social structures and explaining social phenomena, and secondly, a variety of empirical studies based on these theories. The social sciences in general – but class theories more particularly – are products of the self-reflexivity of modern societies and the self-images conjured by their constituents.

Econometric models built on structural equations may provide elegant abstract representations of the characteristics of a society, but in ways that are not readily translatable to the lived experience of most people. Monographs constructed with reference to an abundance of documentary materials and survey interviews may produce elaborate miniatures of particular aspects of a given society, but cannot depict its totality.

In contrast, class studies have endeavored to treat an entire society as the object of analysis while, at the same time, attempting to portray its characteristics in visual representations, posing questions such as: Does the society in question have the shape of a pyramid, a cylinder, a barrel (fat in the middle), or a dumbbell (heavy at both ends)? To what extent are there textural differences in density and color among the top, the bottom and the middle of that society? In what direction is it facing and moving? Class studies aim to address these kinds of problems, both reflecting and producing self-images of society.

The nature of these concerns perhaps renders class studies as the primary field of the social sciences in which non-experts frequently participate. In Japan for example, bestsellers such as *Kinkonkan*

(Watanabe and Koutari 1984) and *The Enigma of Japanese Power* (Wolferen 1990) incorporate class investigations. A seemingly infinite number of journalistic essays and columns have referred to various aspects of disparity in wealth, income and living standards in Japan. All of these have formed broadly defined 'class studies' in post-war Japan.

The term 'class studies' may induce a negative reaction among many, evoking Marx's *The Communist Manifesto*, the now defunct socialist regimes of the Soviet Union and Eastern Europe and the political propaganda of other leftist parties and organizations. In Japan, even professional sociologists tend to object to conceptions of *kaikyū* (class), preferring the alternative: *kaisō* (stratum). In spite of its history, though, class studies should not be reduced to Marxist political ideology; it remains an important tool in the contemporary social sciences. While it cannot be denied that class studies have been historically associated with Marxism, those who engage in class studies do not necessarily advocate a particular political position. A brief examination of the history of class studies will suffice to establish what they have been dealing with and how they are related to so-called stratification studies.

The birth of class theory

There is no general consensus about the origins of class theory. Those applying narrow criteria claim that it began with Karl Marx, while those employing a broader definition trace the origin back to Plato's *Republic* and Aristotle's *Politics*.[1] We will confine ourselves to theories that have analyzed classes in modern society.

Jean Meslier (1664–1729) was perhaps the first to use the notion of class in a sense similar to its present-day meaning (Tanaka 1992). He was born to a wealthy family in the Champagne area of France, worked as a priest for forty years and secretly wrote a large number of notes which are now in the possession of the French National Library. In these notes, Meslier criticized Christianity, rejected the existence of God and distinguished between the 'rich class' made up of the nobility, the clergy and bankers on the one hand and the 'peasant class' on the other, while advocating that the latter should overthrow the former's oppressive rule. Hand-written copies of his notes were circulated until 1762 when Voltaire began to publish extracts from them underground, thus making Meslier's writings more widely available. Whilst this pioneering and revolutionary work influenced some Enlightenment thinkers, his class categories were too simple and intuitive to be considered as the beginning of modern class theory.

While Sieyes' *What is the Third Estate* (1789), written during the French Revolution, adopts a more sophisticated institutional classification – the first estate (the clergy), the second estate (the nobility) and the third estate (the commoners) – it is not really a class analysis. Despite its references to interest competition and struggles between different groups, it is actually a study of political or revolutionary theory. To qualify as a socio-scientific theory, a class theory must develop a methodology that classifies people into categories in accordance with a theoretical framework of class structures rather than grouping them by naive intuition or by the institutional or customary criteria of a given society.

Quesnay, a French political economist who founded the school known as the physiocrats, classified the population into the production class (peasants), the land class and the sterile class (merchants and industrialists) in his *Economic Tables* and examined the processes by which goods circulate among them. His criteria for categorization were not based on institutional or customary status but on economic functions. To that extent, they can be regarded as social-scientific class concepts. However, Quesnay was not interested in explaining various social phenomena on the basis of inequality between the classes and their competing interests, but instead constructed this three-class model in an effort to schematize the economic circulation process. It therefore does not seem appropriate to credit Quesnay with founding class theory.

Adam Smith is arguably the first scholar to present a class theory in the sense that we understand it today. He pointed out that products, and therefore the value of products, are divided into three categories, namely: the rent of land, the wages of labor, and the profits of stock. Those deriving income in these different ways constitute 'three different orders of people: those who live by rent, those who live by wages, and those who live by profit. These are the three great, original, and constituent orders of every civilized society' (Smith 1776: Book 1, chap.11). Smith did not claim that only these three 'orders' (i.e. classes) exist, but recognized that there might also be other classes such as the 'superior class', 'lowest class', 'lower ranks', etc. Nevertheless, whilst using terms such as 'order', 'rank', etc., he attached the utmost importance to the three fundamental classes, arguing that it was from these people that the revenue of 'every other order is ultimately derived' (ibid.).

More importantly, Smith observed that conflicting interests between classes shape the legal system, state mechanisms and the nature of political conflict. According to Smith, a society without ownership or without classes does not require a state; the state was born with the birth of class society as a violent apparatus to protect the owners of material possessions. Thus, politics and institutions are products of ruling class interests. What politicians call the national interest is nothing other than their personal interests and the interests of the ruling class to which they belong. Because the ruling class defends its vested interests, political and institutional systems do not easily collapse even if they lose relevance in the course of social transformation. As a consequence, the lower class – although forming the 'far greater part of every great political society' and being essential to the production of wealth – often suffer poverty. Based on these insights, Smith formulated a scheme to construct a society in which the interests of the working class are reflected in politics such that they might enjoy wealth in a three-class society.[2]

The Marx of *The Communist Manifesto*

Karl Marx emerged as both a successor to and a critic of Smith, but one might ask 'To what extent are Marx's theories unique?' His letter to Joseph Weydemeyer – a member of the Communist League and a participant in leftist labor movements in the United States – suggests an answer:

> My own contribution was: 1. to show that the existence of classes is merely bound up with certain historical phases in the development of production; 2. that the class struggle necessarily leads to the dictatorship of the proletariat; 3. that this dictatorship itself constitutes no more than a transition to the abolition of all classes and to a classless society. (Marx 1852; Marx to Joseph Weydemeyer in New York)

After Lenin cited this letter in *State and Revolution* (1917) it became widely known and regarded as a 'sacred document' concerning Marx's class theory. The substance of the letter sharply reflects *The Communist Manifesto* (1848) written four years earlier.

It is well known that Marx never left a systematic description of class. Chapter 52, the final chapter of the third volume of *Capital*, which was supposed to provide his definitive statement on class – is entitled 'Classes' and begins with a three-class scheme *a la* Smith. But the published chapter ends abruptly with a comment inserted by Engels that reads: 'Here the manuscript breaks off.' *The Communist Manifesto* has often been cited to fill the gap, with both Marxists and anti-Marxists regarding it as the authoritative source for understanding Marx's class theory, despite its oversimplification and the inordinate exaggeration arising from the fact that it is a political document full of rhetoric and polemics. In short, *The Communist Manifesto* has generally been regarded as containing the essence of the Marxist theory of class.

In his letter to Weydemeyer, Marx states that he has added only three points to the already existing theories of class. Summarizing these points in contemporary terminology we can see that, for Marx: first, classes are neither constant nor unchanging but vary subject to the mode of production at any specific stage of historical development. This point differs from Smith's formulation of landlords, workers and capitalists as invariable categories. In Marx's formulation, class structures change in accordance with changes in the mode of production. Class structure and the conflictual relations between classes condition other social phenomena. Second, class struggle in capitalist society will necessarily produce socialist revolution in which the dictatorship of the proletariat materializes. Third, the proletarian dictatorship demolishes private ownership and leads to a classless and communist society.

The first proposition has long provided a basis and essence of a class theory from which we can engage in analysis of the class structures of capitalist and other societies. In contrast, the second and third propositions – which we might respectively call the 'working-class socialist revolution thesis' and the 'inevitability of communism thesis' – differ markedly from the first proposition.

In a forceful style, *The Communist Manifesto* describes the processes through which the initially divided proletariat is repeatedly defeated by the bourgeoisie, gradually organizing themselves into a unified force that through sheer numerical superiority will inevitably overthrow the existing order and establish their own dominance. This narrative is both evocative and inspirational, but completely lacks theoretical underpinnings. Four years before the *Manifesto* Marx wrote:

> The proletariat, on the contrary, is compelled as proletariat to abolish itself and thereby its opposite, private property, which determines its existence, and which makes it proletariat. It is the negative side of the antithesis, its restlessness within its very self, dissolved and self-dissolving private property. (Marx and Engels 1844)

This story about how the proletarian dictatorship leads to the abolition of class society is not only incomprehensible, but sophistic, in spite of Marx's appropriation of Hegel's 'dialectics'.[3] Whilst the first proposition is an expression of a theoretical and methodological position, the second and third are not logically derivable from it; they are prophecies about what might happen in the future. Despite Marx's claim that he proved their logical necessity, they are the products of a transcendentally fired imagination.

In addition to the three points that Marx identified as his own contributions to class discourse, he actually contributed two other elements that had a significant and enduring influence – albeit negative – on class studies: the 'polarization thesis' and the 'absolute immiseration thesis'.

The class polarization thesis is explicit in *The Communist Manifesto* where Marx reiterates time and again that, in capitalism, a variety of pre-modern middle classes – i.e. small tradespeople, shopkeepers and peasants – would slide down into the proletarian class; the entire class structure would then become a simple system made up of two major classes – the bourgeoisie and the proletariat. He states: 'Our epoch, the epoch of the bourgeoisie, possesses, however, this distinct feature: it has simplified class antagonisms. Society as a whole is more and more splitting up into two great hostile camps, into two great classes directly facing each other – bourgeoisie and proletariat' (Marx and Engels 1948).

Furthermore, Marx contends that the proletariat will become incessantly impoverished: 'The modern laborer sinks deeper and deeper below the conditions of existence of his own class. He becomes a pauper, and pauperism develops more rapidly than population and wealth' (Marx and Engels 1948). However, the progress of immiseration endangers the very existence of society whose basis is supported by the work of the proletariat, until at last: 'Society can no longer live under this bourgeoisie' (Marx and Engels 1948). This argument provided the grounds for his claims about the inevitability of the socialist revolution and came to be known as the 'thesis of absolute immiseration'.

As just described, the Marx of *The Communist Manifesto* defined the various classes in accordance with their relationship to the mode of production, his representations of modern society must now be seen as fanciful, grotesque and preposterous, although their power to inspire and galvanize people must also be acknowledged. The images are akin to a series of religious paintings: the workers who are daily subjected to harsh labor, become poorer and poorer with wage cuts and cannot sustain themselves anymore; independent proprietors are defeated by the capitalist offensive, lose their basis of existence and fall into the proletarian camp; the class structure is fraught with darkness and misery; and the silver lining in the dark cloud – the proletariat shakes off the blackness and wretchedness, establishing their own control with wisdom and intelligence, thus liberating the entire society into a classless utopia. But no matter how dazzling and animating the narratives may be, they were simply spectacles developed with inadequate theoretical reasoning and virtually no supporting evidence.

The other Marx

Both the polarization and immiseration theses have been empirically refuted. In advanced capitalist societies, the self-employed independent proprietors and the peasants have remained robust groups while the working class has internally diversified. While some workers are poverty-stricken, it cannot be said that workers as a whole have been increasingly destitute. As to the working-class socialist revolution and the inevitability of communism theses, we need not waste our time in discussing them; today even most committed socialist parties around the world have abandoned these doctrines.

However, rejecting these four theses does not mean that we must abandon the first thesis of Marxist class theory: the changing mode of production is the basis of class formation and is a determinant of other social phenomena. This most fundamental proposition deserves serious attention. Since the working-class socialist revolution thesis and the thesis of the inevitability of communism were not logically derived from it, their refutation does not entail that the initial, basic proposition must also be rejected. It should also be pointed out that neither the polarization thesis nor the absolute immiseration thesis necessarily follow from it. The former is an oversimplification and the latter is in clear contradiction to Marx's own argument that the reproduction costs of labor power determine wages.

It is clear that Marx did not naively believe his own prophecies. Although he understood the polarization of class structure as a broad, basic trend, he also recognized the existence of opposing tendencies. With the rise of productivity, the level of labor demand declines with the consequence that labor mobility from agriculture to modern industries stagnates. This leads to a situation in which the peasantry remains large. In addition, many petty mercantile capitalists emerge with the progress of commerce; 'officers' and 'sergeants' who engage in supervisory and managerial labor between the capitalist class and the working class increase in number, as do commercial workers who engage in bookkeeping and accounting work; and these middle functionaries earn relatively high wages. Marx's points along these lines are most clearly articulated in his *Theories of Surplus Value*:

> What [Ricardo] forgets to emphasize is the constantly growing number of the middle classes, those who stand between the workman on the one hand and the capitalist and landlord on the other. The middle classes maintain themselves to an ever increasing extent directly out of revenue, they are a burden weighing heavily on the working base and increase the social security and power of the upper ten thousand. (Marx 1861–63: chap.18)

These observations and predictions are full of foresight and have figured large in class discourse in recent years, especially since the 1970s.

Moreover, contrary to the widespread misunderstanding that Marx believed that classes automatically and solely determine other phenomena of society and directions of social change, he distinguished between: (1) class-in-itself, comprising those masses that are simply integrated into the economic structure and (2) class-for-itself comprised of people who are aware of their common interests and participate in collective action (Marx 1847: chap.2, part 5). Unlike his simple narratives for political agitation purposes, he clearly pointed out that while competition and conflict between classes determine the general direction of social change, past historical circumstances, non-class factors and contemporary political situations intervene in and transform these concrete processes in complex fashions (Marx 1952).

Nevertheless, Marx's work in this respect was never systematically organized. It thus remains our task to formulate his great insight into a systematic theory and to refine it as a tool for comprehending social dynamics. This will be our objective in chapter 3.

Weber's class theory

Although often situated in opposition to Marx, Weber adopted Marx's class theory in many respects. Weber formulated a conception of class in a more complex manner and developed the notion of 'status' separately from class. Weber defines class in the context of the market:

> ...this is the generic connotation of the concept of class: that the kind of chance in the market is the decisive moment which presents a common condition for the individual's fate. "Class situation" is, in this sense, ultimately "market situation". (Weber 1958: 182; cf. Wright 1985, Crompton 1993)

While this approach might initially appear to differ from Marx, closer consideration reveals that Weber agrees with Marx's classification of classes on the basis of the ownership of the means of production, maintaining that '"property" and "lack of property" are, therefore, the basic categories of all class situations' (Weber 1958: 182). However, the relationship between Marx and Weber is not simple. Weber's references to class tend to be fragmentary, coming close to Marx on some points and diverging from him on others.

Nevertheless, it is mere obfuscation to argue that Weber presented class concepts in opposition to Marx simply on the grounds that Weber formulated class in terms of the 'market'. Within Marx's framework, the capitalist class participates in the market with their own capital as the economic agent, while the working class takes part in the market with their labor power also as the economic agent. In this sense, as Giddens points out, 'it is easy to exaggerate the degree to which Weber's view departs from that of Marx, especially since, in broadening the concept of "market situation", Weber's argument could be expressed by saying that marketable skills constitute a form of "property"' (Giddens 1973: 78).

Rather than opposing Weber to Marx we should recognize that Weber added three major points to Marx's conception of class. First, Weber opened the way for a plurality of classes by proposing three dimensions of classification: property classes formed on the basis of the ownership of properties; commercial classes shaped on the basis of their functions; and social classes classified on the basis of their social mobility (Watanabe 1997: 35–6). As Watanabe and Giddens each point out, Weber left class categories both complex and tangled. His theory 'implies the recognition of an indefinitely extensive number of "classes"' (Giddens 1973: 78). One criticism of Weber's class theory is that it is characterized by such an elaborate conceptual refinement that it does not provide any concrete description of class structure. Metaphorically speaking, while precisely outlining the silhouette of a portrait, Weber leaves the task of completing the details to his followers.

Secondly, Weber distinguished between 'class situation' and 'class action'. Although recognizing class as the basis of communal class action, Weber argues that the effects of any particular class situation depend upon a variety of factors and, therefore, the existence of class does not necessarily generate class action. On this point, Marx had fluctuated between a belief in the inevitability of class action and the recognition that such action was conditional upon a complex set of other circumstances.

Finally, Weber introduced the distinction between status and class, examining the relationship between the two. This point profoundly influenced class studies and social stratification studies in later years. Weber defines a status group as a collectivity that follows a particular lifestyle. It is a kind of community that imposes its specific way of life on those who want to join it. This seems especially true of those who enjoy privileged status, who tend to exclude 'parvenu', even if the latter's style of life faithfully replicates the formers' lifestyles. 'They will only accept his descendants who have been educated in the conventions of their status group and who have never besmirched its honor by their own economic labor' (Weber 1958: 192). This reveals, Weber contends, that status is generationally continuous and durable.

According to Weber, class situation is by far a more basic determinant than status formation, because the ranges of possible status-based lifestyles are economically conditioned (Weber 1958: 190). However, the relationship between the two changes depending upon historical and social circumstances.

> When the bases of the acquisition and distribution of goods are relatively stable, stratification by status is favored. However, every technological repercussion and economic transformation threatens stratification by status and pushes the class situation into the foreground. Epochs and countries in which the naked class situation is of predominant significance are regularly the periods of technical and economic transformations. And every slowing down of the shifting of economic stratifications leads, in due course, to the growth of status structures and makes for a resuscitation of the important role of social honor (Weber 1958: 193–4).

Accordingly, modern society, which is fraught with rapid technological and economic change, is generally the type of society in which class conditions prevail. Weber provides concrete illustrations of various classes in modern society. For instance, as social classes, he lists workers, petty bourgeoisie, intelligentsia and professionals, and those privileged with property and education. In contrast, with respect to status, he refers only abstractly to status categories such as pedigree status and ecclesiastical status in premodern society and provides little specific description of status categories present in modern society. One suspects that this is indicative of the fact that Weber did not believe that clear status distinctions existed in modern society.

It follows that Weber's class theory is not in direct opposition to Marx's class theory. Though Weber introduced the notion of status as distinct from class, he regarded class as more important than status in modern society. As Marx also recognized the importance of status in pre-modern society, it is a mistake to assume that Marx is the founding father of class theory and Weber is the creator of stratification theory as many texts on stratification tend to proclaim. Parkin explains the strength of this misinterpretation thus:

> ...some of Weber's key ideas have undergone a strange metamorphosis in the process of being incorporated into American stratification theory. The Weber who emerges from this theory is hardly recognizable as the

author of *Economy and Society*, a disfigurement due largely to his being called upon as main standard-bearer of the movement against materialism or economic determinism or the monocausal interpretation of class, or some equivalent term for what passed as Marxism during this period. It is a Weber who has been thoroughly de-Marxified and so rendered fit to assume duties as the ideological champion of the classless society of American capitalism. (Parkin 1978: 604)

In other words, the notion that Marx and Weber are in rivalry is a product of the efforts of American sociologists to use Weber as theoretical support for their own ideologically constructed self-representations of America as a classless society.

The concept of social stratification

These misleading images of Weber have been further exaggerated, becoming the standard framework of social stratification studies. In *Economy and Society*, Weber introduced a notion of the 'parties' in contrast to both class and status; parties are organized groups that 'live in a house of "power"' (Weber, 1958: 194). It would be fair to understand that 'the party represents a state of affairs that is one step more advanced than class or status' (Watanabe 1997: 20). Nevertheless, some social scientists came to think that power should be incorporated into stratification analysis as a determinant of social strata and developed a now widely held view that, in contrast to Marx's one-dimensional economic determinism, Weber assumed a multidimensional approach, paying attention to lifestyles and power.

These views are widely accepted in Japan, primarily through the formulations of a prominent theoretician, Ken'ichi Tominaga, who argued that social stratification studies

> inherit the Weberian multidimensional theory which is based on the trichotomy of power distribution – class (economic power, namely, position in the market), status (social honor, namely, position in terms of prestige) and party (political power, namely, political position). This model opposes the Marxist unidimensional theory which defines class in terms only of material possession. (Tominaga 1979: 7)

Tominaga later refined the three dimensions of social positions, formulated them as material resources (income and property), cultural resources (education and cultivation) and relational resources (power and prestige) and developed an original stratification theory of his own (Tominaga 1986, 1995). Broadly speaking, stratification studies in Japan have adopted the Tominaga thesis. In his empirical studies, Tominaga used income, educational background and prestige as the representative variables of the three dimensions. Leading the early phases of the Social Stratification and Mobility (SSM) Survey, he analyzed large data sets and endeavored to demonstrate that Japanese society is characterized by a large number of people who exhibit status inconsistency and that the number of status-inconsistent individuals has been increasing (Tominaga and Tomoeda 1988, Tominaga 1992). In essence, he maintained that Japanese society has neither clearly marked upper and lower strata nor clearly defined rank orders, with social positions being multidimensionally diversified. These are the most polished self-representations of postwar Japanese society that have been generated.

The relationship between class studies and stratification studies

Class theories came into existence at the same time as the establishment of the modern social sciences. Marx gave specific substance to the theories, which Weber later advanced in parts. While it is arguable that those who developed stratification studies either distorted or transformed Weber's theory, we are nevertheless left with at least three different perspectives from which to approach questions concerning the relationship between class and stratification studies.

Following the genealogy of social science research, it appears natural to regard stratification studies as an offspring of class studies. Following this line of thinking, some argue that stratification studies form one type of class study, a position of which Tominaga is the best-known advocate in Japan – perhaps to the surprise of some observers. As Tominaga argues:

> Among the various theories of class, those sociologists who take quantitative approaches to class analysis and use multi-dimensional indices have gradually referred to strata more frequently than to class. As a result, an area called stratification studies has been established. Accordingly, stratification studies constitute one form of class study. It

is not appropriate to think of strata as an object of study independently of class. (1998)

Western scholars such as Wright (1979), Crompton (1993) and Edgell (1993) take similar positions and locate various stratification theories as subcategories of class theory.

However, stratification studies deal with dimensions such as culture and lifestyle that conventional class studies either failed to take into consideration or regarded as secondary factors. As a consequence, the notion of stratum has been understood to include a wider range of dimensions than class. From this perspective, one might argue that class studies are a type of stratification study. For instance, Giddens (1989) argued that there are four types of stratification system – slavery, caste, estate and class. Locating class as a subcategory of stratification he regards Marx and Weber as two representatives of stratification studies. I previously shared this position (Hashimoto 1990, 1997 and 1999) on the grounds that the stratification studies in contemporary sociology had become so diverse and unqualified that an almost endless stream of stratification concepts such as 'gender class', 'cultural stratification' and 'underclass' came into circulation, a multitude of categories that seemingly could not justifiably be classified under the generic category of class.

A third position argues that class studies and stratification studies are mutually opposing approaches. From this view, class theory is equated with Marxist class theory, regarded as uni-dimensional economic determinism, and found wanting against the multidimensional stratification theory typically identified as 'Weberian theory'. The conventional camp of American sociology adopts this framework and defends the stratification studies thus portrayed, a standpoint which many Japanese sociologists share. Advocates of this position tend to put class studies in general, Marxist class theory in particular, and the theory of socialist revolution all into one basket and dismiss them in one stroke.

The relationship between class and stratification studies is clearly quite entangled.[4] The first context concerns the way in which the class studies originally presented the fundamental problematic of the modern social sciences. Here, class studies precede and include stratification studies. In the second context, class studies inherit classical economics in defining class in terms of the possession of economic resources. The most significant case in point is the

Marxist class theory which emphasizes the means of production as a particular kind of social resource. Here, class studies are a subcategory of stratification studies. The third context is the class studies that shaped those narratives of class struggle and socialist revolution that *The Communist Manifesto* initially spelt out and international socialist movements later expanded in grotesque fashions. Here, class discourse is in stark opposition to all stratification studies.

In Japan, class analysis has been primarily debated in the third context with the result that the term 'class' became associated almost exclusively with the 'leftist vocabulary'. Consequently, with the decline of the leftist movements in the 1980s and later, the signifier for 'class' in the Japanese *termini generales* has been used almost solely in reference to the ranks of the Self-Defense Forces and the police forces or to ranking weight categories in combative sports. This is why the fact that some journalists and scholars began to use the vocabulary of class again in recent years attracted public attention.

Japanese class studies have been shaped by the circumstances particular to postwar Japan in which broadly defined 'class discourse' attracted public attention at various points. In the next chapter, I will examine the history of postwar class discourse conducted by expert sociologists as well as scholars in adjacent disciplines, social critics, essayists and politicians who have debated the structural inequalities of Japanese society.

2 When Class 'Disappeared' from Japan

The controversy over mass society and the middle class

From 1956 until the early 1960s, a heated debate unfolded in the pages of journals such as *Shisō*, *Chūō Kōron* and *Keizai Hyōron*, the so-called 'Mass Society Controversy' (*taishū shakai ronsō*). The controversy was instigated by a group of young political scientists and sociologists who advocated the 'mass society theory' (*taishū shakairon*). Born in Western Europe during the rise of fascism and later moving into the United States by exiled intellectuals, 'mass society theory' developed as a theory critical of advanced capitalist society. In Japan the young scholars who were defending this new theory were opposed by Marxists, including numerous theorists from the Japan Communist Party. One of the crucial points of this dispute revolved around the issue of how to understand the class structure of modern capitalism. The mass society theorists generally argue for a more advanced understanding of class than did the classical Marxians, admitting that they were also internally divided in their interpretations of what such a theory means.

Although a flood of competing terms such as the 'middle stratum' (*chūkansō*), 'middle class' (*chūkan kaikyū*) and the 'petite bourgeoisie' (*chūsan kaikyū*) appeared in Japanese socio-scientific discourse, the adherents of mass society theory generally agreed that the middle class was quantitatively expanding in modern capitalism and was thus becoming more important to the social structure. For instance, Keiichi Matsushita, an early exponent of the mass society theory, distinguished between the working class and the middle class on the basis that they occupied different positions in the production process. He argued that the new middle class 'is a major feature of the population structure during the stage of monopoly capitalism' (Matsushita, 1956: 32–3). Shōzō Fujita argued that in contemporary mass society, 'on the basis of completion of the stage of monopoly capitalism, a leveling-out of social strata in terms of consciousness as well as behavior patterns has occurred through three processes: 1. the technological structuring of society; 2. the concentration of the mass media and its spread throughout the whole of society; 3. the new middle stratum, with the core of management and supervisory workers and distribution system workers becoming an overwhelming majority in society' (Fujita 1957: 218). Dating from 1957, Fujita's prescription might be seen as the prototypical argument about 'the expanding new middle stratum' and the 'equalization of social stratification' which is still being argued today. In conclusion, they argued that in mass society, over-all governance of a uniform mass would be reinforced and the working class would be subjected to the state, so political participation and democracy would be increasingly eroded.

This claim soon attracted some powerful supporters in the newly formed Democratic Socialist Party, established in November 1960 by the Nishio group, which broke away from the Socialist Party. Upon the formation of the Democratic Socialist Party, a platform and basic economic policy was announced which claimed that Japan was generally becoming a 'middle class society' and that the Democratic Socialist Party, in addition to basing itself in this class, would further push for Japan to become a 'middle class society'. While attaining substantial increases in employment, the Party would 'turn all citizens into middle class'. The Liberal Democratic Party also began to advocate the 'rearing of the middle class' and various discussions surrounding 'the increase in the middle class' began to appear frequently in the mass media.

Of course, such claims became the focus for a great deal of criticism. Early in the dispute, Shingo Shibata was openly critical in a paper subtitled 'From the Viewpoint of a Marxist Scholar' (Shibata 1957). He launched a scathing and ideological critique of the theory of mass society, labeling it 'contemptuous of the masses' and 'elitist'. Referring to the *White Paper on Labor* (ed. by Ministry of Labor), Shibata poignantly observed that Fujita's argument that 'the new middle stratum was becoming an overwhelming majority' exaggerated the facts. Shibata recognized that the new middle class was, in fact, expanding; however, he claimed that the expansion of the middle class 'did not mean the decline of the logic of class and the elimination of the contradictions of capitalism, as the proponents of a "mass society" believed, but result from a further deepening of it'. That is to say, on the one hand, the expansion of managerial and supervisory occupations results from an increased need for supervisory labor, indicative of the widening and deepening of the antagonism between capital and the working class. On the other hand, it also derived from the gradual and 'relative increase of poverty' of the working class. From this perspective he argued that the fact that the new middle class is expanding proves the validity of Marxism. There is a strong tendency in his argument to obstinately insist that, one way or another, the working class is becoming poorer and the antagonism between capital and the working class is deepening. Nevertheless, the fact that he appears to clearly distinguish the new middle class from the working class, and recognizes that its size is increasing deserves attention.

Hajime Tanuma is another notable critic of the claim that 'the new middle stratum has become the overwhelming majority' (Tanuma 1957). Following the methodology of C. Wright Mills (Mills 1951), in 1955 Tanuma calculated the composition of the old middle stratum, the new middle stratum and production workers based on the national census and employment status survey. He revealed that the old middle stratum occupied 49%, whereas production workers and the new middle stratum were only 36 and 15%, respectively. Japan was not a new middle stratum society, but rather an old middle stratum society. This clearly differed from the United States, where production workers totaled 55% and the new middle stratum 25%. Tanuma's argument was a strong blow against the trend to directly import American theories, as some of the mass society theorists appear to have done, and draws attention to the fact that such arguments must be based on reliable data.[1]

In response to these criticisms, Matsushita argued that the new middle stratum was playing important political and social roles, despite being a numerical minority (Minobe and Matsushita 1960, Matsushita 1960). He began by rearranging the class composition tables produced by the Japan Institute of Statistics (1958) to show that the breakdown of Japan's class composition was: ruling class – 1.9%, old middle stratum – 50.8%, new middle stratum – 14.3% and working class – 32.9%. Then he raised the following points: 1. according to a survey on occupational prestige, most upper-level positions are new middle class in character; 2. the type of work young females seek is new middle stratum in character, such as office work; 3. it is the new middle stratum that runs the mass media; 4. disparities amongst the working class are widening, and; 5. a 'new middle stratum mood' is permeating upper level workers.

Matsushita suggests that even though they do not constitute a large proportion of the population, the new middle stratum is socially influential and thus 'the challenges for the social sciences today are to formulate categories whereby one might theorize about these changing conditions and to reconceptualize the images of postwar Japanese society that were initially derived from such theories.

At about the same time, Hajime Shinohara, in a round-table discussion with Takahashi and Tanuma, clearly articulated the vagueness of the 'middle class'. Introducing survey results from England and the United States, he showed that there was a big gap between actual class composition and class and status identification, and concluded that 'the middle class is, to a certain extent, a matter of consciousness'. He also pointed out that the criteria characterizing the middle class includes 'income, industrial position and intellectual status' and that 'even if only one of these three criteria is met, there is a mechanism to obtain a new middle stratum consciousness' (Shinohara, Takahashi and Tanuma 1960: 49–50). This is an important point, anticipating the theory of 'status inconsistency' which later emerged.

Akira Hamashima also responded to the problems raised by the mass society theory with an argument based on Marxian class theory. He claimed that the advancement of capitalism expands the new middle stratum in a manner 'that blurs class relations between capital and labor'. He argued that due to the increasingly specialized division of labor, encroaching mechanization and further developments in the management system, both capital and labor are each internally divided and 'class has somehow become a vague existence'. He refers to this as the 'massification of class'. In this sense, contemporary class, to borrow from Marx, is a 'class in-itself' and 'remains the basis of class behavior and class organization' (Hamashima 1957). It is worth noting that Hamashima had previously presented a theoretical approach to class in modern society that was not premised an *a priori* understanding of class as the subjective agent of class struggle, but instead, as an objective existence.

It is thus apparent that this debate was, by 1960, already anticipating important issues that would emerge in later research surrounding the trend of the new middle class and changes in the class structure. If the debate over the new middle class had continued and further research had been conducted to illuminate these changes, research about class in Japan might have developed significantly. Unfortunately, it did not turn out this way. One of the reasons is that the claims of the theory of mass society were still premature. At that time in Japan, the old middle class was a majority, the labor unions had enormous power and the two major political parties, the Liberal Democratic Party which was based on the capitalist and old middle classes, and the Socialist Party of Japan which was based on the working class, were 'class parties'. There were no important roles for a 'middle class' to play. Also, directly after the controversy over the revision of the Security Treaty in 1960, the participation of millions of Japanese citizens gathered around labor unions in political activities was interpreted as evidence that the mass society theory was incongruent with the realities of Japan.[2] However, another and crucially important reason was that class studies were disturbed by a certain political slant.

The 'Ōhashi method' takes an irregular course

In the midst of the mass society controversy appeared a statistician named Ryūken Ōhashi who conducted a full-scale study of class structures in Japan. He was born in Niigata Prefecture in 1912 and his family home was a Buddhist temple in which his father served as the chief priest.[3] In later life, in addition to his position as an associate professor at Kyoto University, Ōhashi inherited the position of the chief priest, though supposedly only nominally. In 1937 after majoring in the history of religion in the Faculty of Literature at Tokyo Imperial University, he entered the Faculty of Economics at Kyoto Imperial University where, upon graduating, he was employed as a research assistant. The following year he was arrested on charges of violating the Maintenance of Public Order Law and was forced to resign from his position at the university. In 1942, he joined the accounts department of Japan Steel Pipes Company (NKK), where he remained until shortly after the end of the war when he participated in the formation of the NKK labor union. In January 1946, Ōhashi was appointed as the union's first chairman, but was forced to resign two months later, after his defeat in the Seisan Kanri Tōsō (self-management movement), which was the main target of Japanese labor unions at the time. After being involved with organizing the workers of small companies in the

Ōmori district of Tokyo, in May 1946 Ōhashi became a full-time lecturer at the Tokyo Institute of Technology. He became an Associate Professor in the Faculty of Economics at Kyoto University in 1949. In 1950 he supported Torazō Ninagawa in his first candidacy for the Kyoto gubernatorial elections, and continued this support during Ninagawa's seven terms as governor. In many respects, his life may have served as a model for left-wing intellectuals who attempted to embody 'the unity of theory and practice'. In 1982, he became ill with stomach cancer and passed away in March 1983 at the age of 71, after surgery and a relapse of the disease.

It appears that his first published work after World War II was a paper entitled 'On the Land-holding of the Largest Temples in Japan' which appeared in the documents of the Department of Religious Studies published by the CIE (the Allied occupation forces' Bureau of Civilian Information and Education) in March 1946. By August that year he had published four articles in this journal, detailing both the assets and income of various temples. He appears to have begun working for CIE at about the time that he left NKK and concurrently with his first appointment as a university lecturer. For Ōhashi, who, as we have seen, grew up in a temple and specialized in statistics, this research for the CIE was undoubtedly suitable work. This position may seem contradictory in light of Ōhashi's later anti-US statements, but we must remember that immediately after World War II, the Japan Communist Party saw the Allied occupation forces as a 'liberation army' (cf. Nakayama 2001: 41). It probably seemed natural at the time.

He continued to publish what might be considered as rather sober papers at a rate of about one per year until 1959, which proved to be a watershed in his career. In 1959 Ōhashi published an article entitled 'The Significance and Limits of Social Class Composition Tables' (Ōhashi 1959). He used census data and an original categorization methodology to present a diagram of class composition while carefully explaining the details and basis of class categorization. This paper undoubtedly marks the beginning of the 'Ōhashi Method' which served as the model for research into class in post-war Japan.

However, the class categories that Ōhashi proposed in 1959 differed in significant ways from the categories of what became widely known as the 'Ōhashi Method' after 1968. The two different schemas are compared in Figure 2.1. Before we examine the details

Figure 2.1 Ōhashi's class categories: comparison between his old and new schemes

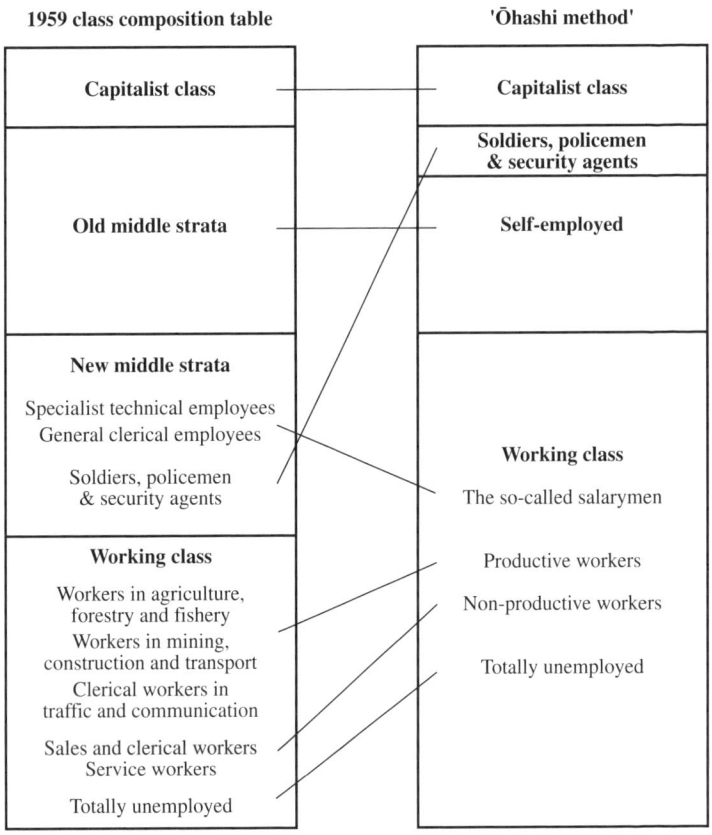

of Ōhashi's two different class definitions, though, we should step back and briefly outline some of the precursors to the 1959 study. There are two significant studies relevant here, the aforementioned 'Compilation of Japanese Economic Statistics' published by the Japan Institute for Statistical Research (1958) and Toshihide Shimada's 'Japan's Class Composition' (1957).

The Japan Institute for Statistical Research's 'Class Composition Table' divides the working population into four categories: 'ruling stratum', 'middle stratum' (individual proprietors and independent, specially skilled workers), 'new middle stratum' and 'workers stratum'. According to this table family employees are included amongst the workers; thus the workers level comprises 60.5% of the total. If these family employees were included in the middle stratum, the results appear to be reasonably similar to Ōhashi's 1959 class composition table. There should be little doubt that Ōhashi referred to this work when conducting his research.

Shimada's paper was published in the Japan Communist Party journal *Zen'ei* (The Vanguard) with the sub-heading 'Reference Materials for Discussing the [Party] Platform'. In the introduction to the article Shimada says, 'when attempting to establish a platform, it goes without saying that the country's class composition forms its basis'. There are two points in this article that we need to focus upon. First, it criticizes mass society theory on the grounds that 'instead of analyzing the facts, it exaggerates one aspect of the phenomenon, declaring that under modern capitalism, both capitalists and workers have become the middle stratum' – a concept it rejects. Second, it presents a class composition table that divides the total working population into five categories: 1. 'workers'; 2. 'working peasants'; 3. 'independent self-proprietors other than peasants'; 4. 'capitalists, managers, high-level bureaucrats'; and 5. 'soldiers and police'. If categories two and three are combined, these categories roughly equate to the 'Ōhashi Method'. Thus Shimada's research appears to have also been influential in the formulation of the 'Ōhashi Method'. Let us turn now to examine Ōhashi's method(s) in more detail.

The class category on the right hand side of Figure 2.1 is the so-called 'Ōhashi Method' (the 'later' 1968 method) which categorizes soldiers, police officers and security personnel separately from the three categories of capitalist class, self-employed stratum and working class on the basis that 'there are doubts about the nature of workers employed in the organs of suppression' (Ōhashi 1971). The left hand side shows the class category that Ōhashi used in 1959, where he placed the capitalist and working classes at opposite ends of the continuum with the new and old middle strata in between. Incidentally, the old middle stratum comprised 53.3% of the labor force and the new middle stratum 13.3% in this research, reasonably consistent to the previously discussed findings of Tanuma and Matsushita. In the later 'Ōhashi Method' the name of the old middle stratum has been changed to 'self-employed stratum', negating its intermediate character. The majority of the new middle stratum has been incorporated into the working class, its uniqueness denied. Clearly Ōhashi's theoretical position has undergone substantial change between 1959 and 1968. Although he never offered an explanation for this change in position, the reasons seem to be quite clear.

At the Japan Communist Party's eighth Congress in 1961 the controversy surrounding its platform was resolved and the party adopted a new platform that stressed two main points: 1. Japanese capitalism's subservience to the USA; and 2. the formulation of a two-stage strategy – a democratic revolution resulting from a united nationalist and democratic front, and a subsequent socialist revolution. It seems most important which class, stratum and social groupings are included in the united front. Indeed, the problem was directly related to the class composition table. Sanzō Nosaka, the Chairman of the Central Committee at the time, explained this point in a 'Political Report from the Central Committee' (*Chūō Iinkai no Seiji Hōkoku*): 'According to the 1955 census, the class composition of the working population was as follows: working class – 44%, peasant stratum – 38%, urban middle stratum – 16% and capitalist class – 2%...Thus, the working class is numerically our country's largest class' (Nosaka 1961). He also argued that 'the central task facing our party is for the working class to become the core, and ally itself with the peasantry to establish and develop a nationalist and democratic united front which gathers together working citizens, the intelligentsia and small business entrepreneurs'. Notably, Nosaka's claim that the working class accounted for 44% of the population counted all employees apart from management as 'workers', including professional and technical workers, and clerical workers. In other words, it rejected the category 'new middle stratum'. Four years later the Japan Communist Party took this position one step further, lumping the 'urban middle stratum' and the peasantry into the 'petite bourgeoisie class' while simultaneously separating Self-Defense Force personnel and the police. The JCP's new class composition table thus consisted of four categories: 'the capitalist class', 'armed forces of the ruling class', 'the petite bourgeoisie class' and 'the working class' (Japan Communist Party Central Committee Economic Survey Department 1965). The concept of a 'middle stratum' had been completely repudiated.

'With the adoption of this platform, research into social class composition became popular in all fields' (Tanuma 1964). In other words, researchers moved in the direction of 'proving' the Japan

Communist Party's revolutionary strategy. Shortly thereafter, Ōhashi's 1959 categorization was subjected to criticism for contradicting the JCP's theory of class. For instance, Nobukuni Mitsumata, after comparing and examining the three different class composition tables – i.e., 1. the Japan Institute for Statistical Research (1958), 2. Ōhashi (1959) and 3. the JCP Central Committee Economic Survey Division (1965) – expressed doubts about the concept of the 'middle stratum' entailed in the first two. He concluded that 'the social stratification and social class perspectives are different in that the former places importance on the sociological perspective or the issue of consciousness while the latter attempts to express class in capitalist society in accordance with its original meaning. In that sense, class composition table 3 is superior to tables 1 and 2' (Mitsumata 1966). As the JCP had enormous authority over progressive intellectuals at the time, having the Party determine that his research methodology was contrary to the Party platform was clearly disadvantageous to Ōhashi.

Yet Ōhashi remained strangely silent for several years, until suddenly, in 1968, he published a revised class composition table which came to be known as the 'Ōhashi Method' (Ōhashi 1968). Although Ōhashi's paper gave no explanation for changing the class categories, it seems obvious that any attempt to explain it would have been tantamount to admitting that he was intellectually subordinate to 'the vanguard party.' In fact, the new 'Ōhashi Method' was virtually identical to the two classificatory schemas proposed by Shimada (1957) and the JCP Central Committee Economic Survey Division (1965). The main difference is that it has been simplified such that a calculation can be made solely on the basis of the cross-tabulation tables for occupations and employment status listed in reports of the national census, and that the internal classifications for the working class have been rearranged. In short, the new 'Ōhashi Method' was a very slightly modified re-articulation of the 'JCP Method'. After a while, with the authorization of the vanguard party, the 'Ōhashi Method' became accepted as an 'established theory' (Hara 1979) and swept through Japanese class research in the 1970s. Consequentially, researchers of class lost interest in the 'new middle stratum'.

Thus, the origins of the 'Ōhashi Method' were very political. Yet in the ensuing years, Ōhashi and the researchers around him became ever more politicized. This politicization reached an apogee in the mid 1970s when Shima, Udaka, Ōhashi and Usami (1976) published the results of their research into class composition.

The stated objective of their class research was 'to specifically analyze postwar Japanese class composition from a working class perspective with the aim of contributing to social revolution' (ibid. 1). This was obviously, anything but an 'objective scientific analysis' of society. Rather, the research explicitly aimed to contribute to a revolutionary change to Japanese society: 'Forces centering on American imperialism and Japanese monopoly capital intend to maintain reactionary forces and revive and strengthen imperialism, whereas forces centering on the working class have a strategic view towards rallying the nation's masses and clearing a path for socialism through a democratic revolution' (ibid). The working class was considered to be the central agent for social revolution. Thus the growth of the working class means 'the growth of social forces in which the rapid build-up of the working class must fight against American and Japanese monopoly capital rule in an uncompromising manner' (ibid, 373). Therefore, forming 'a progressive united front and establish[ing] a democratically allied government is an urgent task. There is a realistic chance we can accomplish these tasks in the last half of the 1970s' (ibid 1976: 387).

During this time many sociologists proceeded with a quantitative analysis of the dynamics of social stratification in Japan. Meanwhile, new developments were appearing in class theory in Western Europe and the United States. Many theorists endeavored to exclude the politicized class theory, develop innovative theories about class structure in contemporary capitalism and analyze class structure objectively. Japanese researchers of class were infatuated with such a fantastic story. Looking globally, we cannot find another school of researchers investigating class under the same ideological schematic of class structure, even in the former Soviet Union and Eastern Europe.

This was ultimately a crushing blow to Japanese class research, for there had been a prevailing image of class as a political phenomenon and class research as a tool for the realization of socialism. If this were true, in the event that labor unions no longer participate in the antiestablishment movement, class will cease to exist and if socialism is undesirable, class research will become unnecessary. In fact, very soon, people arguing along these lines began to appear.

The illusion of the new middle masses

On 20 May 1977, Yasusuke Murakami, a professor at Tokyo University, published a short article entitled 'The Reality of the New Middle Stratum' in the evening edition of the *Asahi Shimbun*. Murakami's article prompted a flurry of comments and counterarguments from eminent scholars such as Shigenobu Kishimoto (9 June), Kenichi Tominaga (27 June) and Michitoshi Takabatake (14 July), marking the beginning of what was later called the 'New Middle Stratum Controversy'. A panel discussion was soon held (22–24 August), chaired by Munesuke Mita, to debate the issues raised by Murakami and his respondents. Before long, numerous articles and books were published about this controversy and the surrounding issues.

Murakami argues that according to a survey on social consciousness, 90% of respondents identified their own standard of living as 'middle', with 60% reporting that they were 'middle-middle'. Throughout Japan's high economic growth periods, living standards had risen, income disparities had been reduced, and the distinction between blue and white-collar workers had become blurred. Urbanization progressed in both the cities and the farming villages and life styles were generally homogenized. The proliferation of the mass media and public education contributed to the homogenization of people's consciousness. For Murakami, this marked the emergence of 'an enormous and homogenous stratum, in terms of living styles and consciousness, occupying a middle position that was neither upper nor lower stratum'. In this regard, Japan appeared to be a more advanced country than the Western Europeans and Americans, where traditional class structure and racial discrimination obstinately survived.

Murakami's article was extraordinary, arguing that 'the section chief, clerical worker, head foreman, foreman, factory worker, shop owner, shop assistant and farmer' constituted a homogenous 'new middle stratum', which effectively denied the existence of most social strata. In fact, in another article Murakami states: 'it can be said that the concept of a new middle stratum plays a somewhat paradoxical role. This is because it is a concept of strata for the purpose of denying the concept of strata' (Murakami 1977, cited in Kishimoto 1978: 104). Of course, this was the focus of numerous critiques. For example, Kishimoto claims that even in contemporary Japan there is no change in the tendency that people are divided into either capitalists or working class. Even if there has been a general 'homogenization' in the sense that a growing number of people have characteristics of both poles, the inequality that has culminated in a few individuals being large stock holders and upper level management has not been eliminated. Similarly, but from a different angle, Takabatake points out that even within the middle stratum as Murakami defined it, if various benefits other than wages are included, a large gap is clearly evident between the managerial workers and 'ordinary white-collar workers'. He observes that if this was not the case, one could not adequately explain various phenomena such as brutal competition over school entrance examinations or duck-shoving in companies. However, we must turn to Tominaga for discussion of the most important points of the debate.

Tominaga's argument presents three main points: First, the fact that many Japanese consider themselves to be 'middle' is ultimately an issue of a 'status identification' rather than their objective social/economic position. It is clearly an exaggeration to claim that 'everyone is the same and everyone is in the middle'. Second, Murakami's terminology conflicted with the established theory in Western sociology from Emil Lederer and C. Wright Mills that calls white-collar employees the new middle stratum, thus inviting confusion. Third, the majority of people appearing to become middle stratum resulted from an increase in 'status inconsistency', a rise in the number of people with high incomes but low prestige, and in the number that were well-educated but had low incomes accompanied by a decrease in the number of unambiguously 'upper' and 'lower' people. In summary, then, Tominaga argued that rather than a process of increasing homogenization, the situation being analyzed actually amounted to a proliferation of 'diverse intermediaries'.

While there is little doubt concerning the first two points, there are several doubts about the third point. I will discuss these later. For the moment I would like to focus on Murakami's response to his critics. Murakami soon accepted the bulk of Tominaga's argument, recomposing his own argument on the basis of the theory of 'status inconsistency'. In the process he replaced the concept of the 'new middle stratum' with 'the new middle mass', explaining that: 'What is developing in post-war advanced industrial society is a decrystallization and destructuration of the process of stratification at each level'. People in the decrystallized strata comprised a majority of the population, including not only white-collar workers, but also many blue-collar workers, farmers and the self-employed. It is this 'enormous stratum' that he labeled the 'new middle mass' (Murakami 1984: 188, 193-4). Anticipating new criticism, Murakami argued that there was some diversity within the new middle mass; namely between white- and blue-collar workers. He claimed that because of the growth of clerical work, particularly the increasing number of female clerical workers, the managerial status of white-collar work was gradually being degraded. Furthermore, with continual technological innovation, blue-collar workers were gradually becoming 'knowledge workers'. He observed that Japanese companies were raising the intellectual adaptability of workers through 'on-the-job-training' (OJT) and 'job flexibility' and argued that 'the lingering distinction between blue- and white-collar work was representative of the inertia of the classical capitalist era'. Thus, even after the reformulation of his stratification theory, Murakami's general depiction of Japanese society was that it was mostly homogenous, both on the surface and at deeper levels.

There are several factual errors and unreasonable inferences in Murakami's argument; I shall discuss only the three most problematic. The first concerns the issue of 'middle class consciousness' which is the starting point for Murakami's argument. The survey result that showed 90% of the Japanese population identifying themselves as 'middle' was virtually inevitable given the way that the questionnaire was worded. In fact, it did not provide any information unique to Japanese society. Conducting a survey in any country using the same questionnaire would result in 90% or more identifying themselves as 'middle' as can be seen in Table 2.1, which compares 'middle class consciousness'[4] for a number of countries. If we exclude Holland where more than 10% identify as 'upper', the percentage of people in each country that identify as 'middle' is around 90%. Similarly the 'middle-middle' reported for Italy is more than 70%, and France is more than 60%. Thus, the stratification that Murakami claims to have identified is not an inherently Japanese phenomenon.

Table 2.1 only contains data from so-called 'advanced countries'. However, there is other data available from a survey of a number of countries conducted by the Secretariat of the

International Values Conference in 1979 entitled 'A Survey of the Values of 13 Countries'. According to this survey, the total percentage of the 'middle' in a number of countries was as follows: Japan – 92.9% (middle-middle – 56%), South Korea – 89.4% (middle-middle – 51%), Singapore – 94.3% (middle-middle – 74.2%), Philippines – 92.6% (middle-middle – 67.1%), India – 91.2% (middle-middle – 57.5%) and Brazil – 87.7% (middle-middle – 57.4%) (cited in Scott and Watanabe 1998: 131). Not only do these figures closely resemble each other, but the fact that some of these countries report a larger percentage of 'middle-middle' than Japan stands out. As per the data presented in Table 2.1, this survey reported approximately '90% middle class' across a number of diverse countries using a questionnaire that divides the total population into three categories – upper, middle and lower – and then divides the middle into three again. The uniformity of the data suggests that such a result could be obtained in almost any country regardless of class structure and levels of economic development, at least in the present age.

Second, concerning the assertion that white- and blue-collar workers are becoming homogenized, it is a fact that the number of female clerical workers is increasing and that much clerical work is losing its managerial characteristics. But it is very doubtful that this trend has had any significant effect on the status of university educated male office workers who, in those days, were management cadets. Management restructuring has become virtually continual, but even today, when meritocratic recruitment and promotion is reportedly being adopted more broadly, the custom of annual intakes of new graduates from prestigious universities as management cadets is deep-rooted. There is no reason to expect that these cadetships will not continue to be the principle launching place for promotion into the higher echelons of the organization, as they always have. Thus, it is spurious reasoning to deduce that because female clerical work has become more prevalent, clerical work in general has become more like blue-collar work.

Furthermore, Murakami provides no evidence to support the claim that Japanese blue-collar workers are becoming knowledge workers through the practice of job rotation. Giving him the benefit of the doubt, it is quite likely that Murakami was influenced by Kazuo Koike's theory of 'intellectual skills,' which

Table 2.1 International comparison of 'middle consciousness'

	Upper	Upper middle	Middle middle	Lower middle	Lower	Total of middle
Italy	2.2	12.5	70.5	10.8	3.0	93.8
France	1.8	10.8	61.2	18.9	6.3	90.9
Germany	0.9	15.9	53.7	21.5	3.4	91.1
The Netherlands	11.2	32.5	44.4	6.5	3.8	83.4
UK	0.4	7.2	53.6	28.1	8.1	88.9
USA	1.5	16.7	54.4	21.6	5.2	92.7
Japan	1.1	10.9	53.6	26.9	5.4	91.4

Note: Year of survey – Italy (1992), France (1987), Germany (1987), The Netherlands (1993), UK (1987), USA (1988), Japan (1988).

Source: Hayashi (1995).

attracted a great deal of attention at about this time. Koike makes the following argument in 'The Skills of Japan' (Koike 1981): In Japan the wage differential between blue- and white-collar workers is small. Moreover, in contrast to Europe and North America, the Japanese operate a seniority based wage system for blue-collar workers. Koike's explanation for this is that Japanese blue-collar workers gain experience through wide-ranging workplace rotation which gives them 'the ability to respond to various changes', 'enabling them to understand how equipment in the workplace is set up and to apply this knowledge'. In this way, Japanese blue-collar workers are 'becoming white-collar' in terms of both wages and the type of work performed. He claims that this is useful when introducing new equipment, as Japanese workers are thus able to adapt to operating new machinery with very little training (Koike 1981: 8–10).

Koike's theory received such a great deal of attention that there were multiple reprints of the book in a very short period of time. Subsequently, Koike further developed the theory using various research materials and survey results. According to Koike, knowledge of the system of production and machine equipment that enabled a worker to carry out 'uncommon tasks' could be called 'intellectual skill'. He argued that a division of labor in which production workers only carried out 'routine tasks' while technicians performed all 'non-routine tasks' is uncommon in Japan. In fact, he claimed, there are many cases where production workers acquire intellectual skills and are responsible for both types of tasks (Koike 1991). If this argument were correct, then it would be fair to say that blue-collar workers were increasingly acquiring the characteristics of white-collar workers.

However, in the 1990s a number of studies appeared that rejected Koike's theory. According to these studies, production workers generally did not acquire 'intellectual skills' as Koike had claimed. Dealing with machinery malfunctions and breakdowns, apart from insignificant cases, was the responsibility of maintenance technicians who had received specialist training. Even though workers did, in fact, become more versatile through job rotation, the level of knowledge and experience was low in both processes, making it merely 'low level multi-skilling'. More recently, multiple authors have raised serious doubts concerning the credibility of the original data that Koike employed to support his theory (Nomura 2000, Endō 1999, 2000). If our assumption that Koike's thesis provided the foundations for Murakami's claim that 'blue-collar workers are becoming knowledge workers' is correct, then Murakami's argument is clearly unfounded.

Finally, concerning the question of 'status inconsistency': Murakami relies almost totally on Takatoshi Imada and Junsuke Hara's article entitled 'The Consistency and Inconsistency of Social Status' (Imada and Hara 1979). This article appeared in a book by Tominaga and other scholars entitled *Social Stratification in Japan*, which collated analytical results of the 1975 SSM Survey data (Tominaga 1979). According to this article, people's status is measured on six dimensions: prestige, education, income, assets, lifestyle, and power/influence. Classifying people based on these status criteria, 11.1% of people were categorized as high status (consistent upper level group) and only 30% of people were low status (consistent lower group). The remaining 60% are of an inconsistent status (inconsistent group). As we have seen, on the basis of this 'decrystallized stratum' Murakami concludes that the 'new middle mass' has been formed.

Again we can turn to numerous critiques that have been leveled at this argument (cf. Shōji 1981, Satō 2000). The most significant of these are: first, highly educated young male professional and clerical workers are included in the inconsistent group, ignoring the high likelihood of promotion which will locate them in the consistent upper-level group. Thus they should be categorized as part of the consistent upper-level group. Adjusting our figures on account of this reclassification, the consistent upper-level group constitutes about 20% of the total. Second, the inconsistent 'group' is only an aggregate of various groups which differ in employment status, income, educational background and lifestyle, etc. One cannot put these groups together and treat them as homogenous. This critique is also applicable to Tominaga's image of Japanese society.

As should be clear from the discussion above, Murakami's theory of 'the new middle stratum' and 'the new middle mass' is not only based on inadequate evidence, but also draws spurious conclusions from the evidence that is employed, thus making the entire schema unacceptable. However, it was undeniably very influential. Furthermore, an OECD report (Sawyer 1976) which claimed that Japan's income differential was the world's lowest seemed to support Murakami's position and contributed to what some time later became known as the 'new middle stratum dispute'. Regardless of the nature and the distortions of the primary materials used in this report, only the study's results became widely known.[5] Subsequently, the notion that 'Japan is a small differential society' and 'Japan is a classless society' became widespread. Although the participants in the dispute held different opinions, they agreed from the outset that Japanese society is increasingly homogenous and that the number of people located in the 'middle' is increasing. Between the two extremes of Murakami, who argued that 'almost everything has become homogenized', and Kishimoto, who claimed an axis of differentiation between capitalist and workers, there was very little difference remaining.[6] In other words, the conclusion appears to have preceded the research in either instance.

The new dogmatism

So what were the class researchers doing during this controversy? Certainly there were a number of articles written and books published that dealt with the issue of Japan's class composition and class theory. However, they could not possibly have been the main actors in this controversy. According to Murakami, 'the response of Marxist scholars was simply to repeat the claim that the new middle stratum was merely the "white-collar proletariat" and would probably be absorbed by the working class. This was far from an effective counterargument' (Murakami 1984: 173). In fact, as late as the 1980s they stipulated that the aim of class research was 'to explain how the working class was formed as a central force that could confront the political and economic control of the government and monopoly capital...during the entire process of the growth of postwar Japanese capitalism' (Tokita and Takagi 1982: 4). They also claimed that when forced to recognize the existence of 'the new middle stratum', limiting this to managerial employees, 'the new middle stratum' is only 4% of the total working population and most employees are working class (Ishida 1984). In other words, when they could no longer ignore the evidence for the existence of this stratum, they persisted in downplaying its significance.

Although they repeated these arguments, most people were not sympathetic to them. To the extent that the Japanese public understood Marxism as they claimed, most people firmly believed that the Marxist theory of class was a theory which argued that society was polarized into capitalist and working classes and that the working class would rise up in a socialist revolution; therefore, it was wrong. In other words, the dogmatic and politicized understanding became the benchmark for understanding – and rejecting – Marxism.

This bias spread, in particular, amongst stratification researchers. The so-called 'collapse of socialism' in 1989 spurred this on. Stratification researchers soon pronounced the 'death' of the Marxist theory of class with confidence, and in the process came to reject the concept of class itself. For instance, 'the fundamental difference between the concepts of class and stratum is that the concept of class has strong theoretical assumptions, whereas the concept of stratum does not' (Seiyama et. al., 1990: 15–16). Put the other way around, the argument is that stratification theory has strong empirical foundations and class theory does not. 'With advancing industrialization, Marx's theory gradually became more problematic. Confident predictions such as "the absolute immiseration of the working class", "falling profit rates", "the proletarianization of the self-employed" and "the intensification of the class struggle" all failed to materialize. During Japan's period of high economic growth (beginning in the 1960s), "class" had lost its social meaning. The decline of progressive parties in Japan was one manifestation of this' (Seiyama and Hara 1999: 10). In effect, they argued that the claims of Marxist class theorists must be identical to the thesis of *The Communist Manifesto*. This is a kind of sacralization of *The Communist Manifesto*, by opponents of class theory that seems to reduce class theory to that of dogmatic Marxism.

Of course, such arguments were not new – they were actually well established criticisms of Marxist theory. However, arguments such as Seiyama et al's were too simplistic when compared to earlier Japanese sociologists' work. For instance, Ken'ichi Tominaga was a disputant second to none when it came to rejecting the validity of the Marxist concept of class in contemporary society. However, after going back to the original texts and examining Marx's and Saint Simon's class theories, he prescribed class as one type of social stratification and distinguished the concept of class from others according to the scale of the disparity and the degree to which it is a closed entity. He did not regard the narrative of *The Communist Manifesto* as absolute and thus did not assume the simplistic position that since the manifesto had been falsified, the concept of class must also be rejected (Tominaga 1986). In a similar vein, Yasusuke Murakami called attention to the fact that Marx had recognized the increase of the new middle stratum in the *Theories of Surplus Value* (Murakami 1984: 198). From this perspective we must ack-nowledge that in spite of the problems with Murakami's theory (discussed above) his multi-faceted stratification research took the concept of class seriously without taking on-board the political dogmatism that too often accompanies Marxian research.

While it sometimes appears as though critiques of Marxist and Marxian theories are overly simplistic, we must bear in mind that it was the Japanese class researchers who treated *The Communist Manifesto* and the platform/pronouncements of the Japan Communist Party as absolute and who continually regurgitated dogmatic political arguments that made such simple counter-arguments possible. People saw their unique form of 'Marxism' as generic 'Marxism' and rejected it because it was not consistent with the empirical evidence. In a sense, it was a natural response. Karel van Wolferen explains: 'There are many points that deserve careful deliberation in Marx's works. He had keen insight. But, today when Communism has come to an end, it is generally considered that there is basically nothing Marx has to say. In some societies his name is still taboo. Therefore, because it was a theme that was emphasized by Marx, the notion of social class has experienced many ordeals. Because Marx was so obsessed with social class, it has definitely become a disagreeable topic' (Wolferen 1999: 70).

The downfall of the myth of equality and the re-emergence of 'class'

However, in the mid-1980s, around the time that Murakami's 'The Age of the New Middle Mass' was being discussed, a certain pessimism was emerging in the '90% middle class', beginning outside of academia. 'Kinkonkan' (Watanabe and Kōtari 1984) considered a large number of occupations that were thought to be at the forefront of society such as designers, stylists, and television directors, etc. They showed with many hilarious illustrations, that these were by no means internally homogenous, but were rather clearly divided into 'Marukin (rich)' and 'Marubi (poor)', and attracted an enormous readership. 'The Age of the New "Stratified Consumption"' (Ozawa 1985), written by a researcher employed by a banking company, also attracted a great deal of attention, arguing that from the 1980s, in addition to people's purchasing power beginning to grow at an ever diminishing rate, there was an increasing disparity in purchasing power which was effectively dividing consumers into an increasingly polarized high- and low-class categorization.

A few years later, what we now identify as the 'bubble economy' raised people's average incomes, but asset disparities grew even more rapidly. Doubts began to emerge concerning the (recently constructed) myth of 'Japan as an egalitarian society'. Despite the rise in incomes, a growing percentage of people reported that their lives 'had become difficult'.[7] Itsuko Teruoka's *What is Affluence?* (Teruoka 1989), which asked whether the apparent Japanese affluence was genuine, became a bestseller. Many similar works exploring the problem of 'affluence' were published at this time. Although public opinion surveys revealed no change in the notion of '90% middle class', many people came to doubt the meaning of 'middle class consciousness'. In this vein, a popular economic journal *Ekonomisuto* ran a feature about 'the end of the myth of equality' (15 May 1990).

As the bubble economy collapsed, any lingering feelings of 'affluence' dissipated. Corporate bankruptcies and mass layoffs occurred in rapid succession, employment instability spread and wages, which had been stagnant, began to fall. From the mid 1990s, many commentators began pointing out the widening disparities in the Japanese economy and the growing social inequality. Amongst these works, Toshiaki Tachibanaki's 'Economic Disparities in Japan' (Tachibanaki 1998) attracted attention for its demonstrative and simple explanation of the rapid progression in the inequality of Japanese income distribution as compared to other developed countries since the late 1980s. It is arguable that this situation increased the objective necessity for a theory of class.

Tachibanaki and others conducted studies in a field of economics called income distribution research. Income distribution research explored, as its name suggests, the distribution of the fruits of production amongst people. This field certainly occupied an important niche in the research into inequality. However, the focus of income distribution research was income, which, even broadly defined, was limited to income and assets, making it a rather narrow field. This research is therefore insufficient unless supplemented by research into class or stratification. In fact, Tachibinaki stands out in the field for having recognized this. Thus, after reporting the results of his research into the distribution of income and assets in the first four chapters of his book, Tachibanaki (1998) examines occupation and educational background in the final chapter to present an analysis of the mobility between strata and educational status. The point, for our purposes, is that Tachibanaki recognized/demonstrated that in order to explain the total picture of inequality, a theory of class in the broad sense is indispensable.

In the year 2000, arguments to the effect that Japan has recently become a 'new type of class society' began to appear. We find representative examples of this argument in the May special feature of *Bungei Shūnjū* (Bungei Shūnjū Henshūbu 2000), and Toshiki Satō's article entitled 'Twenty years Since the Birth of "The New Middle Mass"', which appeared in the May edition of *Chūō Kōron* (Satō 2000a). In June a similar book entitled *Japan as an Unequal Society* (Satō 2000b) was also published. The former pointed out the widening disparity caused by the permeation of a system based on merit and ability, between, on the one hand, a 'winning group' of elite businessmen who were employed by foreign multinational corporations, etc., and received annual salaries ranging from the tens to hundreds of millions of yen, and on the other hand, a 'losing group' of salaried workers whose pay was drastically cut due to managerial crises and restructuring and were forced into retirement. This was referred to as the 'emergence of a class society'. The latter made an issue of the extent to which people follow their parents into a particular occupation. It also pointed out that the generation of people born before 1935 had enjoyed relatively greater chances to become an upper white-collar employee if one made the effort. This tendency had contributed to the development of a 'general middle class consciousness', but more recently, the upper-echelon positions had become far more closed; to the extent that unless a person's father is an upper white-collar employee, it is extremely difficult for them to become one. Satō referred to this as the 'emergence of a new class'.

Both articles emphasized the existence of social inequality and warned of its further expansion. I do not want to deny the significance of these, but am concerned at the potential for generating confusion, as the term 'class' employed in these two articles is significantly different from that used previously in the social sciences.

For example, the *Bungei Shūnjū* article was concerned only with the problem of white-collar workers in large corporations. There is no mention anywhere of factory workers, day laborers, part-time female workers, the self-employed, etc. That is to say, in spite of the widening disparity, it is ultimately merely a problem of a widening disparity amongst white-collar workers in large corporations. It calls the division between these workers 'class', losing sight of the total picture of social inequality. This perspective totally fails to recognize that the 'equal high salaries' of white-collar workers in large corporations up to now were possible only on the basis of the low wages paid to blue-collar and female workers.

Satō employs a distinctive terminology when he questions what he calls the 'emergence of class': the 'increased tendency to follow the same occupation as one's father'. What he calls 'class' is a closed social strata in which there is little inter-generational mobility. Very few social scientists have adopted such terminology. To the best of my knowledge, there are no social science dictionaries or textbooks in which the term 'class' has been defined in this manner. As we discussed in chapter 1, Smith and Marx each defined class according to one's position in the economic structure regardless of what one's father did. It is no exaggeration, then, to say that Satō played a significant role in propagating and disseminating this misunderstanding of the concept of class. From his perspective, provided that the opportunity for people to move to occupations different than their parents is guaranteed, regardless of the existing disparities in incomes and assets, there are no classes in society. In other words, provided the opportunity for mobility exists, inequality itself is acquitted.

Throughout the last quarter of the twentieth century – that is, from the end of the economic 'boom' until the 'bubble burst' – there was a general consensus that 'class' did not exist in Japanese society. Very few people openly discussed class, even in universities. Whether the cause or effect of this situation, it is safe to say that there has been very little agreement about what class *is*. As our discussion of the observations of Satō and *Bungei Shūnjū* has demonstrated, there is a growing awareness that the expanding economic disparity and inequality in Japanese society are problematic. However, these same observers have perpetuated the dismantling of the concept of 'class' which was originally one of the best tools of modern social science.

My objective in this book is to return the concept of class to social science in Japan. It is my contention that this is a necessary concept for social analysis, especially now when disparities and inequalities are once again expanding. Yet, it is also obvious that if we are to reclaim this concept, we must break with the dogma of *The Communist Manifesto* and dismantle the orthodox Marxist conception as it is generally understood. I set about this task in the next chapter.

3 Class Structure in Contemporary Society: From Marxist To Marxian Theory

The significance of class

'Class' refers to a grouping of people who occupy a similar position in the economic structure. In this sense, it is a concept defined in the economic region. However, this does not mean that class analysis is limited to economic disparities and inequalities, because one's position in the economic structure influences one's life conditions and consciousness. Class theories focus upon the ways in which class – as an independent variable – affects other social phenomena. The validity of these theories can be judged by the extent to which they explain social phenomena.

In contrast, some stratification theories attempt to use income, education, property, prestige and power to construct a multidimensional framework of stratification determinants, an approach that tends to blur the causal relationship between variables. These analysts accuse class theories of economic reductionism and determinism. They sometimes provide good insight into various problems of class theories, but make a fundamental error in positing a raft of equally weighted independent variables. This is problematic because, for example, to a considerable extent one's education is determined by the income and property of one's parents and, in turn, determines one's income and property. Similarly, in modern society, prestige and power are generally attained through securing employment, which indicates a particular social position and generates income and property. These cannot, therefore, be regarded as independent variables. The 'multidimensional approaches' ignore the relationships between variables, and are therefore inadequate tools for empirical studies attempting to demonstrate causality amongst social phenomena.

Even more problematic are the many stratification studies that have tried to explain people's work and family life, political attitude, value orientations and view of life by treating an individual's social stratum as the independent variable whose measurable indicator is their occupation. In other words, these studies have hardly adopted a multidimensional approach. One's occupation reflects one's position in the economic structure and can therefore be considered as one of the proxy indicators of class. Put differently, occupation is an empirical and operational variable whereas class is a theoretical concept that points to varying positions in the economic structure. Among the social characteristics of individuals studied in past sociological research, no other attribute is a more suitable independent variable than class. Indeed, Stinchcombe argued that class is *the only* independent variable in sociology (cited in Wright 1979: 3). Social class therefore deserves serious attention. In this chapter, we will develop our understanding of the class structures of modern society and define the various classes.

From Smith to Marx

As discussed in chapter 1, in *The Communist Manifesto* Marx accelerated the development of class theory after Smith and established the foundations of the class theory that remains influential today. But he interwove political propaganda and fantastic predictions into his theory, thereby putting class theory itself into confusion. At first, we will shed the unsustainable elements from Marx's class theory, and refine it to establish a point of departure for analyzing the class structures of modern capitalist societies.

As we have seen, Smith maintained that there are three classes in 'every civilized society': the landlord, working and capitalist classes – respectively corresponding to ground rent, wages and profits as the three forms of income. In contrast, Marx adopted a two-class model particular to capitalist societies: the capitalist and working classes. Although landlords who live on ground rent still exist in capitalism, their significance, Marx claimed, proves much diminished compared to what it had been in pre-capitalist societies. Rent is income usually derived secondarily from the appropriation of the surplus value that capitalists have procured. In the capitalist mode of production landlords can no longer be regarded as significant economic agents. Therefore we can ignore them in our analysis of the fundamental class structures of capitalism.

Marx's class model is based on a small number of people who exclusively 'own' the means of production and a large number of people who do not. The former own means of production far in excess of their capacity to fully utilize them by means of their own labor alone. The latter cannot engage in productive work without some means of production and therefore cannot support themselves independently. Thus, the interests of the owners and the non-owners coincide. This leads to transactions between the two groups in which the non-owners sell their labor power to owners who pay wages in compensation. The economic structure built on the basis of such transactions is called the capitalist mode of production. Each owner of the means of production here is a capitalist, and each non-owner is a worker; collectively they form the capitalist class and the working class.

This 'correspondence of interests' suggests that the two classes involved stand on a par with each other to the extent that each requires the other, and labor and wages are exchanged on an equal footing. However, the relationship between the two is unequal in a number of respects, with capitalists able to assume the dominant position. First, capitalists own many properties and can therefore survive for a period of time without the supply of labor power, while workers cannot support themselves without selling their labor power to the capitalists. Secondly, capitalist societies produce a fluid population of unemployed and under-employed who sustain themselves by stopgap work and are in the market for employment. Marx referred to this as the 'relative surplus population'. Therefore, capitalists can gain an advantage over workers, discriminate between workers, dismissing those who do not suit their objectives and employing others who might. Thirdly, it follows that workers who sell their labor to capitalists are required to work under the capitalists' instructions, which ultimately means that workers are denied freedom of action during prescribed working hours, and their capitalist employers own the goods that they produce. Fourthly, the level of wages usually coincides with the value of the labor power; i.e., the value of consumables required to reproduce the labor power. However, since workers can produce commodities whose value exceeds the value of their labor power, the capitalists can retain the 'surplus value' after wage payments. It is in this sense that we say that capitalist exploits the working class.

...

Whilst the two-class scheme thus formulated is a model that Marx originally constructed in logical abstraction, he later analyzed some of the complexities arising from trying to describe class structures in concrete terms. In this respect, he raised at least three important points.

First, while maintaining that peasants and small producers would degenerate into the working class as described in *The Communist Manifesto*, he recognized that the process of degradation is not a smooth one. As discussed in chapter 1, increasing productivity reduces the demand for labor power, thus reducing the rate at which peasants and small producers are absorbed into the working class, thereby applying a brake to the polarization process. At the same time, the development of commerce produces new self-employed proprietors and small business entrepreneurs, counteracting the process of polarization. Marx observed that 'Capital in the sphere of circulation would become decentralized in the same proportion as it became centralized in the sphere of production' (Marx 1894). Second, the development of capitalism creates internal differentiation of the working class as those engaged in managerial, supervisory and commercial labor increase in number (cf. chapter 1). Marx observed that '... in proportion to the increasing mass of the means of production, now no longer the property of the laborer, but of the capitalist, the necessity increases for some effective control over the proper application of those means' (Marx 1867). In other words, the need for managerial and supervisory labor increases with the progress of capitalism. Thus, capitalists hand 'over the work of direct and constant supervision of the individual workmen, and groups of workmen, to a special kind of wage-laborer' (Marx 1867). Marx called these workers 'officers' and 'sergeants'. Moreover, the expansion of commercial capital increases the number of workers engaged in commercial clerical work. As Marx puts it: 'The commercial worker, in the strict sense of the term, belongs to the better-paid class of wage-workers –

to those whose labor is classed as skilled and stands above average labor' (Marx 1894). It appears then, that Marx anticipated the development of what we call the 'new middle class'.

Third, the capitalist class is also internally divided. Marx distinguished between the 'money capitalists' who own the financial capital, and the 'functioning capitalists' who organize industrial production by investing capital that they have borrowed. These two kinds of capitalist emerged in the development of the credit system. These two types of capitalists have conflicting interests because the surplus value that the functioning capitalist can extract from the commodities produced by wage labor is reduced by the cost of the loan interests that must be paid to money-capitalists. Functioning capitalists receive their income in the form of payments for their managerial work. Profits, then, can be seen as a kind of wage – that is, remuneration for their labor in organizing and managing production. Functioning capitalists thus share some similarities with the managers and supervisors discussed above (Marx 1894). In this sense, Marx recognized the so-called 'separation of ownership and management' as well as the development of some continuity between a type of owner and the new managers.

Beyond Marx

Marx's theory surpasses any other theory of class in the social science tradition from Smith to Weber. Smith left only an ahistorical, three-class model while Weber, despite his achievements in refining class concepts, did not develop a systematic scheme of class structure. In contrast, Marx described the fundamental class structure of capitalism as a particular stage of historical development, whilst keeping its dynamics and future in perspective. However, Marx was constrained by his times and left at least three unfinished tasks.

First, he left unanswered the question of where peasants and small producers are located in the class system of capitalism. While recognizing their long-term survival, he did not clearly detail their locations in the class structure because, as we have discussed, he believed in their eventual disappearance as the classes increasingly polarized. Thus the problem remains for us to determine whether or not they form classes of their own and, if they do, what characterizes them as such.

Second, what location do those engaged in managerial, supervisory and commercial work occupy in the class structure? Marx did not elucidate their characteristics, even though he predicted an increase in their numbers. Nor did he answer questions such as: whether they constitute a class of their own; whether an increase in their numbers undermined/off-set the tendency towards class polarization; and whether they would eventually be absorbed into another class.

Third, there remains the question of the significance of the internal differentiation of the capitalist class for class theory. Marx's distinction between functioning and money capitalists leaves the location of the functioning capitalists ambiguous. Are they capitalists or not? Are the managers and administrators capitalists or workers? Does labeling those who do not 'own' the means of production in their own right as functioning *capitalists* contradict the definition of capitalists?

In short, Marx's is an unfinished class theory: elements of what he regards as the two major classes remain uncertain and those who are not included in these two classes remain ambiguous. In order to redress these deficiencies, we must go beyond Marx's theory and elucidate matters that he never adequately considered. It is worth noting that in the history of class theory since Marx, whenever someone has observed shortcomings in Marx's work and developed new formulations and fresh schemas to overcome them, others go 'back' to Marx's large body of work, scouring his notes and drafts for evidence to support their *ex post facto* claims that Marx had already addressed those questions. We aim to abandon this cult of personality and, while acknowledging the sound foundations laid by Marx, produce our own class theory on the basis of contemporary social scientific research data.

New developments in class theories

Work to theorize the class structure in contemporary societies has accelerated since the 1970s. In this section, we will briefly outline the studies of Nicos Poulantzas, Harry Braverman, John Roemer and Erik Olin Wright – four major contributors to this field, each of whom has accepted part of Marx's fundamental conception and effectively remedied some of the problems in his theory. Through various processes they have each developed an original class theory that we can draw on to provide a basis for developing our own understanding of class structure today.

Nicos Poulantzas

Marxist theories faced a significant turning point in the 1960s when the French philosopher Louis Althusser and his young disciples directed their radical criticisms at orthodox theories and proposed fresh interpretations from the perspective of what came to be known as 'structuralist Marxism'. They refuted what they regarded as the established 'economism' in which the economic 'base' (i.e., the particular mode of production), was assumed to unilaterally condition the superstructure (i.e., law, politics and ideology). They also criticized 'Marxist humanism' as an unjustifiable ideology attempting to overcome a dogmatic orthodoxy through reference to the scattered writings of the early Marx. They produced new conceptual devices such as 'levels of structure', 'overdetermination' and 'ideological state apparatus' to renovate Marxist theory.

Nicos Poulantzas built his class theory upon the framework developed by Althusser and his colleagues. Poulantzas' major points are that three levels – economy, politics and ideology – are to be distinguished in social formations, that multiple modes of production coexist and are articulated in modern capitalist societies, and that there are various types of 'ownership', the fundamental concept in Marxist class theory.

In modern capitalist societies, Poulantzas argues, the capitalist mode of production is dominant but not universal; 'simple commodity production' continues as a remnant form of the feudal mode of production. Thus two different modes of production are in effect simultaneously, with the consequence that the 'traditional petit bourgeoisie' exists alongside the capitalist class and the working class. Although Marx expected this group to be absorbed into the working class and did not elaborate on its characteristics, it is still with us today and shows little sign of disappearing. It has its own foundations in the economic structure of capitalist society.

Poulantzas also defined conceptual boundaries of the capitalist class that Marx had left ill-defined, maintaining that there are three distinguishable ways in which one might 'own' the means of production: (1) economic ownership – the power to assign the means of production to given uses and dispose of products obtained; (2) possession – the capacity to put the means of production into operation; and (3) legal ownership – ownership recognized by law. Within this framework, employers of wage labor who do not 'legally' own a company and 'functioning capitalists' who do not legally 'own' financial capital nevertheless belong to the capitalist class because they 'own' the means of production in the sense of 'economic ownership' and 'possession'.

Poulantzas further argues that class location is determined not only by economic factors, but also by political and ideological factors. The class to which managers, labor supervisors and professionals belong cannot be adequately identified with reference only to economic criteria. Managers and supervisors exercise political control over workers, while professionals affect ideological control over workers through their monopoly of knowledge. Accordingly, these people belong to the 'new petit bourgeoisie' – distinguishable from both the capitalist class and the working class in that they have power to exert control over the working class but do not own the means of production. Poulantzas also maintains that the 'traditional petit bourgeoisie' and the 'new petit bourgeoisie' are ideologically akin to each other and can be grouped into one class (Poulantzas 1973, 1974).

The particulars of Poulantzas' theory have been subject to extensive criticisms and roundly refuted. Yet, his contributions have provided a lasting influence on class theories in boldly revising the conventional theories of Marxism and grasping class structure in contemporary societies from an innovative viewpoint. Contemporary Marxist theorists have adopted many of his ideas; in particular, that there are multiple modes of production shaping class structure and that ownership manifests in multiple forms.

Harry Braverman

To label Harry Braverman a 'class theorist' does not seem adequate. Upon dropping out of university, he worked at the Brooklyn Naval Shipyard as a coppersmith and was later employed as a steel worker doing layout and fitting at different steel companies. During this period, he started participating in a socialist movement and later became a director of Monthly Review Press, a socialist publisher. Among his own publications, his major work *Labor and Monopoly Capital* (1974) offers profound insights into manual labor in contemporary capitalism, combining his own experience as a manual worker with his studies of the labor process.

Braverman's point of departure is the first volume of *Capital* in which Marx articulated how the accumulation of capital altered the production process and the labor process and subjected workers' labor to the machine. However, Marx did not consider the labor processes of clerical, sales and service workers and did not anticipate the changes in labor processes that accompanied the growth of these occupational categories. In an endeavor to scrutinize the changes that had taken place since Marx's era, Braverman introduces an important axis: the separation of conception and execution.

Braverman argues that human labor comprises (1) labor itself, namely, 'execution' and (2) 'conception' which precedes and governs it. Human labor differs from animals' in that it is governed by prior conception. However, conception and execution are separable; 'the conception must still precede and govern execution, but the idea as conceived by *one* may be executed by *another*' (Braverman 1974: 35). In this way, only a small number of people engage in conceptual work such as designing, planning, measuring and recording, and thereby take part in managing and supervising large numbers of other workers. The introduction of scientific technology into production accelerated this tendency, making the labor of a majority of workers simple and monotonous, and creating – between the capitalist and working classes – the 'new middle class' who supervise and organize workers and represent the interests of the capitalists even though they themselves are workers.

For Marx, clerical and commercial workers were considered to be relatively highly paid skilled workers involved in both the conception and execution of their particular type of work. However, Braverman argues that the continuous expansion of firm size and the rationalization of work have made it possible for conception and execution to be increasingly separated here, too, such that most office workers now engage in simple and mundane work. In the retail and wholesale industries as well, most workers are engaged in simple work such as unloading goods, putting commodities on display on shelves and showcases and, with the introduction of mechanical equipment, operating cash registers, while knowledge- and skill-based work is increasingly concentrated in managerial positions. Thus, Braverman contends, with the exception of a small number of those who engage in 'conceptual' work, an overwhelming majority are subjected to the 'degradation of labor' (Braverman 1974).

Questions can be raised about whether changes in the labor process indicate a unidirectional degradation of labor, and the extent to which the development of technology replaces simple manual work with machines that might eventually abolish it. Yet, Braverman's theory has influenced class theories substantially, challenging the established class theory which had defined classes unilaterally in terms of the ownership of the means of production and introducing the analytic 'separation of conception and execution'. In other words, classes are defined not simply on the basis of the ownership of the means of production but by differences in the labor process, a point which suggests that those workers who provide only execution labor are more intensively alienated. These formulations appeal to the intuitive understanding of 'class' among ordinary people and, in that sense, had unique persuasive power. Thus, Braverman's ideas provide an important perspective for the analysis of class structure in contemporary societies.

John Roemer

A novel theoretical position known as 'analytical Marxism' has attracted attention since the 1980s. It critically examines and eventually abandons the dubious theories and propositions of conventional Marxist theory – for instance, dialectics and the labor theory of value. The new current also incorporates a variety of theories and methods developed outside of the Marxist tradition – such as the general equilibrium theory, game theory, and mathematical and quantitative methodologies – into Marxist analysis. The field has accumulated much scholarly achievement in economics, political science, sociology, philosophy and other disciplines. John Roemer is among the main architects of this development. His studies cover a diverse range of areas, but perhaps his most important contribution is the reconstruction of the 'exploitation theory' which constituted the core of Marxist economics and the proof of a theorem that he calls the 'Class Exploitation Correspondence Principle' (CECP). In this process, he established a micro foundation for Marxist economics, demonstrated its theoretical coherence and provided a clear basis for class theory.

Roemer also developed a taxonomy of exploitation by incorporating game theory into the model of developmental stages derived from historical materialism and formulated a 'general theory of exploitation' that, he argued, was applicable to various phases of society from pre-capitalist to socialist. He identified four kinds of exploitation attributable to four different types of properties: the labor power of others, the means of production, privileged status and skills. He then discussed the developmental stages from feudalism through capitalism to socialism in terms of a process in which particular types of exploitation are overcome from an initial phase in which all types of exploitation coexist.

In feudal society, landlords exact corvée from serfs on the basis of the former's enforcement of property rights to the latter's labor power. Feudal exploitation is based on the ownership of the labor power of others. In the capitalist economy, feudal exploitation has been abolished. Capitalist exploitation is based on the unequal distribution of the means of production. The class that had carried out the bourgeois revolution achieved control of the means of production and now profit through the exploitation of the working class. They have thus become the 'dominant class' of the capitalist economy.

The purpose of a socialist revolution is to abolish capitalist exploitation. Many argued that this could be achieved by the equal distribution of the means of production. However, in past and existing 'socialist societies', bureaucrats exploit workers, using their privileged status in the state and party organizations. Thus, even if the equal distribution of the means of production is achieved, what Roemer calls 'status exploitation' remains. Moreover, even if status exploitation is abolished with the democratization of 'socialist societies', what he labels 'socialist exploitation' persists because of the disparities of skills amongst people and the prevailing 'pay according to work' principle, in which skilled workers exploit other workers to the extent that they secure higher remuneration per unit of time for themselves. According to Roemer, in socialist societies skilled workers are dominant. However, if an equality of results were achieved and there were no longer any disparities in rewards, socialist exploitation might be abolished, but with the possible consequence that there would be no incentives to motivate people to work, which might reduce the general living standard of the people, including those who are most exploited. Accordingly, Roemer suggests that some exploitation, what he calls 'socially necessary exploitation', should persist (Roemer 1982, 1986 and 1988).

One cannot help feeling troubled by Roemer's use of the hackneyed model of 'development stages'. Even though what he calls 'socialism' may differ greatly from past and existing socialism, opinion remains divided over his views in these respects, a point we will examine in chapter 9. Putting aside the controversial aspects of his study, however, his formulation is useful as a hypothesis of class structure in contemporary capitalist societies; to the extent that there are concurrent forms of exploiting the means of production, status and skills, it is possible to formulate a complex class structure on the basis of three types of exploitation rather than a simplistic bi-polar class model. Roemer, however, did not produce any concrete schema of class structure, a task that Wright took up.

Erik Olin Wright

Erik Olin Wright attracted international attention with *Class, Crisis and the State* (1978), which begins with a telling anecdote:

> As a graduate student in sociology I constantly confronted the hegemony of an empiricist, positivist epistemology in the social sciences. In virtually every debate over Marxist ideas, at some point I would be asked, 'prove it!' To the extent that Marxist categories could be crystallized into 'testable hypotheses', non-Marxists were willing (sometimes) to take those ideas seriously; to the extent that debate raged simply at the level of theory, non-Marxists found it relatively easy to dismiss our challenges. (Wright 1978: 9)

Following these experiences, Wright's class studies invariably shuttle between theory and empirical analysis. His empirical analysis differs from the conventional Marxists' tendency of selectively assembling facts and numbers to defend their theoretical position. In contrast, Wright is at his best in unambiguously examining his hypotheses through the methods of rigorous quantitative analysis prevalent in mainstream sociology.

His theory has two faces: (1) Wright-I inherits the achievements of Poulantzas and Braverman, and (2) Wright-II stands up as a colleague of Roemer promoting analytical Marxism. Wright's early work emphasized the former, but after some self-criticism, he moved to the latter position. Yet both faces reveal significant accomplishments in class theory today.

Wright-I accepts Poulantzas' postulation of the coexistence of two modes of production: the capitalist mode of production where the bourgeoisie (capitalist class) and the proletariat (working class) are located; and simple commodity production where the petite bourgeoisie is located. Wright then moves a step further, adopting Braverman's ideas that the bourgeoisie is characterized by their 'control over labor power', as well as what Poulantzas calls their 'economic ownership' and 'possession' of the means of production. Between the three fundamental classes – bourgeoisie, proletariat and petite bourgeoisie – Wright argues, there are 'contradictory class locations' which share some characteristics with two of the three major classes. Specifically, between the bourgeoisie and the proletariat, there are 'managers and supervisors' who are employees (i.e., workers who sell their labor power) but who also, like capitalists, have the capacity to

Figure 3.1 The relationship of contradictory class positions to class forces in capitalist society

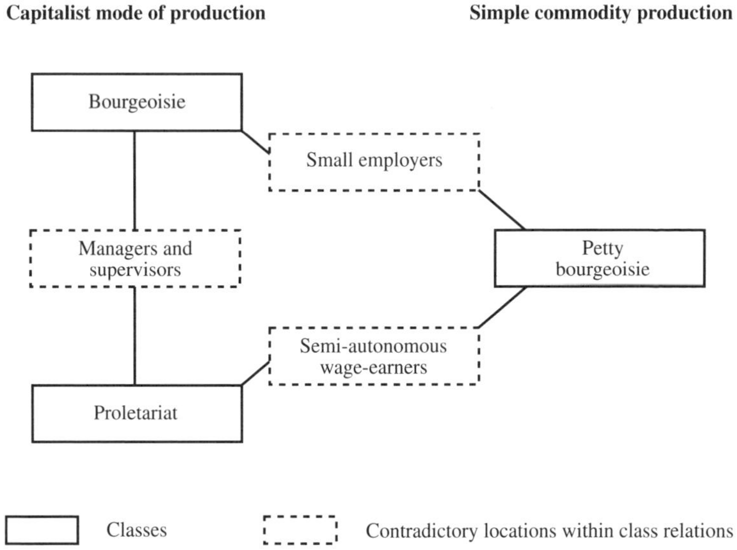

Capitalist mode of production   **Simple commodity production**

```
    ┌─────────────┐
    │ Bourgeoisie │
    └─────────────┘
           │         ┌ ─ ─ ─ ─ ─ ─ ─ ─ ┐
           │         │ Small employers │
           │         └ ─ ─ ─ ─ ─ ─ ─ ─ ┘
           │                                    ┌──────────────┐
  ┌ ─ ─ ─ ─ ─ ─ ─ ┐                              │    Petty     │
  │ Managers and │──────────────────────────────│  bourgeoisie │
  │  supervisors │                              └──────────────┘
  └ ─ ─ ─ ─ ─ ─ ─ ┘
           │         ┌ ─ ─ ─ ─ ─ ─ ─ ─ ─ ┐
           │         │ Semi-autonomous   │
           │         │   wage-earners    │
           │         └ ─ ─ ─ ─ ─ ─ ─ ─ ─ ┘
    ┌─────────────┐
    │ Proletariat │
    └─────────────┘
```

☐ Classes   ⌐ ─ ─ ┐ Contradictory locations within class relations

Source: Wright (1978)

control and exploit the labor power of others. Between the bourgeoisie and the petite bourgeoisie, are 'small employers' who own the small-scale means of production and control the labor power of a small number of workers. Between the petit bourgeoisie and the proletariat are 'semi-autonomous wage earners' who are only partially controlled because of their possession of expert skills. Figure 3.1 illustrates these class locations, whose empirical validity Wright demonstrated through various survey data.

Wright's early class theory and empirical studies elicited various scholarly responses. Some analysts examined its validity through an application of his approach to Asia and Europe.[1] Many criticisms of his work soon appeared. After several years, in fact, Wright withdrew his class typology, explaining the change of position with two major self-criticisms: (1) 'Contradictory class locations' exist only between polarized classes with conflicting interests, not between two modes of production as he had tried to show in the cases of 'small employers' and 'semi-autonomous wage earners'; and (2) His earlier model had overemphasized the control over the means of production and labor power, and had underestimated the significance of exploitation. With this new understanding, he endeavored to develop a new class typology (Wright-II) based on Roemer's theory.

Wright-II is quite complex, postulating three types of exploitation in capitalism based on: ownership of the means of production, organizational assets (status in Roemer's model) and skill/credential assets. Taking these three types into consideration, Wright sets up three axes for a class taxonomy, finally distinguishing a total of twelve classes (Wright 1985). This schema is represented in Figure 3.2.

The class typology presented by Wright-II has, for a number of reasons, not been widely accepted. First, with three axes being juxtaposed as independent of each other, it remains unclear what the most fundamental criterion for class distinction is in this model. Secondly, it has been argued that if 'ownership' is not restricted to the narrow sense of 'legal ownership', but means instead the capacity to exert control over the means of production, his distinction between exploitation based on the ownership of the means of production and that based on organization seems somewhat redundant. Thirdly, skills can be regarded as a part of the capacity to control the means of production, instead of an

Figure 3.2 Typology of class locations in capitalist society

	Owners of means of production	Non-owners (wage labourers)			
Owns sufficient capital to hire workers and not work	1 Bourgeoisie	4 Expert managers	7 Semi credentialled managers	10 Uncredentialled managers	+
Owns sufficient capital to hire workers but must work	2 Small employers	5 Expert supervisors	8 Semi credentialled supervisors	11 Uncredentialled supervisors	>0
Owns sufficient capital to work for self but not to hire workers	3 Petty bourgeoisie	6 Expert non-managers	9 Semi credentialled workers	12 Proletarians	−
	+	>0	−		

Assets in the means of production (top) / Skill/credential assets (bottom) / Organisation assets (right)

independent basis for exploitation. Finally, on a rather practical methodological level, the twelve class typology is too complicated to apply to many empirical studies;[2] especially any class analysis that focuses on women and families, which must employ a system of classification that can account for both the husband and wife in a household. Consequently, although Wright-II attracted a lot of attention, very few scholars have conducted research aimed towards validating this model.

From Marxist class theory to Marxian class theory

It should be reiterated that our objective is neither to prove that Marx was a great thinker nor to propagate the political thesis of *The Communist Manifesto*. Whilst building on the foundations provided by Marx's basic ideas, we aim to produce our own theoretical scheme with the aid of the material provided through the work of Poulantzas, Braverman, Roemer, and Wright. Our task is to explain what is happening in our world today, rather than to justify or validate any particular ideology. Thus, while drawing on some of Marx's insights, we endeavor to be liberal with his ideas in order to develop theories that can explain ongoing changes.

The term 'Marx*ism*' has been overused by Japanese social scientists who have found some inspiration in Marx's work. I suggest that the term 'Marx*ism*' should be abandoned except by those who still embrace Marx*ist* political dogma, which like Stalin*ism* and Lenin*ism*, is the product of the propaganda of individual political actors. To clearly distinguish our critical social study as a social scientific approach with its roots in the theoretically meaningful parts of Marx's work from every form of orthodox or dogmatic political Marx*ism*, we shall call our theoretical position Marx*ian*, thus locating Marx as but 'one amongst social theorists', much as some economists define themselves as Keynes*ian* or Ricard*ian*.

Class structure of contemporary capitalist societies

With its clarity and applicability to empirical studies, Wright's class typology provides a good departure point for our work.

As discussed, though, Wright-II has some problems, particularly in its identification of three mutually independent types of exploitation. In reality, those in high positions of organizations and possessing skills have practical control over the means of production and thereby engage in the exploitation based on it. Put differently, exploitative relationships based on the means of production enable high-ranking and high-skilled individuals to earn high wages. Thus, there are no grounds for classifying 'non-owners of the means of production (wage laborers)' into nine different categories.

Another problem with Wright's model is that the bourgeoisie and petit bourgeoisie are lumped together as 'owners of the means of production'. Wright-II follows Roemer in assuming that capitalist societies have abolished feudal exploitation and rejects his earlier recognition of the continuing existence of simple commodity production as a surviving form of the feudal mode of production. However, in Japan and many other societies there remain a considerable number of low-income farmers and self-employed proprietors as well as low-income and unpaid family workers. Any class analysis that aims to depict these societies must account for the place of small business structures, in particular, the remaining feudal type of exploitation based on the patriarchal family model.

Roemer's explanation of poverty in the un(der)-developed world is instructive with regards to the relationship between the capitalist mode of production and simple commodity production. He observes that disparities in per capita quantities of capital and in labor productivity between advanced and un(der)-developed countries are so large that exploitation through unequal exchange eventuates. The same kinds of disparities exist between the capitalist means of production and simple commodity production, producing similar kinds of exploitation within a developed (or developing) nation.

Thus, accepting Wright-II's self-critique of the under-evaluation of exploitation, one finds that (1) exploitative relationships between the capitalist class and the working class based on the means of production and (2) exploitative relationships between the capitalist mode of production and simple commodity production in the form of unequal exchange, must both be accounted for in an effective class theory. Thus, between the capitalist class and the working class, we can locate the 'new middle class', comprising people who are exploited somewhat more moderately, and who sometimes exploit the working class through exercising control over the means of production and the labor power of others. Outside of this tri-fold relationship we posit the 'old middle class' comprising peasants and other small commodity producers who continue to exist alongside of, and interact with, the capitalist mode of production. Figure 3.3 is our class scheme based on these considerations.

Measurement of class location

Having constructed a scheme of class structure, we must now translate class categories into operationalized categories that can be employed in the analysis of empirical data. To examine the existing statistical data and survey results, we need a procedure through which we can identify the class location of each individual under investigation and to estimate the size of each category in contemporary Japan.

The Ōhashi method discussed in chapter 2 provides, perhaps, the best starting point for these purposes due to its elegant simplicity; combining occupation with employment status enables researchers to scrutinize statistical data compiled within the framework of other theoretically developed class categories. Following Ōhashi, we

Figure 3.3 Class structure in contemporary capitalist society

(a) Class structure of capitalist societies

Class	Effective control of the means of production	Capitalist exploitation	Quantity of corporate capital	Inter-sector exploitation by the means of production
Capitalist	+	Exploiting Mildly	+	
New middle	+ ~ minimum	exploiting or exploited	+	Exploiting
Working	0	Exploited	+	Exploited
Old middle	+	Not relevant	minimum	

(b) Basic class structure scheme

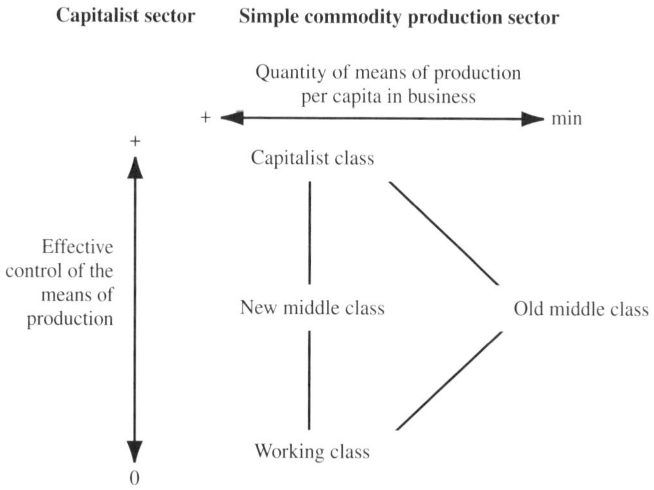

combine occupation with employment status but also introduce firm size as a variable to categorize the capitalist class and the old middle class and thereby distinguish the following class categories, a model that I initially formulated in Hashimoto (1985) and whose validity has been tested by Hashimoto (1986 and 1999) and Hara (1994):

> *The capitalist class*: Executives and directors of enterprises whose number of employees is five or more; and self-employed independent proprietors and family workers in business enterprises of the same scale.
> *The new middle class*: Employees who engage in professional, administrative and clerical work (excluding female clerical workers).
> *The working class*: Employees other than professional, administrative or clerical workers (but including female clerical workers).[3]
> *The old middle class*: Executives and directors of enterprises whose number of employees is less than five; and self-employed independent proprietors and family workers in business enterprises of the same scale.

Three explanatory notes are in order.

First, we have drawn the boundary between the capitalist class and the old middle class at the enterprise size of five employees. Whilst there can be no absolute grounds for this, our consideration is based on the observation that the incomes of business executives and directors comprise two parts; one part derived from their own labor and the other derived from the exploitation of workers. Those whose income is substantially derived from their own labor can be considered to have the characteristics of the old middle class. The larger the exploitative part of their income, the more they assume the characteristics of the capitalist class. The 1995 SSM data[4] show that the income of the executives and directors of companies with less than five employees is 1.6 times greater than that of their employees. The ratio goes up to 2.0 in enterprises with five to nine employees, and increases to 2.5 in corporations with ten to 29 employees. We have selected the doubling point as the dividing line between the capitalist class and the old middle class.

The second point concerns the distinction we have made between male and female clerical employees. This is not posited as a universally applicable distinction between women and men in all capitalist societies, but rather as descriptive of the particularities of contemporary Japanese society. On one hand, institutional structures locate most male clerical employees as potential managerial candidates, thus providing them with relative access to managerial positions. On the other hand, most female clerical employees do not have access to such status, being situated primarily as unskilled workers whose social characteristics – such as educational background, income and social consciousness – resemble those of employees in sales and service jobs.[5] With our definition of the new middle class as those who exercise relative control over the means of production and the labor power of others, it is inappropriate to classify female clerical workers without these characteristics as members of this class. We must therefore locate these employees in the working class, a situation which might change in the future if the position of female clerical employees improves or those of male clerical employees decline.

Finally, we should acknowledge some of the limitations of our proposed procedure. The class categories presented here are constructed through the use of empirically acquired occupational variables and therefore cover only those who are formally employed. Those who are not formally employed – for instance, capitalists whose income is derived entirely from their shareholding and are not employed in any form – are therefore not included in our capitalist class category. The same applies to large shareholders who run their own small businesses. Our only excuse is that large-scale surveys such as the SSM do not separately identify the number of large stockholders in their sample. Other studies need to be designed to elucidate the situation of these people.

A similar problem arises with respect to full-time housewives without jobs who are also unaccounted for by the categories presented. This is a serious shortcoming, considering their large numbers. This issue presents a huge challenge to class studies, raising the question of whether or not it can be inclusive enough to account for the place of women in class structures. Chapter 6 attempts to address these points.

Table 3.1 presents a class composition table constructed using our class categories and the SSM Survey data from 1955 to 1995.

Table 3.1 Composition on class categories (%)

Class	1955	1965	1975	1985 Male	1985 Female	1995 Male	1995 Female
Capitalist	5.5	8.4	6.2	6.3	4.0	10.6	6.7
New middle	17.0	23.1	25.9	32.0	8.5	32.1	11.1
Working	19.5	34.4	36.2	37.2	58.8	37.2	59.4
Old middle	58.0	34.1	31.7	24.5	28.7	20.1	22.8
Farming	39.3	18.0	14.3	6.6	11.4	4.9	6.3
Self-employed	18.7	16.1	17.4	17.9	17.3	15.3	16.5

It identifies internal groupings of the old middle class in an effort to describe the time-series changes with some precision.

Focusing on the male population alone to determine long-term changes in class composition,[6] we can observe that the proportion of the population characterized as the old middle class – the farming population in particular – has dramatically declined over the four decades surveyed, while the relative sizes of the new middle class and the working class have increased, each in the order of 190% over the same period. The expansion of the working class occurred primarily from 1955 to 1965 and its percentage has remained rather stable since. Increases in the new middle class were dramatic from 1955 to 1965, slow from 1965 to 1975, sharp again from 1975 to 1985 and stagnated from 1985 to 1995. The proportion of independent proprietors has shown little change over the survey period, while the size of the capitalist class has fluctuated, with a significant rise from 1985 to 1995.[7]

We can only trace changes in women's class composition from 1985 to 1995, but it is noticeable that the population of women characterized as working class is the largest, accounting for almost 60% of the female population. Women working in the agricultural sector decreased substantially, while those in the capitalist class and the new middle class show a slight increase.

Figure 3.4 displays the class composition of the four classes based on firm size (with the old middle class being broken down into independent proprietors and farmers). Class groups exceeding ten percent of the population are (1) working class employees in petty enterprises, small- and middle-sized companies and large corporations and (2) independent proprietors. Of these, the working class in the petty enterprise sector and the independent proprietor sector are particularly noteworthy, each comprising approximately one sixth of the total labor force.

In sharp contrast, the new middle class is relatively small, with the largest group – those employed by large corporations – accounting for a mere 7.7% and those in public bureaucracy and small- and middle-sized companies merely 6.1%. This indicates that popular images of 'Japan as a new middle strata society' characterized by salaried employees in large enterprises are misleading at best. It is also worth pointing out that while the capitalist class constitutes nearly 10% of the total, the owners of petty companies account for approximately 96% of the entire capitalist class.

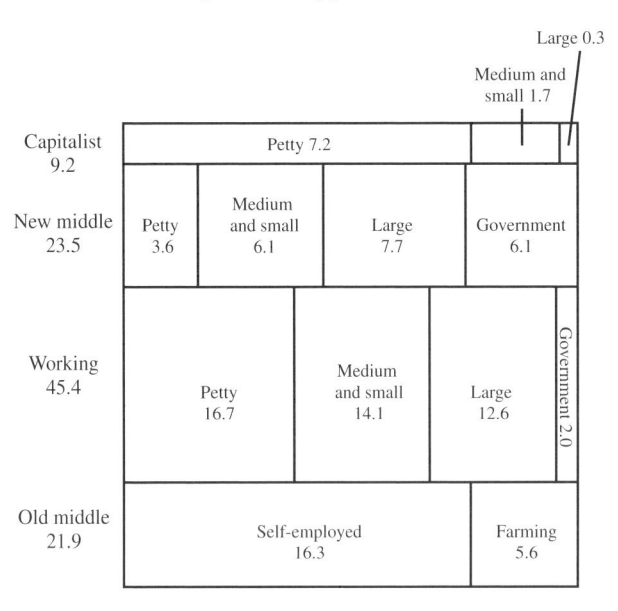

Figure 3.4 Class composition by firm size

Capitalist 9.2	Petty 7.2			Medium and small 1.7	Large 0.3
New middle 23.5	Petty 3.6	Medium and small 6.1	Large 7.7	Government 6.1	
Working 45.4	Petty 16.7	Medium and small 14.1	Large 12.6	Government 2.0	
Old middle 21.9	Self-employed 16.3			Farming 5.6	

Note: Petty = 1.29, Medium and small = 30–299, Large = 300 or more
Source: 1995 SSM Survey data (inclusive both males and females)

The data thus contradicts enduring images that portray an overwhelming number of proletarians in perpetual conflict with a small number of big business bourgeoisie. No matter how small their company may be, those who own the means of production and employ others are capitalists, a point which has often been lost in the evaluation of the capitalist class, resulting in the underestimation of its size and its strength as a social force.

In the following chapters we will study the class structure of contemporary Japanese society by analyzing empirical data from the SSM Surveys in accordance with the class categories set out above.

Promenade: Transgression of Class Borders – Two Versions of 'Tsurumoku Bachelor Dormitory'

'Tsurumoku Bachelor Dormitory' appeared in the youth oriented comic magazine, *Biggu Komikku Supirittsu* (Big Comic Spirits) from 1988 to 1991 (Kubonouchi 1988–92; hereinafter 'TBD vol.*x*') and was made into a film directed by Akiyoshi Imazeki in 1991 (Kubonouchi and Imazeki 1991; hereinafter 'TBDf'). Set in the factory and bachelor dormitory of 'Tsurumoku Furniture, Inc.', it is a story about the love lives and career choices of young workers fresh out of high school. Drawing on his own work experience in a furniture factory in Aichi Prefecture after graduating from a technical high school, Eisaku Kubonouchi depicts the narrative settings and characters with striking realism in the comic; detailing work tasks and regulations, the demands of overtime and participation in small group activities, as well as providing insight into the human relationships that develop in the factory and its dormitories. Dialogues between factory workers discussing their views about work and life occur frequently, and are presumably also based on the author's first-hand experiences. The film version retained the comic's characters and narrative structure, but its ending inverts the original; the main character chooses a different career path and marries a different woman. These two versions thus offer striking contrasts of parallel worlds. In this brief promenade, we will follow the trials of the main character,[1] Shōta Miyagawa, supplementing our discussion of his journey with empirical research and data into the life world of genuine factory dormitories and the career choices of high school graduates.

Shōta goes from high school to the factory

Shōta Miyagawa, our fictional hero, was born in 1969 in Kochi City. He was the oldest son of a furniture shop owner. His family consisted of his parents and one sister, Miku, three years his junior. Shōta began primary school in 1976 and junior high school in 1982 where he graduated in 1985. He then went to the technical high school, apparently studying in the Department of Interior Design. He seems to have had no clear reason for choosing this particular career path, or at least we are led to assume as much in a scene in which Shōta recollects a conversation he overheard between two of his best friends during his technical high school days:

> Friend 1: 'I envy the free time my friends will have at university; four years of good times. What an indulgence! Choosing technical school was a big mistake.'
> Friend 2: 'But you were intellectually inclined to choose the technical high school.' (TBD vol. 10, p. 70)

Sometime after entering technical high school, Shōta began to dream of becoming a world renowned interior designer, but when his classmates heard about it they laughed and jeered.

> Shōta: 'I'll be a world famous interior designer with my own design showroom in New York.'
> Friend 1: 'You'll take over your father's furniture shop, that's all.'
> Friend 2: 'You're dreaming. We're all doomed to mediocrity.' (TBD vol. 1, pp. 58–9)

It should be noted that Shōta's classmates were clearly expressing the dominant view in this debate. But Shōta still had one person on his side, his girlfriend Tomomi who was a year behind him at high school. Sympathetic and supportive, she said:

An ambitious man is groovy. I think it's charming to dream, to think big. (TBD vol. 1, p. 59)

Tomomi did not really have much faith in Shōta achieving his dream; what she wanted was that he would be hers forever. Her love for him was obsessive. For example, when told that Shōta had been given work in the Tsurumoku Furniture factory in Tokyo, Tomomi, in a state of shock and with tears in her eyes, said, 'So, we will be separated from each other' (TBD vol. 8, pp. 140–1). On the day of departure, she came to the station and said, between sobs, 'Even when we're far apart, we have one soul between us. If you're unfaithful to me, I'll wring your neck' (TBD vol. 1, p.9).

In 1988, the year that Shōta graduated, 1.65 million students graduated from high schools in Japan. Of these, 25.7% of all male students and 36.2% of females went directly to a university or junior college upon graduation, while 35.7% of male students and 37.7% of females went directly into employment. In Kochi Prefecture, however, the rate of male students continuing their education at tertiary level was considerably lower than the national average, reaching only 20.8%. The rate of male employment in that prefecture was 43.4%. While only 23.4% of the entire population of Japanese high school graduates who found employment had to leave their prefectures to do so, 41.0% of the male graduates from Kochi Prefecture were employed away from home. This rate reached 53.6% for those employed in the manufacturing sector ('Basic Survey of Schools' (*Gakkō Kihon Chōsa*)). Thus, Shōta's career path is typical of the majority of male high school graduates from Kochi Prefecture.

The Tsurumoku furniture factory 'proudly produces and sells the largest quantity of furniture made in Japan' (TBD vol. 1, p. 24) and employs about 2300 workers. The total number of employees at the manufacturing section where Shōta was assigned was 1550 workers (1180 male and 370 female).[2] Of all high school graduates in 1988, only 20% were employed by large corporations with over 1000 employees ('Statistics of Employment Security Service' (*Shokugyō Antei Gyōmu Tōkei*)). From this perspective, Shōta's employment in a large, successful company might be seen as a relatively privileged position.

Shōta's dream

Upon joining Tsurumoku, Shōta became a resident of a bachelor dormitory where he shared a room with two other men: a 27 year old named Shigeo Tabata and Kyōsuke Sugimoto, aged 21. Shortly after arriving at the dormitory, Shōta met and became friendly with Miyuki Himekawa, a high school graduate (two years ahead of Shōta) and a clerical employee living in Tsurumoku's women's dormitory. As these stories so often go, Shōta gradually came to fall in love with Miyuki.

When he was recruited by Tsurumoku Furniture, Shōta had expected to be assigned a semi-white-collar position within the sales department, but was in fact assigned to the second finishing section of the factory, specializing in the production of sideboards. His job was to transfer manufactured sideboard parts on a handcart from the processing division where they were made to the appropriate section of the warehouse. Sometimes he had to load the parts onto a belt conveyor that took them to the painting process. In short, Shōta found himself doing a very typical blue-collar job. Early in the series he laments:

> I was assigned to work at the manufacturing division that produces sideboards. The job is boring and unrelenting. I just never expected to be doing monotonous assembly-line work. I'm doing physical labor rather than cerebral work because, after all, I'm only a high school graduate. (TBD vol. 1, pp. 24–25)

Shōta's job was a long way from the one he envisaged for himself as a famous interior designer. His, though, is the reality for many. To put Shōta's experience in context, let us look more closely at the nature of employment for new male high school graduates in 1988. Almost half (48.8%) of all high school graduates and 68.5% of all male technical high school graduates who went directly to work were employed as manual workers (technicians and mining, manufacturing, construction workers, and operators). In contrast, 17.3% became sales workers, 10.3% became service workers, and only 3.8% found technical work ('Basic Survey of Schools' (*Gakkō Kihon Chōsa*)). And since Tsurumoku was a large corporation that could afford to employ university graduates in its sales division (TBD vol. 4, p. 12), the odds very much favored Shōta going to work in the factory.

Of course, not all of the workers in the factory are young school graduates. Shōta also came to know some of the elderly workers in the factory, including Ueki who, like Shōta, worked in the second finishing section at the factory. Even on Fridays, when his fellow workers were clocking-off, Ueki would volunteer for overtime to earn extra money for his daughter's up-coming wedding. At one point, Shōta momentarily imagined himself in the future as Ueki, the older man's tired profile and dirty uniform transformed into Shōta's own. The premonition horrified Shōta, who tried hard to deny its predictive power.

> Lives that follow railway tracks – I wonder, will I someday be like him?

No! I am different. I am absolutely different! (TBD vol. 1, p. 62)

Shōta's hatred for the monotonous work builds, until one day, having drunk too much at the dormitory caretaker's birthday party, he abused his colleagues, shouting out:

> I might be constructing sideboards with you now, but mark my words, Shōta Miyakawa will go to Italy at the age of twenty-three and ten years after that will be the Andrea Branzi of Japan![3] Maybe you don't understand my dream. You're only high school graduates and manual workers. In the end, we're just cogs in the machinery of the assembly-line. (TBDf)

Shōta's words aggravated his colleagues. The dormitory leader gently remonstrates Shōta, but Shōta responds by mocking and teasing him. Eventually Shigeo becomes very angry and forces Shōta from the pub. Unsteady on his feet, Shōta falls down on the roadside, murmuring, 'No one understands me'. Miyuki comes out of the pub and runs after him, his only companion.

In a later scene, Shōta meets Satoshi, a guitarist and singer in a popular band called 'The Boobies'. Satoshi had worked at Tsurumoku a few years earlier and had lived with Shigeo in the room that Shōta now occupied. Satoshi had also been Miyuki's lover. Then one day Satoshi suddenly declared, 'I'm pulling the plug on this worthless life as a salaried worker. I'm going to pursue my dream'. He quit his job, left Miyuki, and set out on the road to stardom.

Later, Shōta and Shigeo attended a Boobies concert and after the show, Satoshi explained to Shōta why he had quit his job and decided to make a living from his music.

> Satoshi: 'I've always wanted to get ahead in life and dreamed of making a living with my guitar. But I'm just a high school graduate, so it's not worth working at Tsurumoku. So I just decided I had to hunt for my treasure.'
> Shōta: 'Treasure?'
> Satoshi: 'Yes, my own treasure! After a while you realize life as a salaried worker is like walking on a paved, straight road. As long as you walk there you're safe, but you're also bored and boring.
> Life is too short to be dull. I figure that as long as we're born into this world we might as well explore it a bit, deviate from

the straight and narrow road – take a risk! The alternate routes, of course, carry dangers. Horrible beasts lie in wait for you. You might be found dead on the road. But if you don't go you'll never find your treasure. When you find the treasure, then you'll realize your purpose for being born. Since I'm living a life, I might as well make it a rewarding one!' (TBD vol. 2, p. 96–97)

Shōta was greatly influenced by Satoshi's words and example. Satoshi had followed his desires, quit his monotonous job and achieved his dream through the force of his own will. Shōta's dream was different, but the issues were the same. Satoshi's example gave him hope, something to follow, to aim for.

For obvious reasons, Miyuki's feelings towards Satoshi were more mixed. While in public she feigned indifference, in the privacy of her bedroom she still had a photo of the two of them together and kept a scrapbook of magazine clippings that traced his rise to fame. One day Miyuki asked Shōta, 'Can you kill Satoshi?' She pretended it was a joke, but on some level he suspected that she was serious.

Enduring monotonous labor

Despite Satoshi's inspiration, the reality of the life confronting Shōta was as grim as ever. Everyday he woke up to face another shift of monotonous labor. One time, when he tipped over the handcart and damaged some parts, he was bawled out by his superior. Subsequently, in spite of himself, Shōta spoke straight from his heart to Ueki.

> Shōta: 'Well, Mr Ueki, do you enjoy your present job?'
> Ueki: 'What?'
> Shōta: 'I do the same job on the assembly line, day in, day out. I don't feel like I am making furniture, it doesn't feel real. It doesn't motivate me to work. We're just numbers in this factory, aren't we? I'm number 2360. I feel like a cog in the machine.'
> Ueki: 'It may be true. You are still young, your future is still full of possibilities. Live a way of life that you believe in, so you don't regret your life. But you know, if even one cog is missing, the machine won't work. Don't forget, even the cog can have pride.' (TBD vol. 2, pp.23–25)

Shōta's words point to the essential problems of the monotonous labor inherent in mass production processes. Mass producing furniture involves a series of manufacturing processes: planning, design, producing parts, assembling them, then giving the completed item a finish. For reasons of 'efficiency', this complex series of tasks can be and is separated and broken down into simpler tasks that are assigned to different, isolated individuals. It was as one of these isolated individuals, a mere cog condemned to the relentless repetition of meaningless tasks in an inhuman machine, that Shōta lamented that his work was just a continuous 'repetition of the same simple process'.

As we discussed in chapter 3, Braverman observed that the relationship between the conception of a task and its execution is one of the qualities that differentiates humans from other animals. Yet, integral to the division of labor in modern manufacturing processes lies the fact that the conception and execution of tasks are separated. 'The conception must still precede and govern execution, but the idea as conceived by one may be executed by another. The driving force of labor remains human consciousness, but the unity between the two may be broken in the individual and reasserted in the group, the workshop, the community, the society as a whole' (Braverman 1974: 35).

When the execution of labor is separated from its conception, the work ceases to belong to the worker and, as such, becomes alienated labor. It is for this reason that Shōta doesn't feel like he is making furniture, that 'it doesn't feel real'. Having no part in the conception of his own labor process, he doesn't feel motivated by it.

There is a fundamental line dividing workers who are engaged in the conception of labour and those employed for their labor to execute the conceptions of others.

> A necessary consequence of the separation of conception and execution is that the labor process is now divided between separate sites and separate bodies of workers. In one location, the physical processes of production are executed. In another are concentrated the design, planning, calculation, and record-keeping, so that conception is concentrated, insofar as possible, in ever more limited groups within management or closely associated with it. (Braverman 1974: 86–7)

We have called the group of workers who are engaged in labor related to the conception of production tasks the new-middle class, and the group of workers employed to physically execute productive tasks as the working class. Viewed this way, Shōta's agony can be understood to result from his new-middle class dream of being an interior designer being frustrated by his entrapment in a working class job.

In one sense, Ueki's reply to Shōta's question is brilliant. Admitting that their work is monotonous and worthless and understanding Shōta's desire to find more engaging work, Ueki nonetheless insists that this monotonous work is irreplaceable and important. This response is valid, but also deceptive. While it is true that if one cog is missing the machine will cease to function, this doesn't make monotonous work any more worthwhile or painless. And for the machine to keep running, the 'broken' cog can easily be replaced with a new one. In spite of this, Ueki recognizes a value to monotonous labor when he says that 'even the cog can have pride'. This type of statement is a reflection of the dominant ideology, affirming a manufacturing system that enforces alienated, monotonous labor on many workers who are discriminated against on academic grounds and are condemned to this type of work. While Shōta did not concur with Ueki's opinion, he had no response, either.

Management of private life and QC activities

Shōta's co-workers in 'Tsurumoku Bachelor Dormitory' tried to adapt to their monotonous tasks in many different ways. For example, Yazaki, who was one year junior to Shōta, was arrogant and had a bad attitude about work. He refused to follow his supervisors' instructions. When the company organized a function for new employees, he left early, complaining that the party was boring and that he disliked socializing. But he was always friendly to the girls, offering them rides in the car that he bought on loan immediately after joining Tsurumoku. One day when Yazaki was being cautioned by a more senior worker about his attitude, they started to quarrel and Yazaki struck the other. Shōta intervened with an angry look, restraining Yazaki, who said:

> We are only factory workers! I don't have expectations or hopes about my future, that's why I enjoy my life now, as it is! I know what my salary

will be in ten years time. My retirement benefits are fixed. As soon as I got the job at this company I could see my life ahead, couldn't I! So we'd better take it easy in life. Take it easy at work, get paid, enjoy ourselves – that way, life's more fun. (TBD vol. 5, p. 136)

Yazaki's attitude to life reflects a form of privatism. In this context, privatism means a pattern of behavior in which people abandon any hope of self-realization in the productive or public domain and seek to recover their sense of self and self-worth in the private realm (Tanaka 1974). Hence, their private life takes precedence over all else and their labor is considered no more than a necessary means to obtaining the income required to sustain their private activities. Seen as a necessary evil, labor must be endured, but the worker can try to make it as easy to endure as possible. This kind of privatism gives rise to two prevailing attitudes: one, a 'negative view of labor' which sees workers restrict their mental and physical exertion as much as possible; the other, an 'individualism' that results in workers not caring about their colleagues (Kumazawa 1996). Even though Shōta was angered by Yazaki's attitude, he could not deny its validity because he was also tempted to retreat into privatism. Kyōsuke also revealed himself to have some sympathy for Yazaki when he responds to Shōta's reflection:

> Shōta: 'I was shocked when Yazaki said, "I enjoy my present life because I can see my future". I found I was living this kind of life before I knew what was happening.'
> Kyōsuke: 'As I became older I came to know my limitations and I began to realize that my dream would not be fulfilled. It's a sad life, but it's the same for everyone. That's why I decided that it's not a bad idea to enjoy "my present life".'
> (TBD vol. 5, p. 142)

Yazaki's character went through a number of testing events that, while they didn't alter his view of life, did enable him to reconcile with Shōta and to more successfully conform to the demands of his work place. Nevertheless, for Shōta, Yazaki continued to represent an alternative life choice.

Privatism, the 'negative view of labor' and the 'individualism' created by alienated labor processes, inevitably result in workers having low motivation and therefore increased inefficiency. Tsurumoku, however, is vigorous in its efforts to control such discontent and has implemented various mechanisms to control the workers' behaviors and increase their motivation and work commitment.

The bachelor dormitory is one such mechanism. Here new employees share rooms with more senior employees who act as advisers, listening to their problems and, when necessary, warning them about bad working attitudes. The quarrel between Yazaki and one of the senior employees occurred in the dormitory. From Yazaki's perspective, we might understand his displeasure at being criticized about his work attitude during non-working hours. In a sense, the public domain had invaded his highly treasured private realm. The dormitory organized various events, such as a welcoming party for new employees and a trip to a hot-spring resort. Every morning in the courtyard there was a morning roll call at 7:30. The female dormitory had an evening roll call too. When individuals violated dormitory regulations they were punished by, for example, being confined to the dormitory. In these and other ways, the bachelor dormitory operates as a system for controlling workers' lives, tracking their movements and 'educating' them about the company's prescribed attitudes and behaviors.

'Tsurumoku Bachelor Dormitory's' depiction of dormitory life appears to be fairly accurate, especially when compared to the regulations for the bachelor dormitory of NK Store, which state:

- Room assignments are decided by the company based on the occupant's request and the contents of the work;
- Occupants will rise at 6am. Bedtime is 11pm;
- In general and on principle, meetings with visitors will take place at an appointed location;
- When the company organizes events such as training sessions and recreation activity, etc., boarders will be notified of the planning and method in advance. Boarders are expected to participate in these events as much as possible.

Similar rules and regulations at the MN Industry dormitory include a timetable outlining three meal times, the closing time of the dormitory, the bedtime and a time for putting out the lights. Additional rules and regulations at MN Industry were expressed in a variety of edicts such as:

- Please strictly observe the closing time of the dormitory in order not to hinder the following day's work;
- Please clearly indicate on the name board whether you are in or out of the dormitory;
- You may not drink alcohol for reasons of health and the maintenance of moral order;
- Please occasionally air bedding in the sun. Wash underclothing frequently. Maintain a habit of wearing clean clothes. (Oka 1986)

As these rules and regulations suggest, employer provided accommodation facilities are often designed to control a workforce by depriving boarders the freedom of an individual, private life. It is in recognition of this that International Labor Organization Recommendation No. 115 indicates that 'it is generally not desirable that employers should provide housing for their workers directly, with the exception of cases in which circumstances necessitate'. Section 94 of the Japanese Labor Standards Act says, 'Employers cannot invade the freedom of the private life of the workers who board at the attached boarding facilities of the corporation'. In practice, though, a worker's right to a private life is not protected. Even when company houses are independent dwellings, the occupants' private lives are often infringed upon by company regulations. For further discussion of this phenomena, see Kinoshita's *Corporate War among Wives* (1988), which clearly documents the excessive efforts some companies will go to in order to control their workers.

Let us now turn our attention to QC circle activities. The increased emphasis on the division of labor and the simplification of labor tasks which took hold in the 1960s in the wake of technological innovations regarding equipment, brought with it a new type of labor alienation. Following these developments in Europe and America there was an increase in workplace unrest, frequent wildcat strikes, and a general rise in union militancy. In response to this perceived 'crisis', management introduced a preventive detection method known as QC circle activity (Kumazawa 1996).

QC circle activities have become widespread since the late 1960s. Tsurumoku is not exceptional. Four months after Shōta began working for the company, he was asked by a senior boarder to participate in the QC competition. New employees from each circle represent their circles by preparing and making presentations about quality improvements in their area. The winner selected by the management judges is rewarded with a position in the QC division office, and a 100,000 yen prize. The workers who joined Tsurumoku at the same time as Shōta were very enthusiastic about preparing their presentations and speeches. Of course, preparations for this event were to be made during non-working hours. As with other companies, it is unlikely that participation in QC activity at Tsurumoku was officially compulsory, but it was effectively compulsory because of the importance placed on it in the supposedly meritocratic process of corporate performance evaluation of employees. In many cases the aim of QC programs and the proposals outlined in presentations such as these is to improve productivity through speeding-up the labor processes. Workers sacrifice their precious leisure time in order to advance the corporation's productivity, and in doing so become more enculturated in and committed to the company.

On the day of the QC presentations, Shōta's Tsurumoku contemporaries delivered fervent speeches in their attempts at victory. Meanwhile, Shōta remained a reluctant participant and had trouble deciding on what to say in his speech. Unsurprisingly, he gave a poor performance. While his peers' were rewarded by passing probation or receiving trial appointments, Shōta's QC presentation remained unrecognized. More isolated than ever, he became disheartened. His experience of QC activities is not atypical; while the enforced 'spontaneity' may indeed arouse a spirit of competition amongst the workforce, almost inevitably, some workers remain disaffected; and in compulsory competitions, the disaffected are almost always cast as losers.

Adaptation to/departure from the working class

Some boarders at Tsurumoku did choose different career paths and leave the company. Kyōsuke Sugimoto is a good example to begin with. Kyōsuke met Reiko Shiratorizawa, the only daughter of a company president, in Roppongi where he had gone to pick up a girl. Kyōsuke initially disliked Reiko, a plain woman, but he continued to go out with her in the hope that one day he would acquire her father's company. Eventually he fell in love with her. A playboy with a dignified presence, Kyōsuke knew about restaurants and was assured in his dealings with women. When Reiko was given a restaurant to manage for the family business,

Kyōsuke carried out its renovations, establishing a good reputation for himself in the process. Reiko intended to expand the business, and asked Kyōsuke to join her father's company in a high paid position, assuming, of course, that he would soon become a son-in-law in the Shiratorizawa family. Reiko's parents recognized his ability and presumably welcomed him into the family. Kyōsuke felt like he was walking on air for a while, but gradually his doubts began to grow. Did he really want to take over Reiko's family's company and be forever dependent upon her goodwill? After much agonizing, he decided that he didn't want to become a son-in-law, taken into Reiko's family, but instead had Reiko's name entered in his family register by marriage. Having done this he decided that what he really wanted to do was to run a small coffee shop with his new wife.[4]

Another example of someone who escapes Tsurumoku in order to pursue a different life is the former senior boarder, Tsujioka. One day while visiting his old bachelor dormitory, he explained that he had succeeded his father in running the family noodle (Ramen) shop. Shōta, Shigeo and Kyōsuke accepted his invitation to visit the noodle shop and went there the following day. During their visit, Tsujioka told them the story of how he came to run the shop.

> When I was little, I despised my father for running a small noodle shop. I thought I would start something big. But I recently realized that the noodles he cooks are delicious. He's been making, cooking and selling his noodles for years and years. He's a professional noodle cook. His long experience means he cooks delicious noodles. I recently began to think that such a father is worth imitating. I'm nowhere near as good a noodle cook as my father, but someday I'll cook noodles even more delicious than his. I'll build up the best noodle shop in Japan. What do you think of my dream? Do you think it's big enough? (TBD vol. 7, p. 124)

Similarly, Hajime Hirata, one year junior to Shōta, was expected to succeed his father in the family business; in Hajime's case, an apple orchard in Aomori. Hajime's childhood dream was to become a doctor, but presumably he abandoned such hopes when faced with the reality of his poor academic record. His longing to live in Tokyo, however, remained undiminished. When asked about his motive for entering Tsurumoku, without hesitation he said, 'I wanted to test myself in a large city, in Tokyo'. But born clumsy, he always made mistakes in his work and caused trouble for Shōta and his colleagues. It appears that he may have been failing the 'test'.

One day Michiko, Hajime's girlfriend from Aomori, came to see him in Tokyo. When they met, Michiko told him that his father had broken down from overwork and was now in hospital. Hajime's father hadn't told him about his hospitalization because he didn't want to worry him. And in a sense he was right, because once Hajime heard the news he was worried and immediately returned home. Upon his arrival, his father chastised him, saying, 'You shouldn't come back home for a matter such as this'. Back in Tokyo, Hajime told Shōta:

> My father has an extraordinary artisan spirit. He insists on never using agricultural chemicals and that way produces the best, most natural apples. I deserve to be called a foolish man. I was an only child and was pampered. I said I would be successful in Tokyo, which was untrue. I am just a factory worker and spend my days in meaningless life. And yet my father was so concerned to not disturb his son's important work that he didn't even tell me he was in hospital. The apples he produces really are delicious. (TBD vol. 7, pp. 128–30)

After a while, Hajime resigned from Tsurumoku and returned to Aomori to help run the family's apple orchard. When the day of his departure finally came, he was too shy to speak directly to his work colleagues, so recorded a message for them on video.

> After long consideration, I have finally decided to succeed my father in running the family's apple orchard. While some of you might laugh at me for fleeing Tokyo, I now feel that this is my best chance of leading a meaningful life. I am determined to make the apples from our orchard the best in Japan. (TBD vol. 7, pp. 182–3)

Michiko was at the station to meet Hajime when he arrived in his hometown. Smiling, she held his hand, and they went home together.

Hajime's story is not unusual. In fact, manual workers leaving the companies they work for to succeed in their fathers' businesses is one of the more common forms of intragenerational mobility. According to the 1995 SSM Survey, 16.6% of men whose first job is in manual labor later became self-employed (this includes becoming farmers). However, if their fathers were self-employed, this goes up to 23.7%. Manual workers with a family background in self-employment or farming seem more likely to embrace this as an ideal strong enough to motivate them to escape their manual work and venture into self-employment. In this way, the career paths of Kyōsuke, Hajime and Tsujioka are representative of many manual workers. The story is very different for those who have a family background in self-employment but whose first employment was non-manual labor. For men whose first job was as either a clerical worker or as a professional, only 12.2% and 14.1% respectively later became self-employed (including farmers), only about half as many as manual laborers on the whole. This suggests that non-manual workers, or the new-middle class, have little desire to escape from their present class position.

On the other hand, the path Shigeo chose was to build a happy home as an ordinary factory worker. He said, 'I am not brave enough to venture out like Kyōsuke or Satoshi; plus, I don't have the necessary abilities.' Shigeo held to the conventional dream of being promoted, and was diligently preparing himself for an examination for foreman. It is a company rule that boarders must leave the bachelor dormitory upon reaching the age of 30. Shigeo, who was quickly approaching that mark, searched desperately for an apartment appropriate to his salary. Later on, he started to cohabit with Akemi Nozawa, a naïve female factory worker who he had once rescued from being sexually harassed and then pushed towards resignation by her superiors .

> Shigeo: 'Can you cook my breakfast?'
> Akemi: 'What are you talking about? I cooked the breakfast you're eating now.'
> Shigeo: 'Well, you know I don't mean this.'
> Akemi: 'What then? Speak up if you have something to say!'
> Shigeo: 'Can you wash my underpants? Shall we lie in the same grave? Do you want to change your family name?'
> Akemi: 'Well, what do you mean?'
> Shigeo: 'I'm asking you to marry me.'
> ...
> Akemi: 'Of course, I'll marry you, but you have to make me happy.'
> (TBD vol. 11, pp. 189–91)

Akemi, with a little tear in her eyes, wore a smile on her face which she had never before shown to anyone. Shigeo's conception of marriage is conventional; his wife will do the domestic chores, change her family name and, in death, they will both lie in the same grave. Shigeo's hopes are mediocre and do not extend beyond this traditional image of the happy home. Fortunately, Akemi is the same, her expectation being simply that husbands must make their wives happy.

Before long Akemi quits her job and has a baby. Graphing women's employment rates in Japan against their age typically produces an M-type distribution. That is, there is a high peak in their employment rate immediately after they leave school (18–25 years) which drops away (from 25–35 years) as they quit work to have babies and raise their toddlers. Then, as children become older and spend more time at school, the rate begins to peak again as more women return to the workforce, only to begin to drop away again in their fifties when they begin to retire. According to the 1995 SSM Survey, the M-curve was particularly pronounced amongst women who were employees at the first job and married to male manual workers. At the age of twenty 93.2% of these women were employed, dropping dramatically to 57.2% at the age of twenty-five and continuing down to a 43.3% employment rate at the age of thirty years. The rate then begins to rise again, reaching 49.7% at age thirty-five and 60.4% at age forty, the level at which it stabilizes for about ten years before beginning to drop again with retirement. Chances are therefore very high that Akemi will re-enter the workforce in order to help financially support her family, but her new work is most likely to be part-time and low paid. Most of the family's income will be provided by Shigeo, who will undoubtedly continue to work in the factory to support his beloved wife and future child. Work thus becomes more meaningful; it becomes a means of providing for the family. The alienation and distress of long hours of monotonous labor are compensated by the smiles of a loving family. Thus, to some extent, the family serves as a governing mechanism in the interests of large corporations.

Shōta's two paths

Let us return to Shōta's life story. Shōta was facing two major decisions which would determine the direction of his life: he had to decide whether to marry Miyuki or Tomomi, and whether he would remain a factory worker or follow his dream to becoming an interior designer. In fact, these two options were closely related in several ways.

Born in Nagoya, Miyuki's father was a front-line newspaper journalist, and her mother had passed away. She graduated from one of the most prestigious private high schools, which automatically guaranteed her entrance into university.[5] But, perhaps in rebellion against her father, who she felt had betrayed her mother by not being present at her deathbed, Miyuki rejected the offered university place. Instead, she joined the Tsurumoku company. Miyuki was a beautiful, good-natured person with refined taste in fashion. She was often courted by university graduates working for the company. And her former boyfriend was Satoshi, who had abandoned the factory to successfully follow his dream. All of these factors are indicators that if Shōta weres to marry Miyuki he would not be able to remain a humble factory worker, but rather would have to secure a position commensurate with Miyuki's expectations and her family's high social standing.[6] Miyuki said as much one night when, half-drunk, Shōta climbed through the window of her room in the women's dormitory.

> Miyuki: 'Satoshi was a nauseous man, but he didn't bury himself at Tsurumoku. He made a career for himself. He's different to those who grumble when they've been drinking but can't bring themselves to leave the company.'
> Shōta: 'Leaving the company isn't necessarily a solution, is it?'
> Miyuki: 'What happened to your dream of becoming a designer? You talk about these things, but you never try to make them happen. Am I wrong? If you want to go to Italy, you should go. I'd be happy to send you off.' (TBDf)

But Shōta knows that this would not be an easy path to take. In the 1995 SSM Survey, of the total sample, 790 of the male workers' first job after leaving school had been in manual labor; 540 of these were still employed in manual labor at the time of the survey. Of those who had changed occupations, seventy-four were performing clerical work, fifty-nine had made their way into sales work, and only twenty had found work in a profession. The professional work categories breakdown as follows: construction and civil engineering sectors (six workers), mechanical, electrical and chemical engineering sectors (five workers), the legal sector, certified public accounting, licensed tax accounting, elementary school teaching, high school teaching, religious services, journalism and editing (one each), etc. Hence, while a manual laborer's advancement to the professional sector is not impossible, it is certainly exceptional. This is well illustrated in the two different versions of the 'Tsurumoku Bachelor Dormitory'.

Note that in what follows, 'Shōta A' refers to the comic strip character, while 'Shōta B' refers to the same character in the film version of the story.)

One day Hisako Tsuruya, a niece of the company president, assumed a position as a factory manager at Tsurumoku. This, it turns out, decides Shōta A's fate. Hisako was a graduate of the University of Tokyo and had studied furniture making in West Germany. Returning to her uncle's company, she assumed an active role in the planning, manufacturing and sales sections of Tsurumoku. In recognition of her abilities, Hisako was appointed manager of the factory where Shōta worked. It had been under-performing for some time. Her first initiative was to rearrange the machine layout. We don't know in detail what type of machine layout she adopted, but can safely assume that it was along the lines of the Toyota-style of production management systems. There is no doubt that the adoption of this new process/layout helped to reduce the number of parts in stock and accelerate the transportation of parts between sections. In the process, both the number of tasks assigned to each factory worker increased and the number of times that each task had to be repeated. The workload for Shōta and his colleagues increased by thirty percent, lifting production from 180 to 230 units per day. Overtime increased sharply. The increased stress and long working hours took their toll as workers increasingly fell ill or were injured from overwork. Michiru Hikari, who began with the company at the same time as Shōta, was one of those who became rundown from overwork. Visiting Michiru in hospital, Shōta reluctantly admitted that the changes to the production process were a problem; the new plant layout did not take workers' physical limits into account. Michiru answered:

> It can't be helped. Even if we lodged a complaint, the company managers wouldn't listen; they were the ones who changed the layout in the first place. We're just ordinary factory workers, after all. (TBD vol. 3, p. 92)

In her continuing quest to maximize the efficiency of her workforce, Hisako introduced various company initiatives that incrementally increased the management's interference in the private lives of its workers. Amongst these was the imposition of a ban on consuming alcohol in the bachelor's dormitory. Soon after this rule came into effect, Kyōsuke asked Shōta to go into town drinking with him. On his way home, under the influence, Shōta decides to join the union movement.

> The factory manager can go to hell! Give us back our freedom! I have an idea, I'm going to join the union. It's the only way we can defeat this dictator. Let's start a union rally now! Let's sing our union song; all together now! (TBD vol. 3, pp. 99–100)

The factory manager, however, continued to cleverly devise new ways of harnessing the worker's competitive energies and directing them towards the company's productivity targets. In one of her more successful schemes – at least of the ones that concern our protagonist – Hisako invited the factory workers to enter a furniture design contest. Shōta, of course, was very keen. In contrast to his disinterest in the QC competition, this time he became totally involved. He bought books on furniture and furniture making and studied them carefully. Clumsily at first, he began to draw his own furniture designs. Miyuki cheered and encouraged him in his new venture.

> Shōta: 'Now's my chance to prove myself really capable, so I can stand up to the factory manager! If I stuff this up, I might as well remain silent! I'm going to design furniture so excellent that it leaves her speechless and proves to her that even an ordinary factory worker can do this!'
> Miyuki: 'It's such a brilliant idea. Go for it! I'll support you all the way.' (TBD vol. 3, p. 111)

Miyuki was true to her word. She encouraged Shōta when he became discouraged. She made his lunch so he could keep working on his designs, even on his days off. While ambitious for Shōta, Miyuki did not see herself as a contestant in the design competition. In fact, she doesn't appear to have been personally competitive at all. When asked to do some new task by her superiors, she always said, in a confused way, 'Am I supposed to do this?' No, she didn't want to compete; but she was very happy to act like a newly wedded wife and prepare Shōta's toy-like lunch box.

This lack of personal ambition was not surprising given that in Tsurumoku women were not invited to give QC presentations or to take examinations for promotion to foreman roles (TBD vol. 2, p. 159 and TBD vol. 7, p. 62). The only exception to this rule was Hisako Tsuruya, the factory manager, but she was a member of the company's founding family, one of the super-elite. Thus Tsurumoku provided no stimulation for women's ambition, nor any possible outlets for it – except, perhaps, to assist someone else fulfill their dreams.

Amazingly, Shōta's design won the contest, which brought him to the attention of Yamamoto, an exclusive Paris-based designer for Tsurumoku who happened to be in Japan at the time. Yamamoto was apparently quite impressed with Shōta's designs and undertook to re-draw Shōta's crude efforts.

>Hisako: 'I'll display this new product in the coming exhibition. Tsurumoku's really going to push this product, with Shōta Miyakawa as designer! I will make sure this product becomes a hit, I personally guarantee it!'
>Shōta: 'Thank you very, very much. I have done it at last!' (TBD vol. 3, pp. 186–7)

Even though Shōta's design was adopted and his effort highly valued, the original machine layout was not restored and his workload was not reduced. Shōta, though, no longer cared about these issues – he was a furniture designer.

Two years later, at the invitation of Yamamoto, Shōta left for Paris. One year after that his ability was truly recognized when, having passed his probation period, he was officially employed at Yamamoto's studio. Visiting the bachelor dormitory, he met with Miyuki.

>Miyuki: 'How come you're back all of a sudden?'
>Shōta: 'Well, I came to pick up one thing that I left behind...'
>Miyuki: 'One thing left behind?'
>Shōta: 'A very, very important thing...'
>Miyuki: 'I see...' (TBD vol. 11, pp. 199–201)

We are left to assume that Shōta and Miyuki will begin a newly married life in Paris. Then, one day they'll come back to Japan, by which time Shōta will have become one of Tsurumoku's exclusive designers.

So, what has changed? Shōta has successfully escaped from the working class to the new-middle class. Miyuki, his constant supporter, has probably also escaped to become a full-time, middle class housewife. Thus, the story has a happy ending for both Shōta A and Miyuki.

Kyōsuke, Tsujioka and Hajime probably make successful careers in their own ways as self-employed workers and farmers. Thus they are successful in escaping from the laboring class to the old-middle class. However Reiko, who followed Kyōsuke, dared to descend from the capitalist class to the old-middle class. Thus our fictional narrative reproduces a common misunderstanding, which even social scientists are guilty of, wherein a woman's class position continues to be determined, first on the basis of her father's class, then by the class of her husband.

What then has not changed? The Tsurumoku factory continues to produce furniture, employing a new wave of graduates who continually arise to replace the older workers who have made other career choices. The new machine layout remains, increasing and intensifying the monotonous workload. Ueki and Shigeo are probably still there, putting on a brave front, saying, 'the cog can have pride', and diligently enduring the monotony of their daily tasks in order to support their families. Yazaki will continue to do the minimum required of him while he searches for meaning and self-worth in his private life. Chances are high that this will eventually lead to the creation of a conventional home life. The differences between Ueki, Shigeo and Yazaki are minor. Many surveys reveal a strong tendency for manual workers to seek fulfillment in the private domain, outside of work, and that activities in that domain tend to change from leisure to family with age. When Yazaki is older and has married and had children, it is quite likely that he will work overtime and even take an examination for promotion. If he should ever manage a promotion to the foreman level, he will feel that, to some extent, his job has become more attractive.

What happened then to Shōta B? Neither Hisako Tsuruya nor Yamamoto intervened in Shōta B's life. Instead, the message, 'the cog can have pride', was engraved on his mind. Knowing Miyuki's complicated feelings towards Satoshi, Shōta B visited Satoshi backstage one night and said:

> Shōta: 'Miyuki still loves you, even today. I feel sorry for her in this way. Please go back to her.'
> Satoshi: 'Is this what you want to say? Get out!'
> Shōta: 'How come you are not serious with Miyuki?'
> Satoshi: 'Don't you understand? It's none of your business. Why must you interfere? Leave, now.'...
> Shōta: 'To tell the truth, I'm here to kill you. Miyuki asked me to.' (TBDf)

Shōta took a knife from the table in front of him and pointed it at Satoshi. As the two of them grapple with each other, Shōta is seized by Satoshi's security staff, who rush in just in time.

The next morning, accompanied by Shigeo and Kyōsuke, Shōta emerged from the police station and returned to the bachelor dormitory. Standing on the dormitory roof top, Shōta is disturbed by Miyuki who suddenly appears and cheerfully calls out, 'Good morning'. Shōta then spoke his mind.

> Shōta: 'Do you know that the cog can have pride?'
> Miyuki: 'What do you mean?'
> Shōta: 'Satoshi told me that unless you leave the well trodden path you can never find the treasure. But I'm wondering whether I can make a treasure rather than trying to find one. Do you think that's wrong? I'm going to work hard at Tsurumoku for a bit longer. (TBDf)

Shōta started thinking that he would work as hard as he could in his role as an ordinary factory worker. On his next day off, he visited his home town and dropped-in at Tomomi's house. Upon his arrival, Tomomi ran downstairs and they threw themselves into each other's arms, staying that way for a long time.

Shōta was now determined to follow the path taken by Shigeo and Ueki. He overcomes his childish and impractical dream of becoming a world-famous interior designer and finds dignity in becoming a mature worker who tries to live and work an honest life. Tomomi, after graduating from high school, joined him in Tokyo a few months later. She and Shōta will probably marry soon, and start a family. Isn't this, in its own way, a happy ending?

In the film version, Shōta doesn't escape from the monotony of factory work but instead resigns himself to spending the rest of his working life as a cog in the company's unrelenting machinery. His way of coping is to seek fulfillment in his private, emotional life. While he appears to have choices, the options open to him were few and limited by his particular social structures.

Another path in life

Couldn't Shōta have chosen another path in life? Makoto Kumazawa tells us:

> In sum, one is presented with an "underclass" occupational consciousness, reflecting the pyramidal structure of workplace job assignments; a competitive ethos legitimated by a perceived equality of opportunity; and a traditional aspiration to escape one's class status, intensified by these first two factors. As the life ways and behavior of organized workers in postwar Japan have been molded by these mutually reinforcing social values, they have failed to develop something important: a desire to continue in the status of worker and improve their lives as such. (Kumazawa 1996: 74)

Neither Shōta A nor Shōta B took a path that might attempt to change the class structure. Rather than trying to escape the working class, people like Shōta might try to transform it, so that the execution of their assigned tasks are more closely linked to the conception of them. If this were achieved there might be less need or desire for working class employees to flee into the middle classes, because the distinctions between the two would become increasingly blurred and meaningless.

For instance, Shōta might have suggested that the furniture design contest become a regular rather than a one-off event, and that the workers be given time and money to prepare for it. With regards to the machine layout, he could have argued that the workers' creativity should be a consideration in setting the company's targets; that they not be totally dominated by the goals of efficiency and high productivity This way, both productivity and better working conditions could have coexisted.

Bringing the conception and execution of production tasks closer together might also narrow the gap separating male and female workers. In other words, as the borderline defining the different classes becomes blurred, the gender divides may be more readily breached.

In talking about changing the class structure, we are not necessarily evoking the orthodox dream of a united working class rising up to become the ruling class, the abolition of private property and the eventual establishment of a communist society. Such changes are neither desirable nor attainable.

Shōta is one of us. We could have been Shōta. Shōta could have been us. We all live in and with the problems of the current class structure. Whether we know it or not, we have this in common. And there are reasons to believe that better knowledge of existing class structures might prove useful precursors to any efforts to execute changes to them. For this, we need some imagination and a good class theory.

4 Four Classes: Four Life-worlds

The data: Social Stratification and Sobility Study

We use the Social Stratification and Mobility (SSM) Survey data in this and subsequent chapters to address the theoretical issues under consideration. The survey was initiated in 1955 by a group of researchers headed by Kunio Odaka in the context of rising interest in large-scale surveys and quantitative empirical analysis of social stratification in many advanced countries immediately after World War II. Since the first survey, the SSM has been conducted every decade, interviewing a random sample of Japanese residents aged between 20 and 69 years. The 1995 study was the fifth and most recent.

The SSM Survey inquires about many topics that are essential for studies of social stratification. The key questions in the survey have not been significantly altered since 1955, but new questions have been added over the decades in response to the changing social situation and researchers' identification of new problems. The 1995 survey includes questions pertaining to:

- *Occupation*: present occupation, all occupations that the respondent has taken up since his/her first job (including occupational category, employment status, industrial category, firm size and managerial position), scope of job authority, parents' occupations, spouse's occupations, pathways to getting jobs, the pathway to the present job, occupational prestige and evaluation.
- *Education*: educational achievement, academic record from the respondent's third year of junior high school (9th grade), childhood family environment, experience of extracurricular education to prepare for entrance examinations, parents' educational achievements, spouse's educational achievements, children's educational achievements or the types of schools they

are currently enrolled in, and respondent's attitude to his/her children's education.
- *Family*: sibling order, marital status, family composition, the number and ages of children, and the extent to which household chores are shared.
- *Social life*: leisure activities, and the occupation and social status of the respondent's acquaintances.
- *Assets*: possession of consumer durables, home-ownership, value of real estate owned, value of financial assets, and the value of inherited or donated real estate.
- *Income*: individual income, household income and spouse's income.
- *Social consciousness*: status identification, class identification, perceptions of social justice, views on the sexual division of labor, life satisfaction, value orientations, political consciousness and political party support.

The SSM Survey data has provided the foundation for studies of class and social stratification in Japan for most of the later half of the twentieth century. However, these studies, like most sociological studies in the early postwar years, were androcentrically biased; SSM Surveys included only the male population from 1955 to 1975. Rectifying the distortion, the 1985 survey included a separate survey targeting women in addition to the continuing survey of men. The 1995 survey was the first to cover both men and women within the same sampling frame and using the same questionnaire.

The 1975 and 1995 research included a separate 'prestige survey' to estimate consciousness about occupations and occupational prestige. The 1985 and 1995 studies had questionnaires A and B, which respectively asked different and focused questions in addition to the basic questions common to both. Table 4.1 lists each study's sample size and response rate.

The latest three survey results (1975, 1985 and 1995) have been widely used after coding by the respective research teams. Because the 1955 data set was collected on the basis of three separate samples – metropolitan areas, cities and rural areas – Ken'ichi Tominaga and his group recoded the 1955 data to produce a revised set by re-sampling and adjusting for the relative population size of the three sample groups. The 1965 data was also recoded and a new set produced. Scrutinizing some questionable variables and values, Toshiki Satō and Kaoru Tsuburai recoded it again to produce a

Table 4.1 Structure of SSM Surveys from 1955 to 1995

Year of survey	Survey type	Initial sample	Number of respondents	Response rate (%)
1955	Metropolitan areas	1,500	1,138	75.9
	Cities	1,500	1,230	82.0
	Rural areas	1,500	1,309	87.3
1965		3,000	2,158	71.9
1975	Main survey	4,001	2,724	68.1
	Prestige survey	1,800	1,296	72.0
1985	Questionnaire A	2,030	1,239	61.0
	Questionnaire B	2,030	1,234	60.8
	Women	2,171	1,474	67.9
1995	Questionnaire A	4,032	2,653	65.8
	Questionnaire B	4,032	2,704	67.1
	Prestige survey	1,675	1,214	72.5

corrected data set. We have used the revised data for 1955 and 1965 for this analysis.[1]

In the earlier chapters we discussed the differences between class and status in the context of competing theoretical frameworks. However, Japanese sociologists often use a notion of 'status identification' as a measure of how people identify themselves in terms of a hierarchical social ranking. The SSM Survey uses a five-point scale of status identification, as can be seen in Table 4.2. Similarly the three-class model (**) that the SSM Survey uses is a measure of the respondent's self-identification whereas my four-class model (*) is organized according to the analyst's determination of class location after evaluating the determinate criteria as discussed in our theoretical outline.

Profiles of four classes

The theoretical framework that we have outlined in the preceding chapters includes particular assumptions that are testable against this data, including but certainly not limited to the claims: A person's class location is the location s/he occupies in the economic structure, which determines the type and size of their income, the nature of their work, and the degree of their authority in the workplace at a particular moment. The size and type of a person's income forms the basic framework that defines and limits their life

Four Classes: Four Life-worlds

Table 4.2 Characteristics of four classes as indicated by the 1995 SSM Survey

SSM data categories	Capitalist class	New middle class	Working class	Old middle class
Proportion of the total working population	9.2%	23.5%	45.4%	21.9%
Average age	50.2	41.8	42.8	52.3
Proportion of females	33.1%	21.2%	55.6%	47.0%
Proportion of married	90.5%	78.7%	73.2%	88.1%
Received tertiary education	36.4%	51.9%	15.5%	15.6%
Received only compulsory education	16.2%	4.9%	26.3%	36.3%
Average household income (1000yen)	12,936	8710	6830	8485
Average individual income (1000yen)	7145	5700	2929	3726
Average value of real estate (1000yen)	75,412	26,261	20,009	45,962
Average financial assets (1000yen)	36,578	14,151	9460	20,360
Rate of house ownership	86.7%	74.0%	71.8%	89.4%
Live in company owned dwelling	2.9%	9.4%	3.5%	0.7%
Ownership of consumer durables				
Dish washers	28.0%	13.5%	10.5%	14.6%
Personal computers or word processors	68.3%	68.3%	47.2%	54.5%
Facsimiles	49.9%	15.0%	11.7%	37.2%
Pianos	40.6%	38.7%	21.2%	28.1%
Drawing room sets	63.7%	44.5%	31.0%	45.6%
Sports club memberships	36.0%	10.3%	7.0%	13.4%
Country cottages/summer houses	8.4%	1.9%	0.8%	1.8%
Artistic and antique objects	31.4%	13.3%	7.8%	19.0%
Satisfaction with life				
Satisfied	26.0%	15.8%	17.2%	22.8%
More or less satisfied	44.8%	49.7%	43.2%	40.5%
Status identification				
Upper	3.3%	0.9%	1.1%	1.8%
Upper-middle	47.1%	35.1%	22.0%	29.1%
Lower-middle	39.6%	48.6%	53.0%	47.4%
Upper-lower	7.2%	12.8%	18.1%	16.4%
Lower-lower	2.7%	2.6%	5.8%	5.3%
Class identification**				
Capitalist class	5.8%	2.9%	3.3%	2.8%
Middle class	55.5%	38.2%	21.2%	35.1%
Working class	38.7%	58.9%	75.5%	62.2%
Political party support				
LDP	40.2%	18.3%	17.5%	35.9%
Progressive parties	3.7%	9.2%	10.5%	6.1%
Others	10.5%	9.7%	10.8%	9.5%
No party	45.6%	62.8%	61.2%	48.5%

Note: 'progressive parties' include the Socialist Party of Japan and Japanese Communist Party (cf. note 5 for further discussion of this terminology).

chances. The nature of work and the degree of authority pertaining to it greatly influences the individual's quality of life, affecting the extent and nature of their personal relationships, values, and social consciousness.

Accordingly, the four classes differ from each other not only in the positions they occupy in the economic structure, but also in other quite distinct social characteristics. As we sketch the profiles of the classes' different characteristics, we will attempt to answer: What sort of people actually constitute each class? How is gender distributed across the four classes? How are the different classes distinguishable? and, How different are they from one another in matters of social power and influence?

Capitalist class

The capitalist class is the smallest of the four classes. Almost one-third are women, an unexpectedly high result, explicable by the large number of family workers in small and medium sized enterprises. The average age is 50.2 years, second highest after the old middle class. Marriage is the dominant norm in every class, but even more so amongst the capitalists. They come second to the new middle class in terms of tertiary education qualifications, but have more than three times as many people who have completed only a compulsory education.[2] Thus it is apparent that there are substantial internal variations in the class. Their average household income is the highest of the four classes, indicative of their status as the most economically privileged.[3] They are also the largest owners of assets, with more than one-third of the capitalist class owning real estate valued at more than one hundred million yen and more than ten percent of them owning more than one hundred million yen in financial assets.[4] The rate of home ownership is marginally lower than the old middle class, but the difference is almost negligible once we consider the number in each class who live in company owned housing. And as one might expect, the people in this class own many more durable, high priced consumer goods than the average person in Japan.

Members of the capitalist class reported the highest ratio of the four classes in terms of their satisfaction with life. The one-fifth who reported that their living standard had improved in the past ten years – also the highest of the four classes – suggests that members of this class are more likely to have experienced recent (or continuing) economic success. More than half of this class identified themselves as being either 'upper' or 'upper-middle' status, with relatively few responding to 'upper-lower' or 'lower-lower'. Similarly, the percentage identifying themselves as belonging to either the 'capitalist class' or the 'middle class' are strikingly higher than in any other class. Politically, the capitalist class is overwhelmingly conservative, with two-fifths supporting the Liberal-Democrats (LDP) and a very small minority supporting progressive political parties.[5] In summary, members of the capitalist class are economically privileged, rich in both assets and consumer durables, satisfied with life, and politically conservative.

New middle class

The new middle class accounts for almost one-quarter of the total working population, and is the second largest class, although only slightly larger than the old middle class. Only about one-fifth of the new middle class are women, making it the most male-dominant of the classes. The average age is 41.8 years, the youngest of the classes. More than three-quarters are married, the third highest of the four. The marital status, however, differs according to gender, with more than eighty percent of new middle class men being married, in contrast to only sixty-eight percent of the women. Since the average age of new middle class women is only three years younger than the men, one can assume that there is a relatively large number of single, career women in this class and that a significant proportion of new middle class men are married to women of other classes. More than half of the class is tertiary educated, significantly higher than any other class. While the average household income is the second highest of the four classes, the difference between this average and the first placed capitalist class is considerable. At the same time, there is only a marginal difference between the new middle class and the third placed old middle class on this scale. The average value of real estate owned by members of the new middle class is third of the four classes, with less than one-in-twenty owning property worth more than one hundred million yen. The average value of their financial assets also rank third, with less than one-in-fifty owning more than one hundred million yen in financial assets. Almost three-quarters of the new middle class own their homes, again third of the four, and only marginally higher than the working class, but almost one-tenth of this class live in company-owned housing (including dormitories and official residences), by far the highest of all the classes. This type of 'fringe benefit' constitutes a substantial difference between the new middle class and the working class. The ownership rate of consumer durables is, in most instances, second highest after the capitalist class and, in the cases of personal computers/word processors and pianos the ownership rates are almost as high as those of the capitalist class, perhaps indicating a strong tendency in the new middle class to invest in items that encourage cultural engagement.

Almost two-thirds of this class responded that they were satisfied with their life, next highest to the capitalist class. When broken down further though, we find that half reported being 'more or less satisfied' and only one-seventh claimed to be 'satisfied'. Almost one-third saw themselves as belonging to the upper or upper middle stratum, and slightly over one-third identified themselves as 'middle class'; once again, second only to the capitalist class. Politically, a good majority of the new middle class, almost two-thirds, did not support any particular party. This is the highest response in this category across the four classes and, although twice as many new middle class support the LDP than the progressive parties, they rank second lowest (the working class is lower) in support for the former, and second highest (after the working class) in support for the latter.

In summary, the income level of the new middle class is intermediate, the assets owned are comparatively few, yet the educational standard is very high. The corporate fringe benefits provided to members of this class enable them to enjoy a relatively high standard of living. Despite this, and in contrast to the capitalist class, they are not automatically conservative, appearing instead to be somewhat disaffected in their political sympathies and affiliations.

Working class

The working class is by far the largest of the classes, constituting almost half of the total working population. More than half are women, making it the only class populated by more women than men. This is indicative of the extent of gender inequality in Japan. The average working class age is 42.8 years and less than three-quarters are married, but unlike the new middle class, this rate does not differ greatly between genders. The working class has the lowest rate of tertiary education of all the classes. Despite this and because of the relative youthfulness of this class, three-quarters of the working class have received high school education, which is more than the old middle class. As one would expect, the working class is ranked lowest of the four classes on all economic indicators. The average working class household income is about two-thirds of the averages for the new and the old middle classes. Real estate owned by the working class is, on average, of relatively little value, while almost one-third do not own any property at all. The average value of financial assets for members of the working class is two-thirds of the average for the new middle class. One-eighth of this class own no financial assets. The home ownership rate is unexpectedly high, but the proportions that live in privately rented houses, flats, or public housing are the highest across the four classes. The ownership rate of consumer durables is the lowest in most cases, particularly with items such as dishwashers, personal computers/word processors, faxes, and pianos.

Only three-fifths of the working class report being satisfied with their life, the lowest of the four classes. Status identification is also generally low: less than one-quarter identified as 'upper' and 'upper-middle' status, far below the average proportion of the other three classes. The majority, fully three-quarters, identified themselves as working class. Politically, three-fifths support no political parties; less than one-fifth support the Liberal Democrats (the lowest across the four classes) and more than one-tenth support progressive political parties (the highest of the four classes). In this party political sense, the working class is clearly the most 'progressive' of the classes. This, though, must be balanced with the fact that one-quarter of the working class affirmed the statement that, 'politics is too difficult for me to understand'; again, the highest of the four classes. In general terms, members of the working class lack knowledge about and motivation for participating in politics. On average, they are economically underprivileged and have a low standard of living. Despite this and other dissatisfactions with life, however, they do not typically seek change through political action or involvement.

Old middle class

The old middle class comprises one-fifth of the total working population, a proportion that has been in consistent decline since the end of World War II, primarily due to the reduction in the farming population. In contrast, the proportion of self-employed has remained fairly constant over the same period. As such, the composition of this class has changed; the once dominant farmers are gradually giving way to self-employed traders and industrialists. There are slightly more men than women, but the old middle class is relatively more gender balanced than the other classes. The average age is 52.3 years, the highest of the four classes. More than thirty percent of them are over 60 years old. The old middle class has the second highest marriage rate and the highest proportion of widows and widowers, reflecting the aging population. It is the least formally educated, with more than one-third having only a compulsory education, the highest of the four classes. Few have tertiary education. The average household income is about the same level as the new middle class. The average individual income, however, is much lower than the new middle class, indicating that the household income of this class is supported by a relatively large number of family workers. Nonetheless, they own substantial assets, second only to the capitalist class in both real estate and financial assets. The home ownership rate is the highest of the four classes. Although the old middle class's ownership rate of most consumer durables is third (above the working class), it ranks second behind the capitalist class in terms of owning sports club memberships and artistic and antique objects.

Almost two-thirds of this class expressed satisfaction with their life, the third highest after the capitalist and the new middle class. Broken down, though, the figures reveal that in fact over one-fifth of the old middle class defines itself as 'satisfied', a higher response than the new middle class. The status identification of this class is slightly lower than that of the new middle class. The combined rate of 'upper' and 'upper-middle' identifications was about thirty percent, while self-identification as 'middle class' was slightly higher, but still third highest after the capitalist and the new middle classes. About three-fifths identified themselves as 'working class', second only to actual members of the working class. Politically, constituents of the old middle class are generally conservative, with almost one-third supporting the LDP, second highest after the capitalist class. Only a small minority favor progressive parties.

The old middle class is comparatively asset rich, the members generally engaged in family businesses. Although the average individual income is not large, the old middle class maintains a level of household income comparable to that of the new middle class by employing family members in its small scale enterprises. This enables them to sustain a good standard of living and appears to foster political conservatism.

...

Having established these brief profiles of the four classes, we will now examine the structural differences between them in more detail, focusing on income differentials, nature of work and work consciousness, networks of personal relationships, and leisure activities.

Income differentials

Average income of each class and its relationship to exploitation

Figure 4.1 schematically illustrates the class structure of contemporary Japan and the average income (for individuals, male and female) of each class. In the previous section we discussed household income as an index of the overall standard of living. In this section, however, we will focus on individual income. In terms of the capitalist mode of production, the ranking order of the capitalist class, the new middle class, and the working class is clear-cut. The income of the old middle class lies between the new middle class and the working class.

From the structure of these income differentials, we can state the following about the exploitative relationships between the four classes: (1) The average income of the three classes located within the capitalist mode of production exceeds the average income of the old middle class by about fifteen percent. Given that the old middle class derives its income from simple commodity production, this income differential supports a hypothesis that those engaged in the capitalist mode of production exploit those involved in simple commodity production. (2) There are substantial income differentials between the three classes within the capitalist mode of production. The average income of the capitalist class and the new middle class exceeds the average income of the three classes combined, while the income of the working class falls below this average. This suggests that the capitalist class and the new middle class exploit the working class. We are not saying that the new middle class is

Class Structure in Contemporary Japan

Figure 4.1 Class structure of contemporary Japan and average annual individual income by class

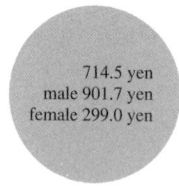

Capitalist class 9.2%

714.5 yen
male 901.7 yen
female 299.0 yen

New middle class 23.5%

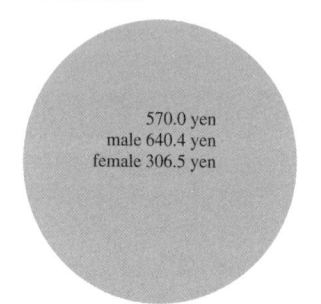

570.0 yen
male 640.4 yen
female 306.5 yen

Old middle class 21.9%

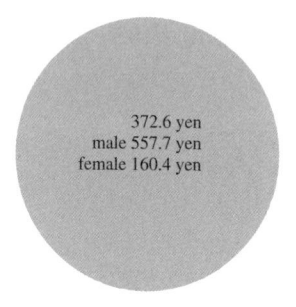

372.6 yen
male 557.7 yen
female 160.4 yen

Working class 45.4%

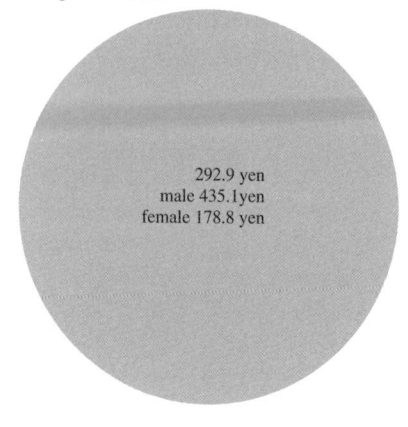

292.9 yen
male 435.1 yen
female 178.8 yen

Capitalist mode of production   78.1%
425.9 yen

Simple commodity production 21.9%
372.6 yen

Average of the total 414.3 yen
(Units: 10,000 yen)

Source: SSM Survey data

uniformly involved in direct exploitation; there are quite large variations in both occupational status and income levels within the new middle class. Nevertheless, it is safe to say that, in general, the new middle class exhibits strong characteristics of an exploiting class and the working class those of an exploited class.

Income differentials between classes and genders

Figure 4.1 indicates that income differentials are greater between genders than between classes. Across all classes, men's incomes are higher than women's. Even the average income of working class men, the lowest of the four classes, is higher than the average income of new middle class women, the highest of the four classes. Although we need to take into consideration that many women are part time workers,[6] this data still describes a situation in which 'men are exploiters and women the exploited'. Having said this, the picture becomes more complex when we acknowledge that the majority of women marry and thereby benefit from their husband's higher income, so that they are both exploited and yet indirectly share in the spoils of exploitation. (Issues concerning household organization and class are discussed in chapter 7.)

The income differential between genders, however, differs depending on the class. The income ratios between males and females by class indicate that new middle class men receive 2.1 times more income than new middle class women, while working class men receive 2.4 times more income than their female counterparts. On the other hand, the gender differential in income is extremely large in the two classes that own the means of production. Men's income in the capitalist class is 3.0 times as large as women's, and old middle class men receive 3.5 times as much as their female counterparts. A detailed examination of women's income in these classes reveals another notable fact. In the capitalist class, 45.2% of women, nearly half of the total, receive an income less than 2.5 million yen (compared to only 5.6% of men). In addition, the combined percentage of women who responded to this question with 'DK' ('Don't Know') and 'NA' ('No Answer'), is abnormally high at 13.0% (compared with 4.3% of male respondents). These tendencies are even more pronounced with women in the old middle class, where 65.6% of women, two-thirds of the total, receive an income less than 2.5 million yen (18.5% of men), 14.1% of women are without any income (0.4% of men), and 13.8% percent of women responded 'DK' or 'NA' to this question (12.3% of men). Almost all of the women without income and who responded 'DK' or 'NA' are family workers. The household income of quite a few of these women exceeds 10 million yen. In other words, many women within the capitalist class and the old middle class are wives, mothers or daughters of proprietors or owners of companies. Despite occupying positions of importance within these enterprises, many of these women receive no or very little direct, individual remuneration for their labors.

Thus, patriarchy largely determines the way income is distributed across genders. Generally speaking, men own the means of production while women (wives, mothers, daughters) work in the enterprises, but men receive the income generated through the women's labor. Hence, in a practical sense, men treat women's labor as their own property. As Wright (1985) accurately observed, it is nothing more than a kind of 'feudal exploitation'. Women are not free from this sort of relationship even when they find a job outside the household. According to a survey conducted by Yoshiaki Yoshida, 72.2% of women from agricultural households who were employed in non-agricultural jobs contributed their entire non-agricultural earnings to the family income pool. Similarly, it is common for young brides to hand over their wages to their mother- or father-in-law and receive a small amount of 'spending money' in return (Yoshida, 1993: 236). The labor of the bride is considered the property of the male head of the household or the household's senior couple. In this way, it is effectively unpaid labor and conforms to standard definitions of feudal exploitation. In short, women in Japan remain generally subordinate to men economically, although the particular forms of subordination vary both across and within classes.

Changes in income differentials

How then have the income differentials between classes changed over time? As previously mentioned, the SSM Survey data provides long-term data only for men's income. Figure 4.2 charts changing trends in male income differentials by class.

Most notable is the fact that working class income levels rose until 1975, but have been in decline ever since. This means that the income differential between the working class and the other classes is expanding. Over the same period, the income of the old middle

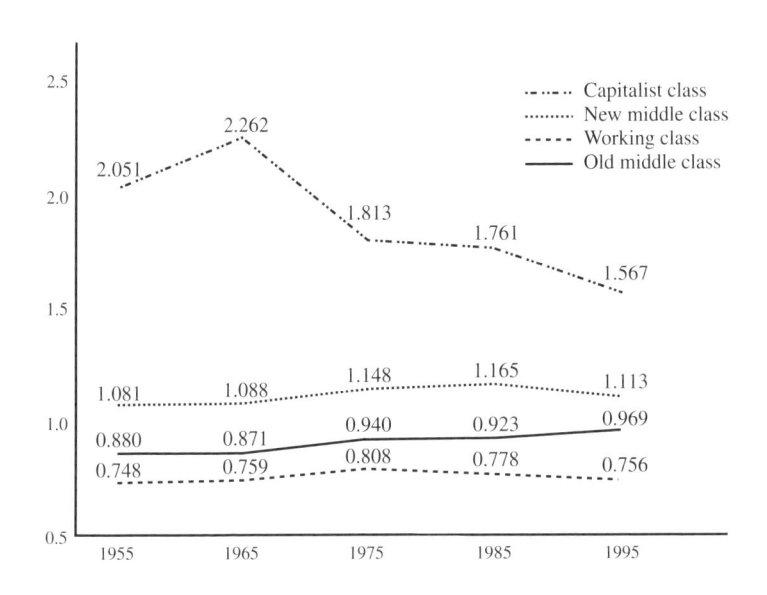

Figure 4.2 Transition of income differentials between classes

```
                              Capitalist class
                              New middle class
          2.262                Working class
                              Old middle class
  2.051
            1.813
                   1.761
                          1.567

                  1.148    1.165
  1.081   1.088                   1.113
  0.880   0.871   0.940   0.923   0.969
  0.748   0.759   0.808   0.778   0.756

  1955    1965    1975    1985    1995
```

Source: SSM Survey data

class has risen since 1965, and by 1995 had reached almost the same level as the average male income for the four classes, which is indexed as 1. The differential between the new middle class and the working class clearly increased from 1975 to 1985. Although the gap shrank slightly in 1995, the overall trend maintains the income differential between the two classes. If we set the income of working class men at 1, the income ratios of new middle class men were 1.44 in 1955, and 1.43, 1.42, 1.50 and 1.47 in the subsequent years of the survey. Since these two classes comprise seventy percent of the total working population, this differential is significant. The income differentials between new middle and working classes are no less significant than the income differentials between the capitalist and working class.

World of work

As Braverman poignantly observed, the labor process differs sharply between the four classes. Following Braverman, a distinction can be made between the 'conception' and 'execution' elements of labor processes. Hence, it is safe to say that the capitalist class is primarily involved with the 'conception' of work, while the working class is engaged in the 'execution' of the process. The new middle class, situated midway between the capitalist and the working classes, participates in both aspects, the balance between the two depending upon the individual's position. Since the old middle class does not generally employ people outside the family, they too tend to be engaged in both the conception and execution of labor processes.

In an attempt to clarify class differences in labor processes, the 1995 SSM Survey included four statements concerning the exercise of work authority. The respondent was to answer either: 'quite applicable', 'more or less applicable', 'not really applicable', and 'not applicable' [7] to the questions:

1 I can determine almost all of the content and the pace of my work.
2 I have the right to be part of the decision-making process regarding changes to the nature of the production and organization of my workplace.
3 My wishes concerning the plan and content of the enterprise are reflected in the decisions made.
4 To a large degree, I decide the content and pace of my subordinates' work.

Figure 4.3 shows the answers to these four statements according to class. The capitalist class responds strongly on all four statements. Around sixty percent answered 'quite applicable' to A, B, and C, and forty percent answered the same for D. Hence, a clear majority of the capitalist class identifies itself as having considerable authority to decide the content and organization of their own work, while two-fifths of them claim to exert control over their subordinates. The old middle class reports even higher levels of authority over the nature of their own undertakings (A, B, and C), although, with fewer subordinates, their responses to statement D were more comparable to the new middle class.

The working class reports the lowest level of workplace authority in response to these four statements, with a particularly notable difference between the working class and the others in response to statements C and D. Only one-fifth of respondents reported 'quite applicable' to A, and very few responded that D (the capacity to exert control over others) was even 'more or less

Four Classes: Four Life-worlds

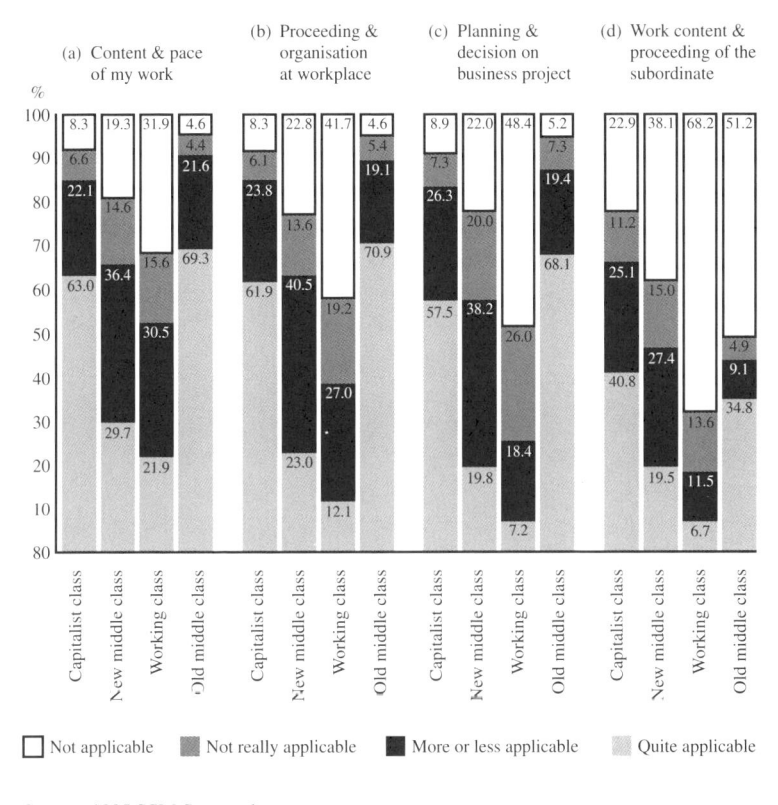

Figure 4.3 Extent of work authority by class

| | (a) Content & pace of my work | (b) Proceeding & organisation at workplace | (c) Planning & decision on business project | (d) Work content & proceeding of the subordinate |

☐ Not applicable   ■ Not really applicable   ■ More or less applicable   ☐ Quite applicable

Source: 1995 SSM Survey data

applicable'. The results indicate that for many workers the content of their labor is totally and unilaterally determined by an employer, supervisor or, increasingly perhaps, a machine.

The new middle class reports an intermediate level of autonomy in their job responsibilities. As indicated by statement D, nearly half of the new middle class report having authority over their subordinates' work. The various respondents to this survey clearly demonstrate that the labor process qualitatively differs between the four classes.

Each class also differs in their prospects and opportunities for promotion. Responses to the question, 'How much prospect is there for promotion in your current workplace?' reveal: 37.1% of the capitalist class reported that there is 'no higher than the current position in the present workplace', and 12.1% responded that the prospect for promotion was 'great'. The perceived prospect for promotion is also quite high for the new middle class, with 14.2% of them believing it to be 'great' and 29.9% thinking there is 'some degree' of possibility. If this proves true, some members of this class will eventually move into the capitalist class. At the other end of the scale, in contrast to the new middle class, only 3.3% of working class respondents reported that their prospect for promotion was 'great', and only 13.7% thought that there was 'some degree' of possible promotion. For the working class, opportunity for promotion, or at least the perception of that opportunity, is very limited; and, as one would expect for the predominantly self-employed old middle class, approximately three-fifths of them reported that there was 'no higher position than the current one'.

These perceived differences in promotional prospects are reflective of other cross-class differences in attitudes towards employment. Following are some of the differences observed:

1. While members of the capitalist and old middle classes try to maintain their current positions and working class people generally tend to be resigned to their modest standard of living, members of the new middle class generally attempt to improve their position in the social hierarchy. This difference appears in the answers to: 'it is more important to retain what one has achieved than to try to gain more' where 33.9% of the old middle class, 27.2% of the capitalist and 24.7% of working class answered 'very applicable' but the new middle class's response on this measure was only 16.2%.

2. Members of the new middle class appear to be under constant pressure to 'improve' their situation. To the statement, 'I am doing well in my everyday life', 43.0% of the capitalist, 36.4% of the working, and 47.1% of the old middle classes answered 'very applicable', but only 27.4% of the new middle class chose this response.

3. Responses to the statement, 'I often sacrifice my home and private life for my work' are remarkably consistent across the capitalist, new middle class, and old middle classes with 40% of each answering 'applicable' (total of 'very applicable' and 'somewhat applicable' answers), in contrast to only 28.5% of working class respondents. These figures are very similar for

both male and female respondents. These results suggest that working class people who perceive little prospect for success (measured as 'career advancement') at work do not sacrifice the quality of their private lives in order to work hard, nor should their employers expect them to.

Networks of personal relationships

Each class exhibits a distinct pattern in the sphere of personal relationships, i.e., the breadth of the network of these relationships. Figure 4.4 graphs the percentages of respondents by class who answered affirmatively to the question, 'Do any of your friends, acquaintances and relatives have the following occupations and/or social positions?' In general, members of the capitalist class have large circles of personal relationships. The percentages of the capitalist class who responded 'yes' to the above question are the highest or near highest for most occupational and social categories, although they have few personal relationships with people in 'agriculture and fisheries'. In particular, they have many more personal relationships with people in socially influential positions than any of the other classes, including 'presidents and executives', 'officers higher than section managers', 'physicians and lawyers', 'members of local government and parliament'. Members of the old middle class rate second on this score, typically having personal relationships with people in all categories except for 'physicians and lawyers'. A high proportion of them also have relationships with 'trade associates and labor union officials' and 'members of local government and parliament'. The new middle class's network of personal relationships is generally smaller, except for contacts with professionals such as 'physicians and lawyers'. As one would expect, the working class has the smallest network of personal relationships with people in positions of power and influence.

Over 60% of people in all four classes have personal relationships with people from the three non-capitalist classes, including 'ordinary salaried men and OL (office ladies)', 'factory workers', and 'retail store keepers and owners of restaurants and cafes'. These position descriptors respectively represent the new middle class, the working class, and the old middle class.[8] Thus, we can say that people of all four classes have personal relationships that extend beyond their own class,[9] but there are huge class differences regarding personal relationships with

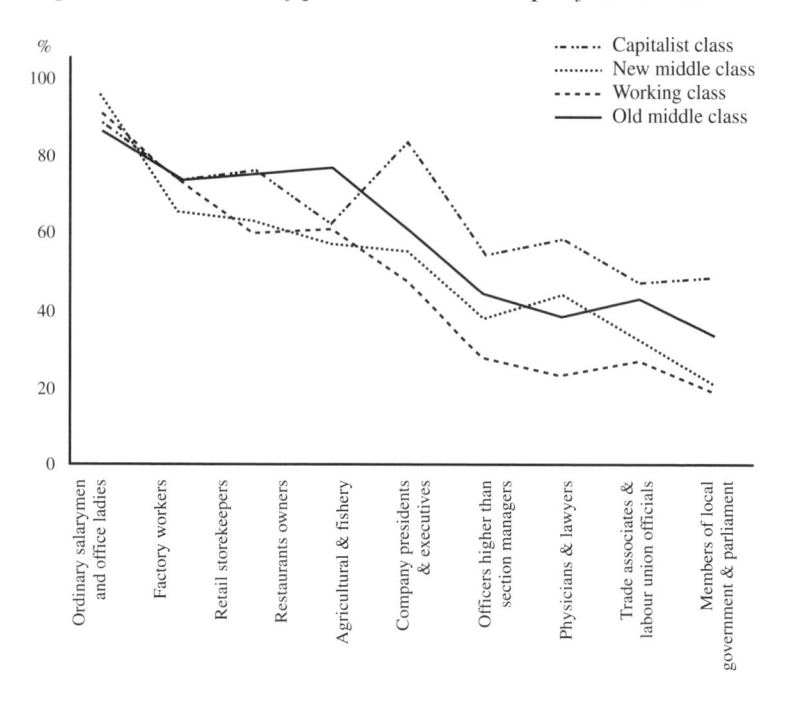

Figure 4.4 Network of personal relationships of each class

Note: Percentage of people who answered 'yes' to the question, 'Have you got any personal relationships with a person of the following occupations?'
Source: 1995 SSM Survey data

people in socially influential positions. The capitalist class is at the apex, suggesting that it maintains its social power and influence through networks of personal connections.

Marxists and other left-wing critics have long argued that the capitalist class is not only the economically dominant class but also a political ruling class. However, this assertion has always run counter to the principles of modern democratic societies. Unlike pre-modern societies, capitalist societies advocate the democratization of political processes. Political rights are in principle equally available to all, and political rule is thus independent of economic control. But Marxists and other left-wing critics have continued to argue that the capitalist class governs politics through various indirect means, without explaining precisely how this occurs. Instead, their arguments have generally proceeded from the assumption that, as Lenin (1917) claimed, 'the state is an organ of class rule'.

Ralph Milliband is one of the few theorists who has attempted to provide empirical foundations to this otherwise ideological assertion. Milliband attempted to demonstrate that pivotal members of the state apparatus (i.e., many politicians and high ranking bureaucrats) originate from the capitalist class and the others who don't have been actively assimilated into the lifestyle and ideology of that class through education and training. Moreover, politicians and senior bureaucrats customarily maintain personal relationships with each other, and often move between these two spheres of political power. In this way, the workings of the nation tend to serve the profit-oriented interests of the capitalist class (Milliband 1969). Likewise, many Japanese analysts have detected similar patterns of association between politicians, bureaucrats and the capitalist class.[10]

Yet, there remain many opponents who argue that networks of personal relationships alone cannot explain the functions of the state and that Milliband and his followers have ignored the fact that other classes are also represented in the state apparatus.[11] However, both sides of the debate agree that networks of personal relationships do influence politics. On the basis of the SSM Survey data, we can examine the personal relationships of capitalists who primarily operate small to medium size enterprises, revealing that close relationships are evident between these members of the capitalist class and members of the Diet. Focusing on the capitalists who own enterprises with thirty or more employees, 67.6% report personal associations with members of local government and/or the parliament. From these figures, it seems reasonable to claim that these people exert an influence on political processes over and above their right to vote.

Class differences in leisure activities

The four classes display differences regarding their everyday leisure activities, suggesting that different class positions reflect somewhat different cultures. Figure 4.5 identifies leisure activities by class, but only for male respondents in order to control for the large gender differences in leisure activity choices.

The new middle class is generally the most active in leisure activities. In particular, they are the strongest participants in leisure

Figure 4.5 Class difference in leisure activities (males, 20% or greater participation)

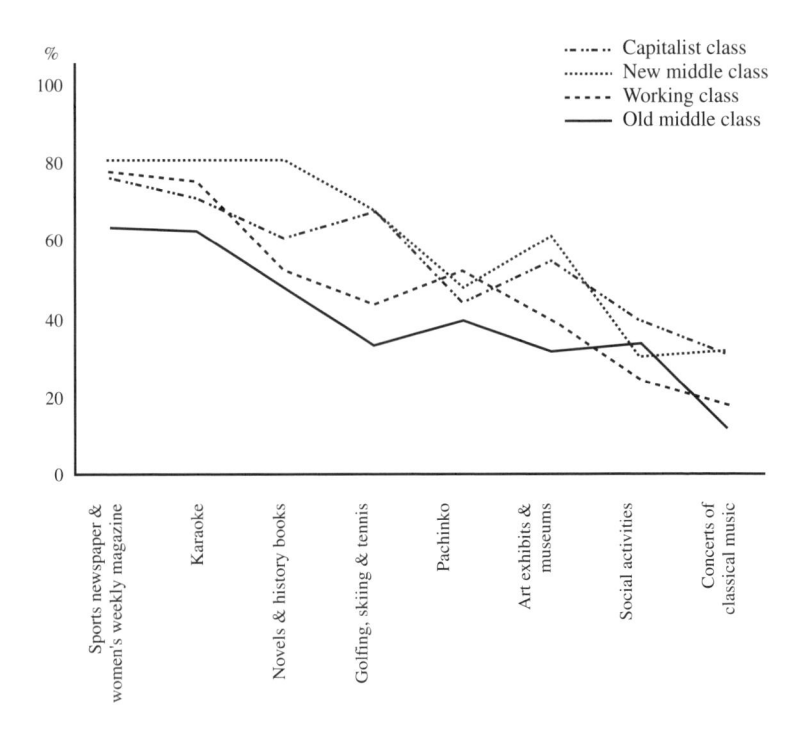

- Capitalist class
- New middle class
- Working class
- Old middle class

X-axis categories: Sports newspaper & women's weekly magazine; Karaoke; Novels & history books; Golfing, skiing & tennis; Pachinko; Art exhibits & museums; Social activities; Concerts of classical music

Note: Percentage of people who performed above in last 5 or 6 years.

Source: 1995 SSM Survey data

activities involving the arts, including reading 'novels and history books', going to 'art exhibits and museums', and attending 'concerts of classical music'. This reveals the intellectual and cultural characteristics of this class. The next most active in the pursuit of leisure is the capitalist class, which is ranked highest in terms of 'social activities'. In most other categories this class is nearly equal to the new middle class. In particular, members of the capitalist class are relatively active in expensive leisure activities such as 'golfing, skiing, and tennis', and attending 'concerts of classical music', indicating the economic power of this class. The working class is ranked highest in playing '*pachinko*' (pinball machines). They exhibit about the same level of activities as the new middle class in reading 'sports newspapers and women's weekly magazines' and participating in '*karaoke*'. They are, however, inactive in most other activities, particularly in 'high' cultural pursuits such as reading 'novels and history books', going to 'art exhibits and museums', and attending 'concerts of classical music'. The old middle class is generally not actively involved in leisure activities. In short, each class's pattern of leisure activities is distinct and reflects particular cultural preferences. These differences are not, however, accidental.

There are numerous cultural genres in contemporary life, each entailing a variety of cultural activities. It is conventional to evaluate these activities as either 'high' or 'low' culture, such that classical music, classical literature, and fine art are judged to be 'high' culture and those who appreciate them are seen to have more refined tastes. At the other extreme, activities like *enka* (traditional Japanese ballads) and popular songs, love stories and cartoons oriented towards the masses, are conventionally considered to be vulgar. Thus the conventionally represented division between high and low (or popular) culture is understood to correlate to the distinction between refined and vulgar taste.

This conventional evaluation of culture, however, is inseparable from the hierarchical order of the social classes. Pierre Bourdieu was the first to systematically analyze this relationship. Describing the relationship through the analysis of various data, Bourdieu argued that each class assumes a different culture, and that these cultures are hierarchically evaluated. The cultural activities of the dominant classes tend to be represented as 'high', while those enjoyed by the subordinate classes are regarded as 'low'. These cultures are transmitted from parents to children, at home and in the community. However, since school curricula are biased towards 'high' cultural pursuits (e.g., classical music, literature, etc.), upper class children who are exposed to these cultural forms in their extracurricular activities have an obvious educational advantage. Bourdieu refers to the cultural skills and knowledge transmitted from one generation to the next through cultural activities as 'cultural capital'. He argues that it is the possession of such capital which ensures that, on average, upper class children perform better educationally and are thereby able to assume positions in upper class occupations, thus reproducing the class intergenerationally. Cultural capital is therefore as important as economic capital in the trans-generational perpetuation of class distinctions and inequalities (Bourdieu 1970; Bourdieu and Passeron 1964).

Although Bourdieu's class categories differ markedly from Marxian class theory, his understanding of the role of class in culture nevertheless greatly enriches and expands the possibilities for class theory. Where traditional class theory tended to emphasize the economic and political aspects of a class at the expense of its cultural manifestations, Bourdieu draws our attention to the fact that class differentiations permeate the cultural and unconscious spheres of everyday life. Figure 4.6 suggests that the relationship between Japanese classes and culture reflect many of the characteristics that Bourdieu ascribed to 'cultural capital'.

In Japan, however, even though it is the capitalist and new middle classes who most enjoy high culture, the extent to which they achieved their class positions through the inheritance of cultural capital from the parents remains questionable. Figure 4.6 combines proportions of respondents belonging to the capitalist and new middle classes and compares them by their 'class of origin' (father's class position) to their level of participation in high culture. Participation in high culture was calculated from the responses to questions regarding leisure activities and is indicated on the horizontal axis. Responses to questions about attending 'classical concerts', going to 'art exhibits and museums' and reading 'novels and history books' are converted into composite scores. At a glance it is clear that, in general, the proportions of the current capitalist and the new middle class are high among those from the capitalist and the new middle classes, but there is no consistent or strong relationship between these proportions and the degree of closeness to high culture. In other words, regardless of their participation in high culture pursuits, people from the capitalist class and the new middle class have a strong tendency to belong to these classes.

On the other hand, for the people of working or old middle class origins there is a strong correlation between the participation in high culture and the upward mobility rate; the more that they participate in high culture, the more likely they are to now belong to the capitalist or new middle class. This suggests that upward mobility is significantly related to the acquisition of high culture, namely, that people from the working and old middle classes acquire high culture in the processes of upward mobility other than direct filial inheritance.

Figure 4.6 Participation in 'high culture' activities by members of capitalist and new middle classes by class of origin

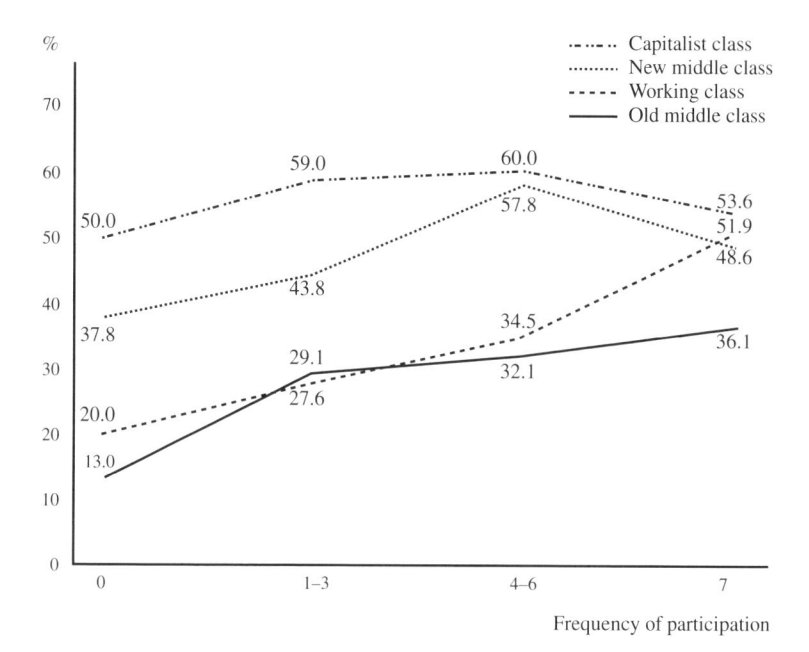

```
%                                      ·· — ··  Capitalist class
                                       ··········  New middle class
70                                     — — —  Working class
                                       ———  Old middle class
60         59.0              60.0
                       57.8                    53.6
50  50.0                                       51.9
                                               48.6
          43.8
40                       34.5
    37.8                                       36.1
30         29.1
           27.6          32.1
20  20.0
    13.0
10

 0
     0      1–3          4–6            7
                              Frequency of participation
```

Note: Numbers indicate percentages of people at each frequency grouping

Source: 1995 SSM Survey data

In the highly competitive Japanese education system, knowledge of classical music, fine art, literature and history is measured by a rigorous examination system. Numerous institutions and processes are in place to facilitate the achievement of high academic results. Therefore, while the upper class children who acquire cultural capital through extracurricular activities have a distinct advantage in passing their examinations in these disciplines, there are mechanisms in place to enable any who study hard to achieve an acceptable knowledge of high culture and good examination results. As discussed, good educational results are demonstrably a key to upward mobility, i.e., movement from the lower to the upper classes. This capacity to learn 'high' culture irrespective of class origins is characteristic of Japanese society and might be called 'cultural social mobility'.

Four life-worlds

Limited as they must be by the numerical data from which they are constructed, the portraits presented above appear to be little more than flat, abstract sketches. Nevertheless, they provide a clear outline of the characteristics of the different classes in contemporary Japanese society.

The capitalist class has relatively high incomes, is the most substantial owner of assets and consumer durables, and tends to enjoy expensive leisure activities, including many classified as high culture. They can generally determine their own work processes and are the most likely of the classes to have the authority to decide the nature of other's work. They also have a wide network of personal relationships with members of parliament, government officials, and other executives, and have substantial social and political influence.

The new middle class, although their assets are not as great, maintains above average incomes and standards of living and participates in many and varied leisure activities, including those considered to be high culture. They have a significant amount of autonomy over their own work, and often maintain a degree of authority over the management of the company's business as well as the nature of their subordinates' work. Their opportunities for promotion are fairly high and, while their network of personal relationships is not necessarily as large as the capitalists', compared to the working class they have more acquaintances with professionals such as physicians and lawyers, government officials, and company presidents and executives.

The working class generally gets by with relatively low incomes and few assets. People of this class are not active participants in high culture or other expensive leisure activities, tending instead to be more involved with 'the pastime activities of the common folks', such as *pachinko* and *karaoke*. Both the content and pace of their work is typically determined by a supervisor or machine process and they are rarely involved in decisions regarding the management of the company's business. Their opportunities for promotion are also very limited. Their circle of personal relationships is narrow, and their acquaintances tend to be confined to members of the same class or people such as salaried men, office ladies, and self-employed people.

While the individual incomes of the old middle class are low, household incomes for this class are relatively high, suggesting that all of the family members are typically employed in the family business and pool their incomes. This class is also asset rich. Being self-employed, members of the old middle class have a high level of autonomy in their work, often exhibiting the characteristics of a 'small feudal lord' who can decide at will the content and processes of their enterprise. While the bulk of their acquaintances are independent business owners like themselves, or salaried men, office ladies, and factory workers, many old middle class people have associations with local government members and officials of trade associations, and hence wield some influence in conservative politics.

This evidence, then, suggests that the people in each Japanese class inhabit quite distinct worlds. Although the classes overlap to some extent in various ways, the available data makes it clear that Japan is in fact a class society.

5 Can Class Borders be Crossed? The Structure of Cross-class Mobility

Freedom from one's class of origin

Can class borders be crossed? More specifically, can a person from the working class move into the new middle class or capitalist class? Conversely, what are the chances of someone from the capitalist class or the old middle class moving into the working class? In modern Japan, where freedom of occupational choice is legally guaranteed, it is undeniable that such movement occurs. The question is whether the possibility for class mobility is so great that people can move from one class to another unimpeded by class borders.

Mobility between classes includes two things. First, it means mobility from one's class of origin – i.e., the class to which one's parents belong – into a new class. Second, class mobility refers to a person's movement from one class to another within the span of their working life. The former is called 'intergenerational mobility' and the latter 'intragenerational' mobility. The central question for understanding intergenerational mobility is the extent to which a person is free to move out of their class of origin; i.e., the class into which s/he was born and/or raised. For intragenerational mobility, the key question to be investigated is whether or not people can change classes once they have commenced employment in a particular class. We will first focus on intergenerational mobility before returning to discuss intragenerational mobility.

Until recently, debate about intergenerational mobility has been dominated by the so-called 'industrialization hypothesis'. Put simply, it claims that as a society becomes more industrialized, intergenerational mobility increases. This corresponds with the common sense notion that in pre-modern status-based society each person assumes the same status as their parents, but in the modern world can choose their occupation freely. There was enough data supporting this hypothesis for it to have remained largely unchallenged throughout the long economic boom (most of the third-quarter of the twentieth century). However, many questions have been raised about it since then.

Certainly in the process of modernization, class mobility increased as the pre-modern status system was abolished, and a large percentage of the population moved from rural areas to urban centers and from agriculture to modern industry. Arguably, however, once industrialization has advanced to a certain extent, the class structure will stabilize and mobility between classes stagnate. For example, a newly established upper class may gradually strengthen their power to stabilize their position, defending the exclusiveness of its own position, and thereby decreasing mobility.

The merits of these two positions are still hotly debated between the advocates of the 'constant mobility hypothesis' and the 'decreasing mobility hypothesis'. Research results so far remain inconclusive. Tominaga (1992) supported an 'industrialization hypothesis' on the basis of his analysis of the SSM Survey data up to 1985, and Imada (1989) argued for a 'constant mobility hypothesis' based on the same data. No study to that point had clearly supported a 'decreasing mobility hypothesis'.

As analysis of the 1995 SSM Survey data progressed, the 'decreasing mobility hypothesis' suddenly gained currency. Since 1998, Hara (1998), Seiyama and Hara (1999), and Hashimoto (1998, 1999) have presented results of analyses that are consistent with the decreasing mobility hypothesis. It is important to note that these studies merely indicate the possibility of, but are so far inadequate to conclusively argue for, the 'decreasing mobility hypothesis'. On the other hand, as mentioned in chapter 2, Satō, in his best-selling book, *Japan as an Unequal Society* (Satō 2000), argues that the exclusiveness of the white-collar workers, especially the upper white-collar, has rapidly increased. Utilizing original occupational categories and drawing on an analysis of intergenerational mobility, he has called this phenomenon the 'emergence of a new class', a concept which has attracted much attention.

Why have various analyses of the same data produced different conclusions? Simply stated, it is because different points of view and methods of analysis have been adopted. The fact is that, depending on the method used, an analysis of the 1995 SSM Survey data can produce results that support an 'industrialization hypothesis'. The vital question then is, which interpretation most accurately reflects social reality? Can we obtain Satō's conclusion that 'class exclusiveness has increased' using the categories of our four-class model? Such questions will be discussed in due course, without going into too much detail. Our focus in this chapter is on class mobility for men, so that we can analyze the data longitudinally (see chapter 4 on the compilation of SSM data).

Structure of interclass mobility

Analysis of intergenerational mobility is based on cross-tabulation of class locations. Table 5.1 (a) shows a man's class of origin (his father's class) on the vertical axis, and his present class position on the horizontal axis. The table demonstrates the relationship between the two, and is commonly called a 'mobility table'. For instance, the numbers on the first row indicate that people whose class of origin is capitalist total 176, and out of those 176 people, 68 remain in the capitalist class, 48 now belong to the new middle class, 36 to the working class, and 24 to the old middle class. The vertical and horizontal totals indicate class compositions of respondents and fathers. For further reference, the percentages presented in each cell are calculated on the class of origin (the horizontal data), in order to indicate the percentage of people from each class of origin who now belong to each class.

The four positions where the present class is the same as the class of origin are indicated in Table 5.1 (a) with bold numbers. These are the numbers of people who have not experienced intergenerational class mobility. There are 68 of these in the case of the capitalist class, which amounts to 38.6% of those whose class of origin is capitalist. Looking at the bottom figure of this column, we see that people in the capitalist class account for 11.0% of the total sample. In comparison, 9.1% of new middle class origins now belong to the capitalist class, 5.7% of working class origins, and 9.0% of old middle class origins. Thus the probability of becoming a member of the capitalist class is less for people originating in any of the other classes than it is for people coming from the capitalist class. In other words, people whose fathers belonged to the capitalist class are more likely to belong to the capitalist class than people of any other class origin. Similarly, as the other boldfaced figures show, 191 people (52.8%) of new middle class origin, 229

Table 5.1 Intergenerational mobility and mobility index

(a) Intergenerational mobility table of 1995 (male)

Father's class (Main occupation)	Capitalist	New Middle	Working	Old Middle	Total
Capitalist	**68** (38.6)	48 (27.3)	36 (20.5)	24 (13.6)	176 (100.0)
New middle	33 (9.1)	**191** (52.8)	102 (28.2)	36 (9.9)	362 (100.0)
Working	25 (5.7)	147 (33.6)	**229** (52.4)	36 (8.2)	437 (100.0)
Old Middle	88 (9.0)	245 (25.1)	338 (34.7)	**304** (31.2)	975 (100.0)
Total	214 (11.0)	631 (32.4)	705 (36.2)	400 (20.5)	1950 (100.0)

Note: Those who did not move (bold-faced) 68 + 191 + 229 + 304 = 792
Non-mobility ratio = 792/1950 = 0.406
Mobility ratio = 1−0.406 = 0.594 (gross mobility ratio)

(b) Intergenerational mobility when mobility is minimum

Father's class (Main occupation)	Capitalist	New Middle	Working	Old Middle	Total
Capitalist	**176** (100.0)	0 (0.0)	0 (0.0)	0 (0.0)	176 (100.0)
New middle	0 (0.0)	**362** (100.0)	0 (0.0)	0 (0.0)	362 (100.0)
Working	0 (0.0)	0 (0.0)	**437** (100.0)	0 (0.0)	437 (100.0)
Old Middle	38 (3.9)	269 (27.6)	268 (27.5)	**400** (41.0)	975 (100.0)
Total	214 (11.0)	631 (32.4)	705 (36.2)	400 (20.5)	1950 (100.0)

Note: Those who did not move (bold-faced) 176 + 362 + 437 + 400 = 1375
Non-mobility ratio = 1375/1950 = 0.705
Mobility ratio = 1−0.705 = 0.295 (structural mobility ratio)

(c) Intergenerational mobility table when present class & class origin are not related (prefect mobility)

Father's class (Main occupation)	Capitalist	New Middle	Working	Old Middle	Total
Capitalist	**19.3** (11.0)	57.0 (32.4)	63.6 (36.2)	36.1 (20.5)	176 (100.0)
New middle	39.7 (11.0)	**117.1** (32.4)	130.9 (36.2)	74.3 (20.5)	362 (100.0)
Working	48.0 (11.0)	141.4 (32.4)	**158.0** (36.2)	89.6 (20.5)	437 (100.0)
Old Middle	107.0 (11.0)	315.5 (32.4)	352.5 (36.2)	**200.0** (20.5)	975 (100.0)
Total	214.0 (11.0)	631.0 (32.4)	705.0 (36.2)	400.0 (20.5)	1950 (100.0)

Note: Those who did not move (bold-faced) 19.3 + 117.1 + 158 + 200 = 494.4
Non-mobility ratio = 49.4/1950 = 0.254
Mobility ratio = 1−0.254 = 0.746 (mobility ratio at perfect mobility)

Gross mobility ratio 0.594   Non-mobility ratio 0.406
Structural mobility ratio 0.295   Mobility ratio at perfect mobility 0.746
Pure mobility ratio 0.594−0.295 = 0.299
Unrealized mobility ratio 0.746−0.594 = 0.152

Source: 1995 SSM Survey data

people (52.4%) of working class origin and 304 people (31.2%) of old middle class origin have remained in their classes of origin. All of these percentages are larger than the percentages of people from other classes. Overall, more than 40% of the men in this survey still belong to the same class as their father. This suggests that there are some restrictions on interclass mobility. The question then is, can we demonstrate the strength of these restrictions numerically? To do so requires some time-consuming calculations.

The total number of men presently located in their class of origin (the bold figures: total 792) divided by the total sample (1950) is the non-mobility rate (792 ÷ 1950 = 0.406): the ratio of people who have not moved between classes intergenerationally. When we subtract this ratio from 1 (1 − 0.406 = 0.594), we obtain the gross mobility rate: the ratio of people who have moved between classes. If all respondents belonged to the same class as their fathers, the gross mobility rate would be zero, whereas if everyone had moved from their classes of origin, the gross mobility rate would be one. In order for all sons and their fathers to belong to the same class, there must be identical numbers of people in two generations for each class, but this cannot possibly occur, since the class structure changes over time. Nor is it conceivable that no son would belong to the same class as his father, unless it was somehow prohibited by an authoritarian power. Therefore, the gross mobility rate is necessarily larger than 0 and smaller than 1.

What, then, is the lower limit of the gross mobility rate? In order to comprehend this we must assume that class compositions of respondents and fathers remain as represented in Table 5.1 (a) and that everyone tries to remain in their class of origin as far as possible. In such a situation a person moves to another class only when a gap between his class composition and his father's forces him to do so − i.e., when the son is in surplus of the numbers required to replace the older generation (replenish the class). Such is the situation in a pre-modern status-based society. Table 5.1 (b) shows this hypothetical situation. The sizes of the capitalist, new middle and working classes have increased in the younger generation, so there are more people in these classes in the son's generation than in the father's. Therefore, all of the sons can remain in the same class as their fathers. This is not, however, the case with the old middle class. Because the old middle class has shrunk in scale − the old middle class contains 975 people in the father's generation and only 400 in the son's − only 400 people in the younger generation can remain in their father's class. In other words, the number of people who can remain in their class of origin is the smaller of (1) the number of their fathers who belong to the class or (2) the number of the respondents who belong to the class. Thus, the balance of 575 people must move to other classes. These people are distributed to the other three classes according to the gap between the numbers of the two generations. Thus 38 people are distributed to the capitalist class, 269 people to the new middle class, and 268 people to the working class. This is the situation where intergenerational mobility is smallest; where the gross mobility rate is 0.295. This, then, is the lowest limit of the gross mobility rate. This mobility is created by the incontestable gap between a person's class position and his father's, and is called the 'structural mobility rate'.

Having established the lower limit of the mobility rate, what is its upper limit? As seen earlier, people tend to remain in their class of origin. This tendency is common to all known eras and classes. An ideal situation is created when people belong to each class with exactly the same probability regardless of class of origin. This situation is called 'perfect mobility'. The gross mobility rate in such a situation is, therefore, considered the upper limit, which is shown in Table 5.1 (c). Regardless of their class of origin, 11.0% of people belong to the capitalist class, 32.4% to the new middle class, 36.2% to the working class and 20.5% to the old middle class. The gross mobility rate in this situation is 0.746, the realistic upper limit of the gross mobility rate.

These lower and upper limits naturally change when changes occur to either the sons' or fathers' class composition. The gross mobility rate fluctuates accordingly. In order to assess whether the gross mobility rate is high or low, we must take the lower limit and upper limit into consideration. Thus, we can suppose that two indices represent the extent of mobility. One comes from subtracting the lower limit of mobility, the rate of mobility that cannot be dismissed, from the gross mobility rate. This is generally called the 'pure mobility rate'. The other comes from subtracting the gross mobility rate from the upper limit of mobility. This indicates how far the actual mobility situation is from the ideal condition where there is an equal chance to belong to each class (perfect mobility). This can be called the 'unrealized mobility rate'. To explain each in simple terms, the pure mobility rate is an index to show how far away the chances for mobility are from the pre-modern status-based society where the chances are closed, while the unrealized mobility rate indicates the extent to which chances for mobility are restricted. Therefore, the more the pure mobility rate increases and the unrealized mobility rate decreases, the greater the chances for mobility. Since these two indices are adjusted by the lower and upper limit of the gross mobility rate, we should be able to compare two mobility tables of different generations (namely, the different class composition of sons and fathers).

Figure 5.1 illustrates changing trends in the pure mobility rate and the unrealized mobility rate calculated from the SSM Survey data between 1955 and 1995. Respondents to the SSM Survey were aged between 20 and 69. If we treat these people as a single unit for data analysis, all movements over the last several decades are mixed, and as a consequence we cannot accurately gauge recent changes. To account for this, the results of 'people aged between 35 and 44' are compared to 'people of all ages'.

We can conclude that until 1975 all four indices indicate that chances for mobility decreased from 1955 to 1965, but that they increased in 1975. Since then, however, a change can be discerned. The pure mobility rate continued to increase for 'people of all ages', whereas it decreased slightly for 'people aged between 35 and 44' between 1985 and 1995. Meanwhile both of the unrealized mobility rates continued to increase. The degree of increase in the unrealized mobility rate is particularly conspicuous for people aged between 35 and 44. Judging by the pure mobility rate for people of all ages, the chances for mobility continue to increase. However this results from the fact that people experienced increased mobility in the aftermath of the drastic population and labor movement that accompanied the postwar economic boom. This, however, does not reflect more recent changes. We can conclude that restrictions to intergenerational mobility in Japan have been recently reinforced.

Trends of intergenerational mobility

Various issues with methods of analyses

Quite a few researchers have analyzed data using the pure mobility rate as we calculated it in the previous section. We have followed the basic conventions of this analysis, but have also introduced a new perspective: the unrealized mobility rate.

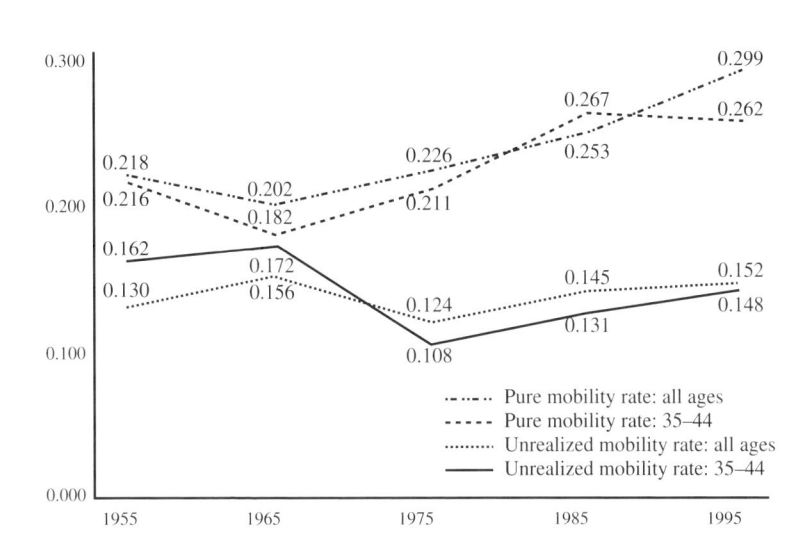

Figure 5.1 Change in pure mobility rate and unrealized mobility rate (male)

```
                                                              0.299
                                            0.267
                                                              0.262
                           0.226        0.253
         0.218
               0.202
         0.216            0.211
               0.182
         0.162
               0.172                          0.145   0.152
         0.130 0.156                                  0.148
                          0.124        0.131
                          0.108

         ·—··—··  Pure mobility rate: all ages
         — — — —  Pure mobility rate: 35–44
         ·········· Unrealized mobility rate: all ages
         ————     Unrealized mobility rate: 35–44

         1955   1965   1975   1985   1995
```

Source: SSM Survey data

However, Satō (2000) offers a sweeping critique of these methods and proposes alternatives. His central argument can be summed up in two points.

First, past analyses failed to account for age differences, treating the data of all age categories as if their present class locations had the same meaning regardless of their age. We have already taken steps to address this problem in the previous section's comparison of the 'all age' data against the class positions of respondents aged between 35 and 44. Nevertheless, it is worth summarizing Satō's argument to add clarity to our analyses.

Analyses that do not distinguish stages of life in some manner are unable to identify intragenerational class mobility occurring amongst those who are presently ordinary employees but will, like their fathers, one day occupy a managerial position or inherit the family business. As such, their present and future occupations do not correspond. Therefore, when we compare the occupations of the younger generation with their fathers' 'main occupations', intergenerational mobility is over-estimated, which leads to a conclusion that the present society is more open than it actually is. In order to accurately compare a person's occupation with his father's, Satō argues, we should focus on the occupation they have at the age of 40.

It is worth noting that it is far from meaningless to analyze the data of people of all ages. Even though the probability of gaining a managerial position in the future may be high for a person from the capitalist class, an ordinary employee's poor living conditions are part and parcel of his current lived reality. In that sense, he has, if only momentarily, moved downward in comparison with his class of origin. Mobility tables encompassing people of all ages are summations of these people's lives at a given point in time. But we also accept Satō's point because it is necessary to make analytic methods consistent for respondents and fathers. Class locations of fathers are measured based on their main occupations, so class locations of respondents should be measured based on their main occupations too, which means we should focus on the occupation at the age of 40 or so.

Satō's second point is that since people in advanced societies choose their occupations on the basis of personal preference, we cannot necessarily attribute any gap between a father and son's occupational status to incontestable structural factors. Therefore, we cannot distinguish structural mobility from pure mobility.[1] To measure chances for mobility, Satō argued, we should use the odds ratio and the coefficient of openness (explained later) instead of the pure mobility rate.

This argument is quite technical and is therefore difficult to explain. People do, in fact, have occupational preferences, but such preferences are certainly not the sole, and generally not the primary determinant of actual occupations (as our Promenade sought to illustrate). If occupational preference were the primary determinant of occupation, we would find far more pilots, stewardesses, professional sportspeople, mass media journalists, tour conductors and employees of Sony or Tokyo Marine Insurance Company (the most popular companies among Japanese job-seeking students). It is not improbable that the class structure changes as a result of people's occupational preferences, but the change occurs within limitations such as those defined by the economic structure. However, it is true that the odds ratio and the coefficient of openness are excellent indices, as Satō suggests.

We will test Satō's findings against an analysis following his method of our own four-class model to see the extent to which the results change when other methods of analysis are employed.

Odds ratio and coefficient of openness

First, we should explain the 'odds ratio' and the 'coefficient of openness', the two indices used for analyzing the data. We will consider the capitalist class by way of illustration. Some people of capitalist class origin come to belong to the capitalist class, while others of capitalist origin do not. Let us take 'A' for the number of the former and 'B' for the number of the latter. Some people from other classes may also come to belong to the capitalist class, while others may not. Let us take C for the number of the former, D for the number of the latter. 'Odds', then, refers to a 'chance of winning', and concretely it indicates a ratio of a 'chance of winning' over a 'chance of losing'. Becoming a capitalist does not necessarily make one a 'winner', but if we assume it to be 'winning', then we can obtain the odds of the people from the capitalist class by dividing 'A' by 'B', and the odds of people from other classes by dividing 'C' by 'D'. The former ratio divided by the latter [(A/B)/(C/D)] is called the odds ratio for the capitalist class. The higher the odds ratio, the more closed the class. In other words, this indicates how advantaged people from the capitalist class are compared with those from other classes. We can similarly calculate odds ratios for all the other classes.

The coefficient of openness is defined in terms of three boldfaced numbers in Table 5.1 (a), (b), and (c). To illustrate the capitalist class, the boldfaced numbers are (a) the real number of 68, (b) the maximum number of 176, and (c) the number at perfect mobility of 19.3. If we divide the number 'who have moved from their class of origin' (176 − 68 = 108) by the number of 'people who would have moved if perfect mobility were realized' (176 − 19.3 = 156.7) the ratio produced is the index of realized mobility (108 ÷ 156.7 = 0.689). This is called the coefficient of openness of the capitalist class. The lower the coefficient of openness, the more exclusive the class.

While the 'pure mobility rate' and the 'unrealized mobility rate' are indices related to the total mobility table and do not directly indicate a trend for each class, the odds ratio and the coefficient of openness indicate the relative chances of mobility for each class.

For example, when mobility increases between certain classes but not others, say between the capitalist and old middle classes but not between the new middle and working classes, the 'pure mobility rate' merely registers the increase in mobility. On the other hand, the odds ratio and the coefficient of openness can provide more detailed understanding of trends in mobility chances.[2]

The capitalist class is becoming more exclusive

In keeping with Satō's method, the sample is divided into four birth cohorts (groups of the same generations), and the odds ratio and coefficient of openness for the four classes are calculated for each cohort. The results are shown in Figure 5.2. Following Satō, adjacent cohorts overlap by 10 years.

The results are clear-cut. The odds ratio of the capitalist class decreases for the cohorts born between 1925 and 1944, but rapidly increases for those born between 1935 and 1954. The odds ratio of the new middle class rises in the cohort born between 1905 and 1924, then remains stable for a while; but it too increases for the cohort born between 1935 and 1954. The sharp rise at the right side of the odds ratio indicates that the capitalist and new middle classes have strengthened their exclusiveness in recent years – they have become more closed. The capitalist class in particular is rapidly becoming extremely exclusive. The coefficient of openness of the capitalist class points to relatively moderate changes in recent years, but their coefficient decreases more acutely than that of the new middle class. Therefore, the basic trend is the same. On the other hand, openness is stressed in the two most recent working class cohorts. This is due to the fact that this class has absorbed a great number of people from other classes, particularly those from the old middle class. No great change is observed in the openness of the old middle class.

Figure 5.3 is reproduced from Satō (2000), representing the odds ratios between a person's occupation at the age of 40 and his father's main occupation by different birth cohorts. By comparing our diagram with Satō's, we can discern that trends for capitalists and UWE (upper white-collar employees), as well as new middle class and LWE (lower white-collar employees) are very similar. This is to be expected as the class categories used here and the occupational categories used by Satō have much in common. UWE include professional and administrative/managerial employees, owners and

Figure 5.2 Odds ratio and coefficient of openness of the respondent's class at age 40 by class of origin and birth cohort (male)

(a) Odds ratio

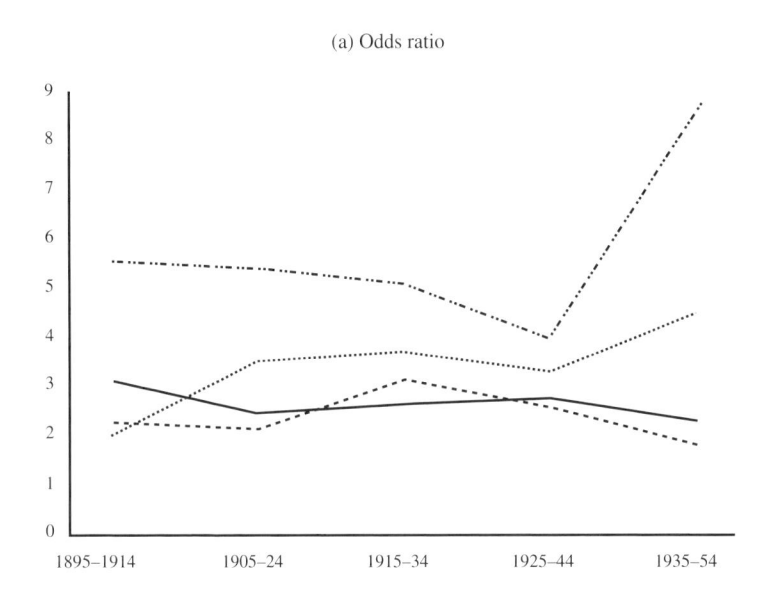

(b) Coefficient of openness

········· Capitalist class
············ New middle class
- - - - Working class
——— Old middle class

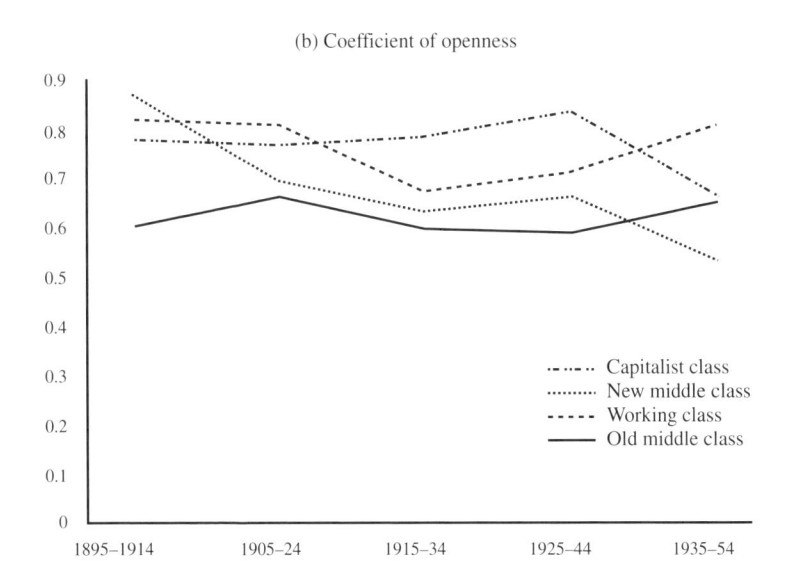

Source: Based on 1965 and 1995 SSM Survey data

Figure 5.3   Odds ratio of the respondent's occupation at age 40 and his father's main occupation by birth cohort (male)

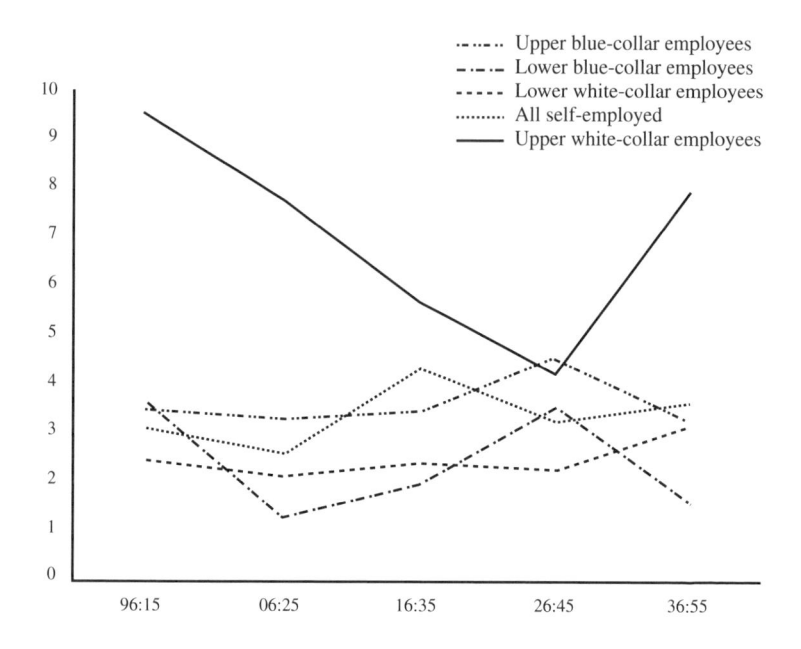

```
·· ··· ··  Upper blue-collar employees
· — · —   Lower blue-collar employees
- - - -    Lower white-collar employees
··········  All self-employed
———         Upper white-collar employees
```

x-axis: 96:15, 06:25, 16:35, 26:45, 36:55

Source: Satō (2000b:58)

executives. These roughly correspond to people in our four-class model who occupy managerial and professional positions within the new middle class and the capitalist class. Similarly, LWE are employees in clerical and sales positions, and coincide with people in this study who are employed in new middle class clerical positions and working class sales positions. Complete replication of Satō's occupational categories proved impossible, but I succeeded in reproducing approximately 97% of them. To understand the relationship between the two, then, 29% of UWE belong to the capitalist class, 63% belong to the new middle class, and 8% to the old middle class. Seventy-three percent (73%) of LWE are new middle class and 27% are working class. Hence, it is not surprising that we have obtained similar results.

There are differences, however. In comparing the odds ratio of the capitalist class with that of UWE we discover that change is greater for the capitalist class than UWE. Why is that so? What Satō regarded as a change for UWE may in fact have been a change within the capitalist class. In fact, it was not the upper white-collar employees that became more exclusive, but rather the capitalist class as a whole.

In seeking to support this explanation and the conclusion drawn earlier, we must now examine the results gained by other methods of analysis. Odds ratios were calculated on the basis of movement between a person's class and his father's class. Drawn from the SSM Survey data of each study year, samples were drawn from people aged between 35 and 44 and between 45 and 54. Figure 5.4 displays these results. The former sample is a cohort aged 40 plus or minus 5 years, and should be roughly regarded as representative of the participant's class when aged 40. Since the latter sample is composed of employees who, at that age, have reached the peak of their careers, it can be safely assumed to be their class location at the time of their 'main occupations'. What, then, is the result?

In both cases the odds ratio of the capitalist class rapidly increases between those born in the 1930s and those born in the 1940s. This, then, confirms the earlier finding that the capitalist class has rapidly become more exclusive. As to the new middle class, however, the odds ratio is unchanged or slightly decreased between those born in the 1930s and those born in the 1940s. This suggests that the earlier finding regarding the new middle class becoming exclusive is derived from a method of analysis based on occupation at the age of 40, and is only an unsubstantiated assertion.[3] The odds ratios of the new middle class, however, reaches 3.0 to 3.4, even though they have declined slightly. This fact nonetheless indicates that this class is, to a considerable extent, closed to people of other classes. It does not, however, indicate that the new middle class has become exclusive, especially not in recent years.

Satō called the UWE an 'intellectual elite', and argued that they have strengthened their exclusiveness and are becoming a 'new class'. In reality, however, the group of people who have most increased their exclusiveness are not the 'intellectual elite' of the new middle class, but the capitalist class, the core of which consists of owners of small and medium-sized enterprises. According to my calculations, 31% of Satō's UWE work for small and petty enterprises with less than 30 employees, and 29% work for medium-sized enterprises with 30 to 299 employees. Owners and executives, that is, typical small and medium-sized enterprise

Class Structure in Contemporary Japan

Figure 5.4 Odds ratio of the respondent's present class and origin class by birth cohort (male)

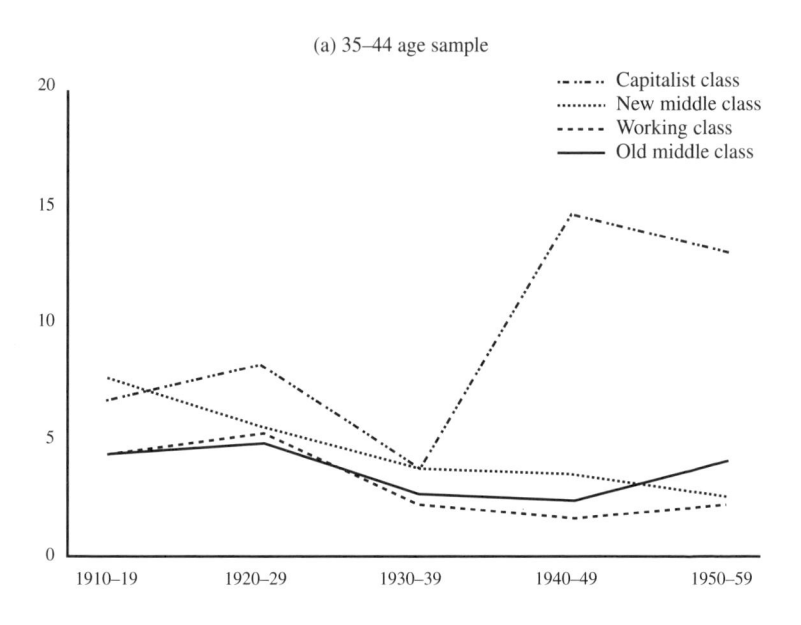

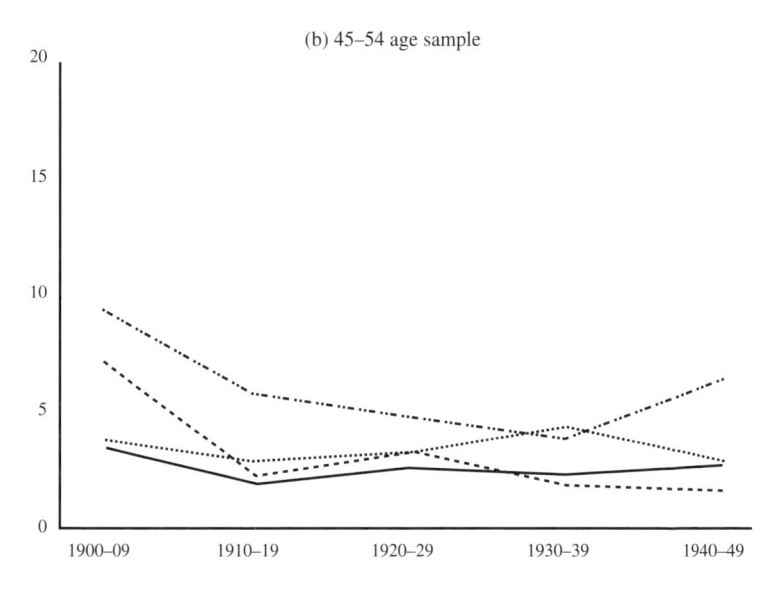

(a) 35–44 age sample

- ·—·— Capitalist class
- ·········· New middle class
- ----- Working class
- ——— Old middle class

(b) 45–54 age sample

Based on SSM Survey

capitalists (or self-employed people approaching this category) accounted for 57% of the UWE employed by small and medium-sized enterprises (34% of the total UWE). The trend that Satō interpreted as an increasing exclusivity amongst an intellectual elite was in fact a sign of the increasing difficulty confronting people aspiring to become self-employed or small-scale capitalists. In reality, while it is indeed difficult to join the 'intellectual elite', the path is virtually closed for an ordinary person wanting to establish a small or medium sized enterprise.

Life-course and intragenerational mobility between classes

Class location is not unchangeable. People can change their class location by being promoted, finding other employment, or inheriting the family business. How often, then, do such instances of interclass mobility occur?

Drawing on the 1995 SSM Survey data, Figure 5.5 illustrates class location at different ages for respondents aged 40 years or older. Almost half of the men began their careers in the working class. However, this figure steadily decreases with age, so that by the age of 50 less than 30% are still working class. As one might expect, the percentage of the capitalist and old middle classes have increased proportionately over this same life span. While accounting for only 3.5% and 14.0% respectively of men at the beginning of their working lives, by the age of 50 they account for 12.3% and 25.0% respectively – i.e., there are almost four times as many capitalists at age fifty as there are people who begin their working lives as capitalists and almost 80% more old middle class. For women the story is very different. More than 70% of women begin their working careers in the working class, but this figure decreases dramatically as nearly one-half become unemployed during the years in which they typically marry and have children, and a small proportion move into the old middle class. As their children reach school age, the proportion of women in the working class increases again and the so-called M-shaped distribution begins to take shape. (See the Promenade chapter for further discussion of the M-shape distribution of women's work.)

This sort of change in class composition has been brought about by intragenerational class mobility, as illustrated in Table 5.2. Taking class location at age 50 to be someone's 'attained class', the table plots respondents' class location every five years up to

Class Structure in Contemporary Japan

Figure 5.5 Class location at different ages (sample of 40 years old or older at present)

(a) Male

Percentage of population

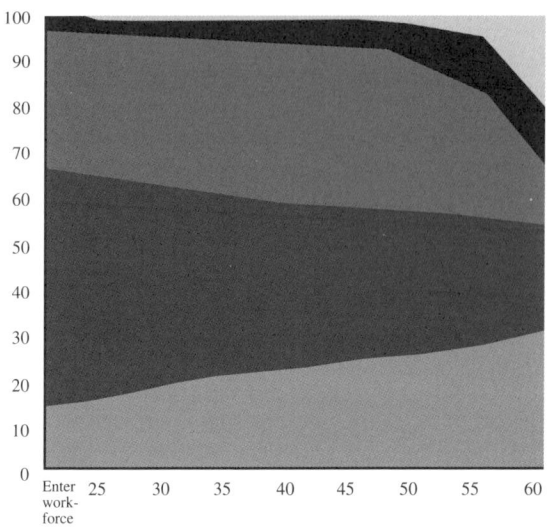

(b) Female

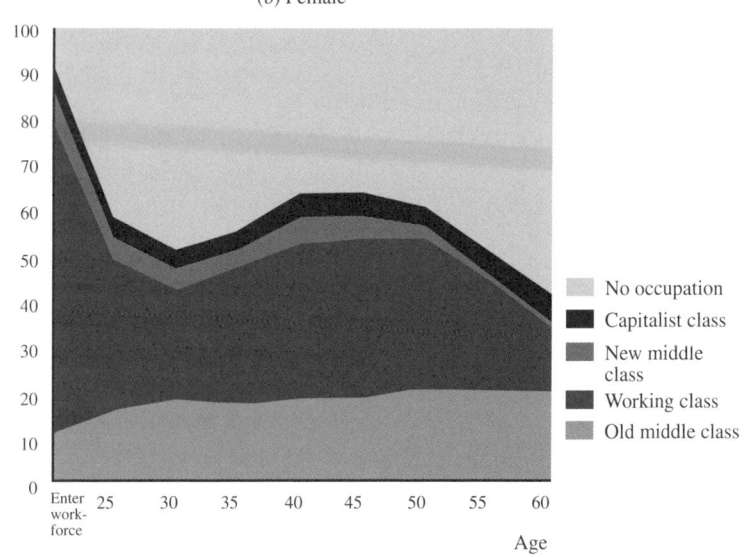

- No occupation
- Capitalist class
- New middle class
- Working class
- Old middle class

Age

Source: Based on 1995 SSM Survey data

Table 5.2   Class location during career for respondents at age 50 (male)

Class at age 50		Entering workforce	25	30	35	40	45	50
Capitalist	C	17.2	32.3	44.4	60.3	71.4	85.9	100.0
	N	35.9	27.4	22.2	19.0	19.0	9.4	0.0
	W	37.5	27.4	25.4	15.9	6.3	3.1	0.0
	O	9.4	12.9	7.9	4.8	3.2	1.6	0.0
New Middle	C	0.6	0.6	0.6	1.2	0.0	0.0	0.0
	N	69.1	75.9	79.1	82.4	98.0	94.5	100.0
	W	24.2	20.9	18.4	15.2	10.4	5.5	0.0
	O	6.1	2.5	1.8	1.2	0.6	0.0	0.0
Working	C	1.3	0.0	0.6	0.0	0.0	0.0	0.0
	N	3.8	3.8	2.5	3.2	1.9	1.3	0.0
	W	82.2	85.9	89.8	91.1	93.6	96.2	100.0
	O	12.7	10.3	7.0	5.7	4.5	2.6	0.0
Old Middle	C	4.5	3.8	4.6	2.3	0.8	0.0	0.0
	N	9.8	8.5	5.3	3.8	1.5	0.8	0.0
	W	45.5	33.8	18.3	12.1	6.8	2.3	0.0
	O	40.2	53.8	71.8	81.8	90.9	97.0	100.0

Note: C = Capitalist Class, N = New Middle Class, W = Working Class, O = Old Middle Class

Source: 1995 SSM Survey data

this point. The table is limited to the data of males in order to consider the continuity in career structures. Of those classified as capitalist class at the age of 50, only 17% began their careers in the capitalist class. The percentage of people moving into the capitalist class increased each year, but the rate of increase was slow, with most coming from the new middle and working classes. The new middle class are slightly older when they change classes, with almost 20% still in the new middle class at age 40. This suggests that people in the working class become capitalists by setting up their own enterprises, whereas people in the new middle class attain capitalist class status by assuming a position on the board of directors after progressing through a long-term career within a given enterprise.

Almost 70% of the new middle class at age 50 began their careers in this class. Far and away the majority of newcomers arrive at a steady rate from the working class, who have moved to the new middle class. Fully 82% of respondents classified as

Figure 5.6   Amount of assets owned by class origin

Class	Monetary assets	Real estate assets
Capitalist class	2600	4850
New middle class	1570	3100
Working class	990	1710
Old middle class	1510	3600

Amount (10,000 yen)

working class at age 50 reported that they began their careers in the working class, and very little movement is observed from other classes. The largest influx is the one-eighth of the people from the old middle class, mostly farmers, who have moved to the working class. In contrast, only 40% of the old middle class at age 50 began their working lives in the old middle class; the largest proportion of people who have joined it have come from the working class. One-third of these people had moved into the old middle class by the age of 25 and two-thirds by the age of 30, but the movement remains steady even after this age. Thus, intragenerational class mobility is most active between the working class and the old middle class. However, more detailed analysis (not in Table 5.2) reveals that approximately 70% of the men who moved from the working class to the old middle class between the beginning of their working life and age 50 were, in fact, 'born and raised' in the old middle class. Thus much of this movement may be attributed to the privilege of those whose families own businesses, but who, for one reason or another, initially sought employment elsewhere than the family business. Similarly, although in shear numbers, quite a few people moved from the working class to the new middle class, at age 50 they still account for less than one-quarter of the entire new middle class. More generally, there was very little movement from the capitalist class to the new middle class or the working class, from the new middle class to the working class, and between the new middle and old middle classes. We might conclude, then, that there are considerable limitations to interclass mobility.

Inherited assets – economic capital and cultural capital

It is evident that, to a large extent, one's class location is inherited from one's parents. How, though, does this occur? As discussed in chapter 4, class location is intergenerationally perpetuated through the inheritance of the means of production (i.e., economic capital) as private property and through differences in educational opportunities. A variant of the former is the not uncommon case of someone who succeeds his/her father as an executive in a corporation even though the family do not own a controlling interest in the company's shares.

To more fully understand the succession mechanism in the class structure, we will analyze the ownership of assets and real estate, processes of inheritance, and differences in educational opportunities by class of origin.

Figure 5.6 depicts the assets owned (monetary and real estate) by a person's class of origin. People from the capitalist class own substantial proportions of real estate and financial assets, and, as might be expected, people from the new middle and old middle classes own moderate proportions, with the latter's property skewed slightly towards real estate. People from the working class own few assets, one significant characteristic that distinguishes them from the other classes. Clearly, asset ownership differs greatly according to class origins.

Figure 5.7 examines changes in the rates of participation in higher education by class of origin. For the cohort born in the 1930s, participation in higher education is extremely low amongst the working and old middle classes, and class disparities are very large. With the subsequent increases in the participation rate for these two groups, class disparity decreased for the 1940s' cohort. However, the disparities increased again for the 1950s' cohort as the participation rate amongst the new middle class increased rapidly and, although less rapid, the participation rate for the capitalist class still outstripped the other two classes.[4] In short, the general upward trend in the higher education participation rate has been greater for the capitalist and new middle classes than it has for the working and old middle classes; the latter are thus relatively more educationally disadvantaged than their predecessors.

We develop a more complete picture of the differences between the classes when we investigate the relationship between class of origin, academic record in the 9th grade, and the proportion of the youngest cohort (born in the 1960s) advancing to higher education. The relationships are shown in Table 5.3. People from the capitalist and new middle classes with superior academic records almost always advance to higher education. Even when their school record is only average, more than one-half advance to higher education and approximately 40% of those with below average academic records still manage to advance to higher education. In contrast, only about one-half of the people from working and old middle class backgrounds with superior

Figure 5.7   Rate of advancing to higher education by class of origin and birth cohort (male and female)

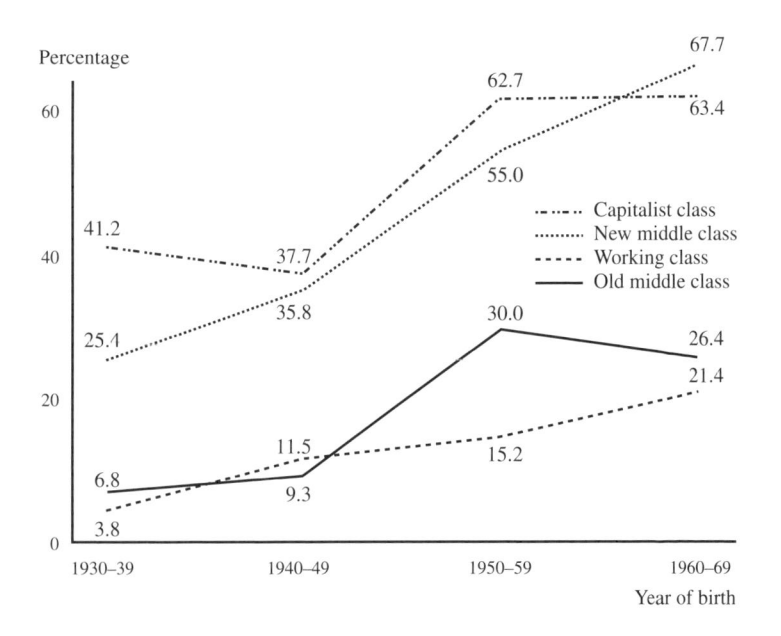

Source: 1995 SSM Survey data

Table 5.3 Ratio of students advancing to higher education by class origin and school record at the 9th grade (male & female cohort born in the 1960's)

Class origin	School record at the 9th grade		
	Superior	Average	Inferior
Capitalist Class	75.0	58.8	42.9
New Middle Class	84.4	55.3	40.0
Working Class	57.7	16.0	3.0
Old Middle Class	40.0	22.6	20.0
Total	65.8	32.3	17.3

Source: 1995 SSM Survey data

academic records advance to higher education, and as the academic standard declines, the proportions advancing to higher education rapidly decrease. In particular, it is virtually impossible for someone from a working class background with a below average academic record to advance to higher education. Affirming Bourdieu's theory that 'cultural capital' is inherited, we find that academic records vary greatly according to class of origin. Across all age groups by class of origin, 45% of the capitalist class and 51% of the new middle class achieved superior academic records compared to only 28% of the working class and 29% of the old middle class. But this difference in academic record between classes of origin still does not explain the even greater differences in the proportions advancing to higher education. Even when the academic results are the same, people from the capitalist and new middle classes have a much higher rate of advancing to higher education. Thus, it appears that the capitalist and new middle classes are able to pass on their class location to younger generations through higher education.

While it is not impossible to cross class borders, there are indeed many obstacles restricting people's capacity to do so. It is difficult to ascertain the direct relationship between educational qualifications and membership in the capitalist class; because, that is, ownership of the means of production plays such a decisive role in determining its membership. In comparison, it is easier to join the new middle class. This, though, is only relative, because with higher educational achievements becoming the primary prerequisite for entry into the new middle class, it is no simple matter for people from working class and old middle class backgrounds to attain the academic results needed to advance to higher education. Thus it seems that each class remains separated from the next by barriers that are not insurmountable, but continue to present significant difficulties nonetheless.

6 Differentiation of the Farming Class in Postwar Japan

Introduction

The first postwar survey to examine Japan's agricultural population, the Population Survey of Agricultural Households, was conducted in April 1946, when Japan still remained totally devastated from WWII. Though one can imagine that the researchers must have encountered numerous difficulties, their findings were remarkable. There were 5.70 million farm households, the total population of the agricultural sector was 34.14 million, and the number of agricultural workers[1] reached 18.49 million, of whom 14.48 million were full-timers (farmers with other jobs 'on the side' numbered 4.02 million). Each of these figures was the largest on record. In particular, the number of agricultural workers increased by some 4.93 million from an estimated number of 13.56 million in 1940, a growth rate of 36.4%.

The expansion of the agricultural population continued for several years, peaking in 1950 when the number of agricultural households and the size of the agricultural population reached 6.18 million and 37.67 million respectively. There were 19.32 million agricultural workers in 1955. This population probably also peaked in 1950, but the data required to confirm this is not available. All of these figures were unprecedented. The farm household population was 45.5% of the total population of the nation and agricultural workers accounted for 46.9% of the entire work force. Thus Japan came out of World War II with a very large agricultural sector.

These trends set the stage for the differentiation of the farming class,[2] the most dramatic transformation that has ever occurred in modern Japan's class structure.

Farming class trends in postwar Japan

The differentiation of the farming class

Immediately after World War II the Allied Occupation Forces implemented wholesale land reforms, bringing to an end the feudalistic landlord-like ownership system in the agricultural sector which had been undergoing change since industrialization began some sixty years earlier. As a consequence of these reforms, independent farmers owning small allotments of land became a majority in the agricultural sector. The 'differentiation of the farming class (*Entbauerung*)' occurred subsequently as these small landowners and other agricultural workers dissolved into the various other classes. Numerous studies have accumulated since the middle of World War II and have become 'the point of culmination, in a sense, of social-scientific studies on agriculture' (Ōuchi 1961: 1).

The differentiation of the farming class concerns the basis of the modern stratification system and its development in at least two ways. First, it is representative of the process that paves the way for the formation of capitalist society. Secondly, it also facilitates the consolidation of the capitalist system where the capitalist mode of production is already predominant, i.e., further reducing simple commodity production and accelerating capitalist production.

The first process relates to what Marx called 'primitive accumulation'. The differentiation of the farming class generates a pool of wage workers, a necessary precursor to the accumulation of capital and the transition from pre-capitalist to capitalist society.

The second process concerns the dynamics of the existing capitalist society where farmers and self-employed proprietors have been engaged in simple commodity production since pre-capitalist days. The capitalist mode of production has transformed this sector, conditioning their class characteristics and reducing their numbers. The differentiation of the farming class sits at the core of this process. We can therefore link studies of the social classes with those of the dynamics of capitalism by scrutinizing this process of differentiation.

Trends in farm households and the farm population

Figure 6.1 charts the changes in the population of the farming sector on three scales: the number of farm households, the farm

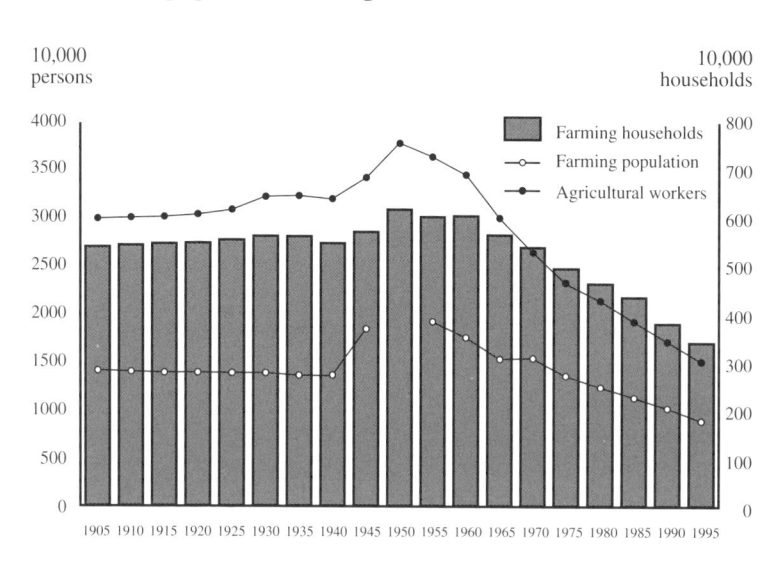

Figure 6.1 Trends of farming households, the farming population and agricultural workers

Note: The numbers of farming households are from *Nōgyō sensasu ruinen tōkei* (Annual statistics of the farming censuses) and *1965-nen nōgyō sensus* (1965 farming census). The farming population figures are based on the estimated figures provided by Umemura, Akasaka, Minami, Takamatsu, Nii and Itō (1988) for 1905–1940 and *Nōgyō sensasu ruinen tōkei* and *1965 nen nōgyō sensasu* for 1946 and thereafter. The numbers of agricultural workers are based on Umemura et al. for 1905–1940 and *Nōgyō sensasu ruinen tōkei* for 1946 and thereafter except 1950.

household population and the number of agricultural workers. A few fundamental patterns are discernible.

First, the numbers of farm households and of agricultural workers were surprisingly stable during the prewar period. During the thirty-five year period from 1905 to 1940, the number of farm households changed only by two percent, hovering around 5.5 million. Similarly, there was very little change in the number of agricultural workers until 1930, followed by a decline of about three-percent during the first decade of the war. This is remarkable stability in view of the fact that the total Japanese population increased substantially – from 46.62 million to 71.93 million – during this thirty-five year period. During this same period, the vast majority of agricultural households were maintained trans-generationally; the cases of whole households deserting their village and establishing branch families were exceptionally rare in most rural areas. On the other hand, the birth rate in farm households was fairly high. Except for those who inherited their families' households, the surplus population moved to industrial areas, supplying almost the entire labor force required for the expanding non-agricultural sector. This emigration amounted to approximately four hundred thousand people per annum, about seventy percent of whom found employment (Honda 1950; Namiki 1955, 1956 and 1960).

Secondly, the numbers of farm households and agricultural workers – especially the latter – substantially increased following Japan's defeat in World War II. This can be attributed to the immigration of discharged soldiers, repatriation from former colonies and occupied territories, and workers who lost their jobs to the devastation of urban industries at the time. According to more detailed data, Namiki demonstrated that the growth caused by these social factors ended around 1947, when the trend turned around. The outflow of population from this sector soon accelerated until, by 1950, the net emigration from farm households had reached about half a million per year. Then, until 1954, the numbers of both farm households and agricultural workers stabilized. This suggests that during these years, the natural increases in the numbers of farm households and the farm household population were absorbed by the non-agricultural sectors at levels consistently higher than during the prewar years (Namiki 1955).

Third, this stability soon dissolved and the numbers of farm households and agricultural workers began to rapidly decrease. The declining birth rate of postwar years led to the number of emigrants from this class peaking in the early 1960s. Yet, the number of emigrants as a proportion of the farm households' population continued to increase, as the agricultural sector entered a dissolution and reorganization phase (Tashiro 1976: 183). By 1995, the number of agricultural workers had been reduced to 9.08 million, of whom only 2.05 million were engaged in farming for more than one hundred and fifty days per annum (1995 Census of Agriculture and Forestry).

Through this process, the shape of farm management was greatly changed. The proportion of farm households engaged full-time in agricultural production peaked at 55.4% in 1947 against a background of wartime disruptions to the part-time employment market. However, this proportion soon began to decline, dropping to 34.3% in 1960 and 15.6% in 1970. Thus, the farm households that combined part-time agricultural production with other income generating employment became an overwhelming majority of the farming class. Initially, there was growth in the proportions of two different types of part-time agricultural production. The first-type engaged in farming primarily with a side job providing secondary income. The second-type were primarily engaged in other income generating employment and farmed on the side. But the first-type gradually stagnated and then declined, while the second-type formed a majority and became the mainstream. The second-type accounted for 50.8% of all farm households in 1970 and exceeded 70% in 1990. In recent years, the second-type part-time households tend to quit agriculture entirely, accelerating the decline in the total number of farm households. Consequently, the percentage of the full-time farm households gradually increased to 14.3% in 1985 and 16.0% in 1995 after a low of 12.4% in 1975. Yet, even in 1995, the second-type part-time households accounted for 69.1% of all farm households.

Immigration and emigration of the farm household labor force

The progressive differentiation of the farming class is reflected in massive intra- and inter-generational mobility. The pattern of this movement can be seen, to some extent, in official statistics. Figure 6.2 graphs the migration of the labor force of farm households between the agriculture and the non-agricultural sector. (Figure 6.2(a) indicates outflow above and inflow below the x-axis and Figure 6.2(b) graphs the proportions taking different avenues of emigration to the non-agricultural sector).

During the twenty-two year period under consideration, the number of immigrants remains stable, hovering around one hundred thousand, whilst the number of emigrants gradually declines until 1970 and rapidly decreases thereafter. The breakdown of the emigrants suggests that 'new graduates' form the largest group until 1965 but their proportion of the total emigration falls away after that. 'Other emigrants' also continue to decline over time. In their places, 'other commuters' and 'new graduate commuters' become the major categories. This means that, whereas emigration from villages to urban areas initially

Figure 6.2 In-flow and out-flow of the farming labor force

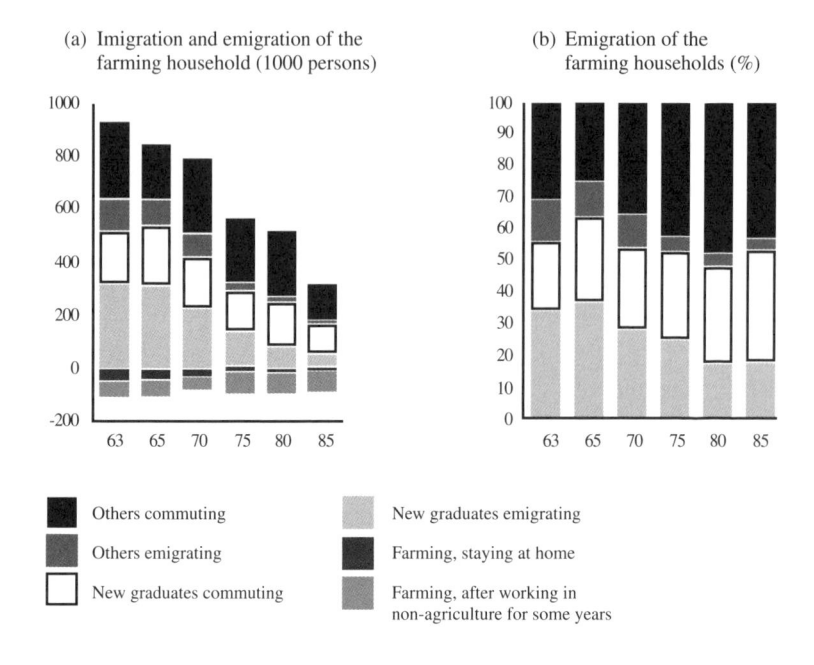

(a) Imigration and emigration of the farming household (1000 persons)

(b) Emigration of the farming households (%)

- Others commuting
- Others emigrating
- New graduates commuting
- New graduates emigrating
- Farming, staying at home
- Farming, after working in non-agriculture for some years

Note: Data based on *Nōka shūgyō dōkō chōsa* (Surveys on employment of farm household members).

constituted approximately one-half of outward migration, those who maintain their primary residence in the village but no longer work in agricultural production as their primary occupation – instead assuming jobs in the non-agricultural sector – later constituted the largest group of farming class emigrants. Thus the formation of part-time farm households became the primary route of outward movement of the farm household labor force.

In this process, the sociological attributes of emigrants have changed. The breakdown of male emigrants indicates that up to 1965 household heads constituted 13.6% of all emigrants from the farming class, household heirs accounted for 36.0% and non-heirs 50.5%. In contrast, in 1980, the proportion of emigrating household heads had increased to 17.7% and heirs to 46.3%. The total of these two groups accounted for some 64% of men leaving the sector.[3] This suggests that the total numbers of non-heir males had decreased with the declining birthrates even whilst the family heirs increasingly abandoned full-time farming. In Japanese farm households, as we have seen before, it was a common pattern that one heir (generally male) would inherit the farm household while the other male siblings would move to non-agricultural sectors. The evidence here, though, indicates that even heads and heirs began to leave the farming sector as commuting workers and part-time farming became the norm.

Limitations of official statistics

Official statistics provide no further information. While there is rich and precise information available about the quantitative structure of the farming population and mobility between the agricultural and non-agricultural sectors at various times, this data does not adequately document emigration from the farming sector, because agricultural census data and official statistics measure households rather than individuals in their data collection. For example, official data collates information about the increasing and decreasing mobility of members of farm households and their inter-occupational movements. Data about their occupations after emigration are limited to broad industrial categories. Therefore, this data does not enable us to examine the careers and final class destinations of individuals of farm origin nor does it enable us to draw any final conclusions about the differentiation of the farming class. We must instead rely on the SSM Survey data.

Intergenerational mobility of persons of farm origin

Overview

Let us first scrutinize the overall structure of intergenerational mobility of those for whom farming defines their class of origin. Table 6.1 tabulates their intergenerational mobility at five points over the forty year period from 1955 to 1995. The tables are based on a modification of the four-class model, using instead five-classes by separating the old middle class into the 'self-employed' and 'farming' sub-categories. The following observations can be made from the tables:

Table 6.1 Intergenerational mobility table by class categories (male)

1955

Father's class	Capitalist	New Middle	Working	Self-employed	Farming	Total
Capitalist	39 (19.8%)	39 (19.8%)	39 (19.8%)	57 (28.9%)	23 (11.7%)	197 (100.0%)
New middle	12 (6.9%)	78 (45.1%)	23 (13.3%)	23 (13.3%)	37 (21.4%)	173 (100.0%)
Working	6 (4.2%)	16 (11.2%)	78 (54.5%)	23 (16.1%)	20 (14.0%)	143 (100.0%)
Self-employed	18 (5.4%)	80 (24.0%)	79 (23.7%)	126 (37.7%)	31 (9.3%)	334 (100.0%)
Farming	28 (2.7%)	106 (10.4%)	136 (13.3%)	122 (12.0%)	628 (61.6%)	1020 (100.0%)
Total	103 (5.5%)	319 (17.1%)	355 (19.0%)	351 (18.8%)	739 (39.6%)	1867 (100.0%)

1965

Father's class	Capitalist	New Middle	Working	Self-employed	Farming	Total
Capitalist	64 (36.2%)	51 (28.8%)	26 (14.7%)	30 (16.9%)	6 (3.4%)	177 (100.0%)
New middle	18 (9.2%)	102 (52.3%)	51 (26.2%)	18 (9.2%)	6 (3.1%)	195 (100.0%)
Working	6 (2.6%)	48 (21.1%)	138 (60.8%)	24 (10.6%)	11 (4.8%)	227 (100.0%)
Self-employed	35 (10.0%)	82 (23.5%)	107 (30.7%)	112 (32.1%)	13 (3.7%)	349 (100.0%)
Farming	30 (3.5%)	140 (16.3%)	279 (32.4%)	106 (12.3%)	306 (35.5%)	861 (100.0%)
Total	153 (8.5%)	423 (23.4%)	601 (33.2%)	290 (16.0%)	342 (18.9%)	1809 (100.0%)

1975

Father's class	Capitalist	New Middle	Working	Self-employed	Farming	Total
Capitalist	29 (22.0%)	43 (32.6%)	25 (18.9%)	31 (23.5%)	4 (3.0%)	132 (100.0%)
New middle	23 (7.1%)	159 (49.2%)	89 (27.6%)	38 (11.8%)	14 (4.3%)	323 (100.0%)
Working	11 (3.6%)	69 (22.4%)	184 (59.7%)	34 (11.0%)	10 (3.2%)	308 (100.0%)
Self-employed	42 (7.8%)	147 (27.3%)	148 (27.5%)	184 (34.2%)	17 (3.2%)	538 (100.0%)
Farming	42 (4.2%)	176 (17.5%)	377 (37.4%)	114 (11.3%)	298 (29.6%)	1007 (100.0%)
Total	147 (6.4%)	594 (26.7%)	823 (35.7%)	401 (17.4%)	343 (14.9%)	2308 (100.0%)

1 The non-mobility rate of the farming population consistently declined from 0.616 in 1955 to 0.167 in 1995. They moved primarily to the working class, peaking at a mobility rate of 41.5% in 1985 and constituting a majority of those who were mobile. There is a rising trend in the rate of movement from farming to the new middle class during this period.
2 Comparing the *real numbers* vertically, we can observe that those of farm origin have consistently accounted for considerable

Table 6.1 Intergenerational mobility table by class categories (male) (cont.)

1985

Father's class	Respondent					
	Capitalist	New Middle	Working	Self-employed	Farming	Total
Capitalist	46 (25.4%)	59 (32.6%)	34 (18.8%)	39 (21.5%)	3 (1.7%)	181 (100.0%)
New middle	20 (6.2%)	193 (59.8%)	79 (24.5%)	29 (9.0%)	2 (0.6%)	323 (100.0%)
Working	9 (2.4%)	122 (32.0%)	202 (53.0%)	44 (11.5%)	4 (1.0%)	381 (100.0%)
Self-employed	23 (5.5%)	122 (28.9%)	127 (30.1%)	144 (34.1%)	6 (1.4%)	422 (100.0%)
Farming	24 (3.5%)	148 (21.5%)	285 (41.5%)	104 (15.1%)	126 (18.3%)	687 (100.0%)
Total	122 (6.1%)	644 (32.3%)	727 (36.5%)	360 (18.1%)	141 (7.1%)	1994 (100.0%)

1995

Father's class	Respondent					
	Capitalist	New Middle	Working	Self-employed	Farming	Total
Capitalist	68 (38.6%)	48 (27.3%)	36 (20.5%)	23 (13.1%)	1 (0.6%)	176 (100.0%)
New middle	33 (9.1%)	191 (52.8%)	102 (28.2%)	33 (9.1%)	3 (0.8%)	362 (100.0%)
Working	25 (5.7%)	147 (33.6%)	229 (54.2%)	34 (7.8%)	2 (0.5%)	437 (100.0%)
Self-employed	48 (10.7%)	119 (26.6%)	146 (32.7%)	129 (28.9%)	5 (1.1%)	447 (100.0%)
Farming	40 (7.6%)	126 (23.9%)	192 (36.4%)	82 (15.5%)	88 (16.7%)	528 (100.0%)
Total	214 (11.0%)	631 (32.4%)	705 (36.2%)	301 (15.4%)	99 (5.1%)	1950 (100.0%)

Source: SSM data

proportions of every class and contributed the largest numbers to the new middle class until 1975 and in the working class until 1985, although these two classes tend to be supplemented by internal reproduction in recent years.

3 Movement into the farming sector from other classes is consistently small. The inflow rate, that is, the proportion of those of non-farming origin in the farming population, only slightly exceeds ten percent each year. This is attributable to the fact that agriculture generally requires the possession of agricultural land, a prerequisite that makes it difficult for outsiders to enter the sector.

4 We have separately calculated the outflow rate and the inflow rate for women only in 1985 and 1995,[4] both of which are higher figures than for men. This supports the claim that few women inherit farm households but a considerable number enter the agricultural class via marriage.

Table 6.2 Intergenerational mobility based on the five-class schema (female)

1985

Father's class	Respondent					
	Capitalist	New Middle	Working	Self-employed	Farming	Total
Capitalist	10 (14.5%)	5 (7.2%)	38 (55.1%)	14 (20.3%)	1 (1.4%)	69 (100%)
New middle	2 (1.5%)	22 (16.2%)	74 (54.5%)	31 (22.8%)	6 (4.4%)	136 (100%)
Working	5 (3.2%)	8 (5.2%)	112 (72.3%)	20 (12.9%)	9 (5.8%)	155 (100%)
Self-employed	5 (3.0%)	11 (6.6%)	94 (56.7%)	44 (26.5%)	11 (6.6%)	166 (100%)
Farming	9 (3.4%)	15 (5.6%)	147 (54.9%)	26 (9.7%)	70 (26.1%)	268 (100%)
Total	31 (3.9%)	61 (7.7%)	465 (58.9%)	135 (17.1%)	97 (12.3%)	790 (100%)

1995

Father's class	Respondent					
	Capitalist	New Middle	Working	Self-employed	Farming	Total
Capitalist	30 (23.4%)	8 (6.3%)	61 (47.7%)	27 (21.1%)	1 (0.8%)	128 (100%)
New middle	17 (5.5%)	58 (18.9%)	186 (60.6%)	42 (13.7%)	3 (1.0%)	307 (100%)
Working	18 (5.0%)	36 (10.1%)	250 (70.0%)	44 (12.3%)	8 (2.2%)	357 (100%)
Self-employed	22 (6.7%)	35 (10.7%)	179 (54.9%)	81 (24.8%)	8 (2.5%)	326 (100%)
Farming	16 (4.2%)	25 (6.5%)	207 (53.9%)	55 (14.3%)	80 (20.8%)	384 (100%)
Total	103 (6.9%)	162 (10.8%)	883 (58.9%)	249 (16.6%)	100 (6.7%)	1498 (100%)

Source: 1995 SSM Survey data

The process of the differentiation of the farming class

Table 6.3 shows the class locations of people of farming class origin every ten years from 1955 to 1995 in a cohort-based format. We can observe the movement of each cohort at each age bracket and develop an overall picture of the differentiation of the farming class.

Table 6.3 (a) displays the proportion of respondents of farming origin who remain in the farming class, that is, the non-mobility rate. Two points can be observed. First, it is unambiguously clear that the younger the cohort is, the lower the percentage of the farming class, with the exception of the 1920–29 cohort. This cohort had a consistently high non-mobility rate. When they were middle aged in 1975 (i.e., aged 45–54 years) they reported a non-mobility rate of 39.6%, higher than the corresponding rate for the 1910–19 cohort in 1965. This may be attributable to the limited employment opportunities available to this group toward the end of and immediately after World War II, when they completed their

Table 6.3 Class locations of persons of farm origin at various time points by cohort

(a) Percentage belonging to the farming class (non-mobility rate)

Cohort born between	Male 1955	1965	1975	1985	1995	Female 1985	1995
1890–99	66.8						
1900–09	61.5	52.9					
1910–19	53.3	35.5	44.3				
1920–29	60.3	36.4	39.6	34.4		25.7	
1930–39		28.3	21.7	14.3	19.6	21.2	18.8
1940–49			19.2	8.9	11.0	8.8	8.7
1950–59				4.5	7.6	3.4	6.3
1960–69					6.1		5.3

(b) Working class

Cohort born between	Male 1955	1965	1975	1985	1995	Female 1985	1995
1890–99	7.0						
1900–09	9.4	12.5					
1910–19	14.5	33.5	22.1				
1920–29	19.0	26.3	26.8	29.3		24.8	
1930–39		43.3	42.2	43.3	30.7	43.4	24.0
1940–49			49.4	48.9	44.5	47.5	46.2
1950–59				51.7	38.7	34.5	46.8
1960–69					36.4		28.9

(c) New middle class

Cohort born between	Male 1955	1965	1975	1985	1995	Female 1985	1995
1890–99	5.3						
1900–09	9.8	11.8					
1910–19	13.6	15.7	15.0				
1920–29	14.3	22.8	17.9	17.2		0.0	
1930–39		13.7	17.3	18.2	14.7	0.9	1.6
1940–49			20.3	24.4	26.0	6.3	4.6
1950–59				32.6	39.5	12.1	9.5
1960–69					39.4		5.3

Note: Male figures are based only on those in active employment whereas female figures include those who are not employed.

Source: SSM Survey data.

education and went into the job market. This cohort also had some difficulties in securing employment in the post-recovery period when large numbers of younger people found employment outside of the agricultural sector as new graduates. Consequently, the 1920s' cohort became the driving force of agriculture in postwar Japan.

In contrast, of the 1940–49 cohort, not quite 20% remained in farming in 1975, and that already low rate was more than halved ten years later. The proportions remaining in the farming class hovered below ten percent for later cohorts. The almost landslide differentiation of the farming class is obvious.

Available data and, therefore, observable patterns are limited concerning women. Yet, the proportion of female farmers resembles male farmers among the 1930–39 female cohort and those who followed them; women who entered the job market around 1960 when male employment outside of agriculture increased. This suggests that females of farming origin form a central force in agriculture today.

The second point is that for each male cohort born in or after 1910, the percentage remaining in the farming class gradually declines as they age, but later increases again. In other words, the relationship between age and farming for these cohorts is curvilinear. The turning point for the 'recovery' is 1975 for the pre-1929 cohort and 1995 for those born later. This means that many who originated in the farming class returned to agriculture after working for some years in a non-farming sector.

The 1995 SSM Survey data also traces the classes to which emigrants from the farming class moved. Table 6.3 (b) and (c) reveal the proportions of people of farming class origin who moved to the working and new middle classes respectively. The figures are small for both groups in 1955. However, in 1965, the percentages emigrating to the working class dramatically increased among those in the younger age brackets, marking a rapid movement away from farming, particularly among new graduates. The trend continued in 1975, followed by another sharp increase among the middle aged in 1985, indicating that those who had been employed in agriculture were moving away from it. At the same time, the younger cohorts were increasingly moving to the new middle class rather than to the working class, entering the job market as fresh graduates, whilst older cohorts continued to move into the working class in large numbers. On the whole, only small proportions of women moved to the new middle class, but much larger proportions moved to the working class. Though female figures include those without employment, women moved to the working class in similar proportions to their male counterparts, an indication that women with farming backgrounds are a major supply source for the working class.

Emigrants' destination class

We can clearly see the differentiation of the farming class through a detailed examination of farming emigrants on the basis of a sample of the 40–59 year old age bracket (born between 1935 and '54) in the 1995 SSM Survey data. Following the 1925–34 cohort, who had shouldered agriculture in postwar Japan, the next generation found themselves in the middle of the differentiation of the farming class which had begun in earnest during Japan's high-growth period. Because of their age at the time of the survey, we can more or less judge where they ended up in terms of their class locations. As a group for comparison, we select those in the non-farming sectors who came from a non-farming background. Our analysis shows:

1 Generally, the educational background of the emigrants from farming class is lower than the average of all of the non-farming sectors. Some 39.2% of the emigrants completed only compulsory education (compared with 19.5% for the non-farming sectors) but merely 8.2% finished higher education (compared to 25.3% for the non-farming group).

2 The emigrants are more likely than those from a non-farming background to belong to the working class. At their first jobs, 75.4% of farming class emigrants become members of the working class (66.3% for those of non-farming origin), and only 14.7% join the new middle class (compared to 23.4%). In their current jobs, 47.0% – nearly one-half – of the emigrants belong to the working class (compared to 35.2%), with only small percentages belonging to the capitalist and new middle classes. Of non-employed married women, some 47.5% of their husbands had working class jobs at the time of the survey, a much higher rate than for the non-farming classes (compared to 34.7%).

3 The internal composition of the working class shows that emigrants tend to concentrate in small and petty enterprises (72.9% compared to 64.9% for non-farming origin), are numerous in semi- and non-skilled jobs (44.3% compared with 32.9%) and scarce in clerical and sales jobs (22.3% versus 39.4%).

Table 6.4 Non-mobility rates of persons of farming class origin by various attributes

		Male 1965	Male 1995	Female 1995
Sibling order	1st son/daughter	52.7%	26.9%	13.0%
	2nd and 3rd son/daughter	22.4%	8.9%	12.4%
Sibling order at first job	1st son/daughter	58.5%	27.5%	13.5%
	2nd and 3rd son/daughter	36.9%	12.0%	14.9%
Educational qualification	Primary and middle school	41.1%	21.4%	17.0%
	High school	21.4%	14.8%	8.7%
	University and college	6.8%	9.1%	9.5%
Educational qualification at first job	Primary and middle school	53.3%	24.9%	25.9%
	High school	29.6%	15.8%	5.3%
	University and college	6.5%	8.2%	2.5%
First sons and daughters by education	Primary and middle school	58.8%	35.9%	20.0%
	High school	35.2%	25.2%	7.1%
	University and college	21.4%	11.8%	13.0%
Second and third sons and daughters by education	Primary and middle school	27.1%	12.6%	15.4%
	High school	10.5%	6.3%	9.9%
	University and college	0.0%	6.3%	5.3%

Note: Male figures are based only on those in active employment whereas female figures include those who are not employed.

Source: SSM Survey data.

These observations suggest that the farming population has played an important role in supplying a pool of labor to the working class, particularly the lower working class.

Factors that determined whether farmers left or remained in agriculture

Who remained in farming?

What factors conditioned the choices of whether to leave the farming class or not? Table 6.4 lists different non-mobility rates by various individual attributes. Data is available for a comparison of the male samples from 1965 and 1995.

First sons record the highest non-mobility rate in 1995 with 26.9%, but the rate for first daughters was 13.0 %; it was 12.4%

for second and third daughters. In fact, if we look at a sub-sample that excludes non-employed women we find that 20.8% of first daughters and 21.3% of second and third daughters inherit farming class positions. This indicates that women of farming origins make significant contributions to agriculture.

In contrast, while merely 8.9% of second and third sons remain in the farming class, this is an unexpectedly high figure in view of the popularly held view and 'dominant thesis' that first sons are the inheritors of agricultural households. Over time, the non-mobility rate decreases for first sons as well as for second and third sons, but the rate of decline is most noticeable at the time of the first job for second and third sons. In 1965 the proportion of second and third sons who chose farming as their first job was 36.9%, significantly higher than the proportion in farming at their present job (22.4%). This indicates that the practice of 'appreciation apprenticeships' – where non-inheritors assisted with the household's farming for a limited period of time upon graduation – was quite prevalent in 1965, whereas in 1995 only 12.0% of second and third sons in agricultural households took up farming as their first job, a sharp decline.

On the whole, the lower the educational background of those of farming origin, the higher the proportions remaining in farming. However, although only a small proportion of women with high school and university education had taken up farming as their first job, nearly ten percent of them were engaged in it as their present job in 1995. This suggests that some highly educated women tend to initially find employment in non-agricultural sectors but return to farming after a while.

Revisiting the 'dominant thesis'

A dominant thesis about the social mobility of the farming class is that, while first sons inherited their households and farms, second and third sons were given greater educational opportunities in recompense and moved to cities where they formed a supply pool for the urban industrial workforce.

Nojiri (1942) provided the prototype of this line of argument after conducting case studies of several villages in the Tohoku region and Saitama Prefecture. He demonstrated that a majority who left the village and found employment in cities were second and third sons; and the latter's educational qualifications were higher than the first sons'. This view became widespread during the 1950s and '60s when a public debate heated up over the so-called 'second and third son problem'. New civil codes issued after WWII defined equal rights for children regardless of sex and sibling order. However, many people pointed out that second and third sons in farm households could not inherit agricultural land and were thus disadvantaged. Ishiwata (1958: 195), for instance, argued: 'There were various methods of camouflaging the inequitable inheritance. The most prevalent method was to provide second and third sons with educational chances, a measure more cost-effective than establishing branch families and giving them an equal amount of land.'

The thesis continued to gain acceptance among social mobility researchers and educational sociologists. Tominaga (1990: 356), for example, maintained that a majority of those who moved from villages to cities during and after the 1920s to become modern industrial workers were 'second and third sons who had no alternatives but to leave their villages because of the primogeniture system'. Adding that the educational qualifications of second and third sons were higher than those of first sons, Hirota (1991) presented the most polished version of the thesis. Referring to the Taisho period (1912–26), Hirota argued that first sons did not require high educational qualifications and there were concerns that they would not come back to the villages if they were given education in cities. Therefore, this argument concludes, educational opportunities were reserved for second and third sons. Although first sons began to advance to secondary or higher education in the Showa period (1926–88), Hirota pointed out that it was still assumed that they would be the successors to their households, a belief that continued to restrict their pursuit of formal education even into the 1960s and '70s. However, the 'dominant thesis' appears to be extremely doubtful when some preceding studies, official statistics and the SSM Survey data are considered.

In the first place, whilst it was the dominant practice in eastern Japan for first sons alone to inherit their households and properties; this was not common in other areas of Japan (cf. Kawashima 1957, Takeda 1974, Toshitani 1974 and Tsuburai 1995).[5] The SSM data shows that the proportion of first sons inheriting farms is surprisingly small. According to the 1995 data, only 70 of 105 farmers in the sample are first sons (66.7%

– two thirds). If we expand the sample to include those whose spouses engage in farming, only 87 of the total of 148 men (58.8%) are first sons. Thus approximately 40% of inheritors are second and third sons. Admittedly, they may include those whose eldest brother died young, those who were adopted and those who established branch families immediately after World War II when there was a rapid increase in the total number of agricultural households. Still, these factors are not sufficient to explain the significant proportion of farm households inherited by second and third sons. This data clearly refutes the dominant and popular view that the successors to farm households are always first sons.

In the second place, there is no evidence to suggest that second and third sons have higher educational qualifications than first sons. The 1995 SSM data reveals that the rates of students of farm origin continuing to vocational high schools and above are 18.5% for first sons and 16.3% for second and third sons for the 1900–09 cohort; 15.5% and 17.8% respectively for the 1910–19 cohort; and 28.8% and 26.0% respectively for the 1920–29 cohort, showing no discernible differences between the two groups. For the postwar years, the 'Trend survey of new graduates of farm origin' (conducted by the Ministry of Agriculture, Forestry and Fisheries) provides data on the different levels of educational achievement for male inheritors/male non-inheritors/daughters. Until 1975, the proportions advancing to high school and beyond were consistently higher amongst male inheritors than male non-inheritors. The proportions of male non-inheritors who went on to high schools were lower than daughters. Furthermore, the employment data suggests that those with higher educational backgrounds tend to stay in their residences of origin. Though only a small proportion engaged in farming, the numbers who worked outside of farming without moving away from their native homes tended to be larger. In other words, though the highly educated were not inclined to work in the agricultural sector, they did not opt to immigrate to a different location. Accordingly, at least with respect to the postwar period, the 'dominant thesis' that second and third sons were given education instead of inheriting land is totally unfounded. Instead it appears that farm households give their first sons preferential treatment, providing them with educational opportunities in an endeavor to keep them at home.

The upshot of all this is that the proportion of first sons remaining in farming is greater than second and third sons, although the proportion of first sons inheriting farm households is smaller than commonly believed. Some forty years ago, Kawashima (1957: 71) argued: 'A vague view that the primogeniture system in which first sons inherit land alone prevails throughout the country, but this is an illusion that contradicts the reality.' The illusion, together with additional speculations about the supposed relationship between sibling order and educational opportunities, gave rise to much confusion in studies on the differentiation of the farming class and social mobility as researchers themselves became captured and prejudiced by the ideology of the 'family primogeniture system'.

Forms of existence of the farm household population

Occupation and income of farm households

What are the conditions for those who remain in agricultural households whilst so many others are emigrating away from farming? To address this question, we will examine farm household members including the spouses of people engaged in farming.

Farm household members are skewed sharply in favor of the middle-aged and older, with 52.8% being sixty years or more. If we include people in their fifties, the percentage jumps up to 78.9%. Some 69.4% of farm household members currently engage in farming, with 13.7% belonging to the working class, 1.0% to the capitalist class, 1.6% to the new middle class and 2.3% to the self-employed. The latter three categories total only 4.9%, and the remaining 12.1% are without employment. Thus a majority of employees outside farming in those farm households that combine agriculture with other jobs are members of the working class. Women comprise a significant proportion of the population who are without occupations, but the non-employed constitute only 18.4% of women in all agricultural households. About 67.7% of women engage in farming, and 12.7% belong to the working class.

The average annual incomes of employed farm household members are 5.25 million yen for men and 0.95 million yen for women. Women's income level is noticeably low when compared to the average income of employed non-farm household members

(6.36 million yen for men and 1.87 million yen for women). The income of women in agricultural households is less than one-fifth of the income of men in the same category and approximately one-half of the income of women working in the non-agricultural sectors. Examining the wage distribution of women who are directly engaged in farming (N = 107) reveals that 37 (34.6%) have no income, 45 (42.1%) earn less than 2.5 million yen per annum, 19 (17.8%) belong to the DK (do not know) or the NA (no answer) group, and the average income is only 0.77 million yen. In comparison, the average income of men who engage in farming amounts to 5.39 million yen. This means that most women in farming engage in work without compensation whilst men reap the rewards of female labor and enjoy a relatively high income. We can call this 'patriarchal income distribution', reflecting the 'feudal exploitation' pointed out by Roemer (1982) and Wright (1985).

Does the 'agricultural surplus population' exist?

Some studies have claimed that the farming population contains a 'surplus population' which moves back and forth between the agricultural and non-agricultural sectors in accordance with business fluctuations (Ōkōchi 1950; Eguchi 1978). Other studies, including Namiki's research discussed above, argue that the 'agricultural surplus population' has constantly moved into the urban labor market, relatively unaffected by the business cycle. On this point, the 1995 SSM Survey data reveals some intriguing points.

We divide the entire sample of the A Questionnaire (see Table 4.1) into three categories: (1) those who have at some point been directly employed in agricultural production; (2) those who have at some point been self-employed but do not belong to the first category; and (3) others. Respondents in the second category recorded the highest job mobility over the course of their careers, averaging 2.71 different employers each, compared to 2.37 for the first category and 2.1 for the third group.[6] The second category also constituted the highest proportion (22.3%) of those employed by four or more establishments in their working lives, compared to 14.7 for the first category and 11.7 for the third. In summary, people who have worked in farming experience higher job mobility than those in the 'other' category but not as high as those who have been self-employed.

Furthermore, of the 191 people of farm origin who had worked at more than one job, 76 had moved between farm households (39.8%). Out of the remaining 115 people (60.2%) who have worked in jobs other than farming, 59 (30.9%) have had only one job outside of farming, 46 (24.1%) have had two or three, and only 10 (5.2%) have had four or more. In contrast, of the 389 individuals who have been self-employed, 314 (78.9%) have also worked as employees (that is, neither farmers nor self-employed). Of these, 121 (30.6%) have been employed by two or three establishments, and 46 (11.6%) by four or more.

The job histories recorded in the SSM Survey include neither *dekasegi* (seasonal work away from home) nor the additional non-farm employment that farmers undertake as side jobs. This makes it difficult to draw conclusions, but if we limit the scope of analysis to those who have been employed on a long-term basis, it is safe to say that farmers' mobility between the agricultural and non-agricultural sector is not nearly as high as the 'agricultural surplus population' thesis maintains. Such fluidity was more prevalent amongst the self-employed.

As discussed earlier, the Namiki thesis suggests that the outward movement of the farming workforce before World War II was rather constant, unaffected by economic fluctuations, and that this pattern continued for a while after the war with the number of both farm households and emigration from the farming class increasing. The 1995 SSM Survey data on the mobility of individuals of farming class origin shows a clear pattern after the number of farm households begins to decline: they tended either to secure long-term non-agricultural employment upon graduation or to find employment initially in farming before later settling into long-term non-agricultural employment. They did not generally move back and forth between the agricultural and non-agricultural sectors. The differentiation of the farming class constituted a constant emigration away from farm households.

The present state and future prospects of the differentiation of the farming class

Let us summarize the research that describes the present state of the differentiation of the farming class.

The numbers of farm households and agricultural workers remained high for a while after World War II but started to decline in the 1960s and recorded sharp decreases from the 1970s onward. Initially, emigrants consisted mainly of new graduates. However, the proportions of emigrating household heads and inheritors increased also, even whilst many farm households engaged in non-farm employment on the side and others found full-time employment, reducing their farming to a side job. In the process, the rate of emigration from the farming class rapidly increased, exceeding 80% in 1985. Emigration became the mainstream for people of the farming class, regardless of their educational background, sibling order and other sociological attributes.

Nevertheless, sibling order and educational background did affect whether they would emigrate or stay in farming. Generally, second and third sons had higher outward mobility than first sons, as did those with high educational qualifications compared to those without. However, the differences based on sibling order were not as substantial as the 'dominant thesis' claimed. Second and third sons accounted for a surprisingly large 40% of agricultural household successions. The 'dominant thesis' that inheritors of farm households are primarily first sons while second and third sons almost always emigrate is conclusively refuted.

About 70% of the population of agricultural households engage in farming, and a majority of the remainder belong to the working class. Thus most of the farm households that have side jobs or that do farming on the side are cross-class households, combining the farming and working classes. Amongst this group, the income of the farming class women is so low that the continuation of a patriarchal income distribution structure, i.e., 'feudal exploitation', is undeniable.

The working class constitutes the largest destination group of emigrants from agricultural households. Furthermore, a majority of non-employed emigrant women are married to men of the working class. Comparatively high percentages of emigrants from the farming class move into the lower strata of the working class in terms of firm size and occupation. In short, they have provided an important supply pool for the working class, particularly for the lower strata. However, since 1985, one generation after the commencement of the rapid differentiation of the farming class, the proportion of people from the farming class in the working class has declined. In 1995, the working class itself became the largest supplier of its own membership. The farming class is no longer the main supplier of new members for any other class. Thus, the differentiation of the farming class in postwar Japan has come to its final phase.

In 1995, the national average age for agricultural workers was 59.9 years. Some 46.3% of them are 65 years or older.[7] The 1920s' cohort who had consistently formed the core of the agricultural work force throughout the postwar years were in their seventies. Upon their retirement and death, the number of farm households will drastically decline. About 435 thousand out of 1.17 million farm households whose head is sixty years or older do not have successors living with them. Out of 2.85 million commercial farm households, 696 thousand do not have successors altogether.[8] It is inevitable that most of these farm households will disappear in the near future.

We have confirmed the landslide differentiation of the farming class in postwar Japan on the basis of various statistics and the SSM Survey data. Already in 1995, the system founded on self-sustaining small farmers was close to a complete breakdown. The 2005 SSM Survey will probably describe the differentiation of Japanese farming class in its final stage.

7 Women in Class Structure

Women and class

Class location mediated by family

How are women related to the class structure?

While on a certain level this question seems discriminatory – we never ask, 'How are men related to the class structure?' – it must nevertheless be asked, for women's relationships to the class structure are far more complex than men's.

For instance, consider the case of full-time housewives. Since they do not engage in paid work they are not directly involved in the capitalist mode of production. Therefore, they do not have their own class location. Are they then unrelated to class? Of course not. Family relations connect them to the class structure. Family is a basic unit of livelihood and daily life. Accordingly, the family transmits the effect of each class location from one member to another. An increase or decrease in her husband's salary, a change in his working conditions, etc., directly affects a woman's life. Her husband's views about work, including the values he has developed in his working life are, at least partially, shared by her. In short, full-time housewives are directly affected by their husband's class location. It thus seems safe to say that for many women 'class location is mediated by family'.

To a lesser degree, this also applies to employed women. Consider a woman who works in sales or as a clerk, occupations that we have characterized as working class, but whose husband's occupation locates him in the new middle class. While her work life may be low paid and have low status, her life is not entirely defined by the working class's characteristics. Instead, she enjoys a higher standard of living on the basis of her husband's much higher income. Hence, her own class location is not the key determinant of her living standard, consciousness or values.

Likewise, women generally experience class society differently to men.

Gender and class

From the above discussion, it is arguable that women share a common economic position as a house worker. The sexual division of labor typified by the statement 'men working; women tending family and home', is not simply a personal issue about the division of labor between a woman and a man in the privacy of their own home and marriage. The man's engagement in 'productive' work outside the home expends his labor power. In order to reproduce this labor power, domestic labor, such as cooking, washing, cleaning, etc., is required; and in the typical sexual division of labor the wife shoulders this domestic burden. Yet in spite of their best efforts, the man's mental and physical ability will decline over time, and society will need to replace his labor power. Domestic work is therefore necessary to produce new labor – to reproduce labor power trans-generationally. The wife also carries this domestic load. Thus, the sexual division of labor between a husband and a wife within their home has also become a social division of labor, defined as 'the man engaging in productive work and the wife in reproductive work'.

However, a decisive difference between the two sorts of labor is that a wage is paid for the husband's 'productive labor', but no wage is paid for the wife's 'reproductive labor'. Thus, domestic labor is unpaid work, suggesting that the husband and wife occupy totally different economic positions, leading some to argue that men and women belong, in fact, to different classes. From this perspective it doesn't matter which class their husband belongs to, a woman engaged in unpaid domestic labor belongs to a particular class called 'women'.

Christine Delphy is a prominent advocate of this position. Delphy argues that there are two modes of production in capitalist society: the 'industrial mode' and the 'family mode'. Ordinary goods are produced by the industrial mode, but services within the home and child rearing are produced through the family mode. Almost all women engage in domestic work in the family mode as a 'wife' of someone; they thus constitute a class of their own. Therefore, their class location cannot be reduced to their husbands' class. Delphy goes so far as to claim that 'it is about as accurate to say that the wife of a bourgeois man is bourgeois as it is to say that the slave of a plantation owner is himself a plantation owner' (1970: 72).

Although I do not want to dismiss the significance of this proposition, it seems confusing to characterize the relationships between men and women in the domestic sphere in class terms which, as we have seen, conventionally refer to the sphere of production. For one thing, such a classificatory schema would serve to obscure the fact that many women are treated as secondary labor in the 'industrial mode' because of the burden of domestic labor that they carry in the 'family mode'. To maintain clarity about the interdependent relationship between the two, it is more appropriate to consider them as separate mechanisms, calling one 'class' and the other 'gender'. Besides, treating all women as belonging to the same class is to deny the differing access to power and the different interests within the broad population of women. Thus, paraphrasing Delphy, it seems more accurate to say: to regard bourgeois women and proletariat women as belonging to the same class is only accurate in the same sense that the slave of a plantation owner is himself a plantation owner. Some women are the wives of wealthy capitalists, some are executives of small and medium-sized enterprises, others are the wives of agricultural households, of the new (white) middle class, black women laborers and so on. If we treat all of these women as belonging to the same class simply on the basis of their engagement in domestic labor, we commit an extreme form of gender reductionism, one which ignores the diversity of classes and ethnicities that are also significant determinants in women's lives.

While earlier studies of class have tended to ignore women's problems and have not sufficiently dealt with the inequalities between men and women (cf. Hashimoto 1997), we cannot resolve these issues by categorizing all women as belonging to a single class of their own. Rather, we must regard class and gender as two mutually influencing and frequently overlapping factors.

Differences in interclass mobility

In chapter 5 we established that men tend to remain in their class of origin and attributed this to constraints in interclass mobility. That discussion, though, was confined to men's class mobility to

Table 7.1 Intergenerational mobility in 1995 (female)

Father's class (main occupation)	Respondent's class (present occupation)				
	Capitalist	New Middle	Working	Old Middle	Total
Capitalist	**30** (23.6%)	8 (6.3%)	61 (48.0%)	28 (22.0%)	127 (100.0%)
New Middle	17 (5.6%)	**58** (19.0%)	186 (60.8%)	45 (14.7%)	306 (100.0%)
Working	18 (5.1%)	36 (10.1%)	**250** (70.2%)	52 (14.6%)	356 (100.0%)
Old Middle	38 (5.4%)	60 (8.5%)	386 (54.5%)	**224** (31.6%)	708 (100.0%)
Total	103 (6.9%)	162 (10.8%)	883 (59.0%)	349 (23.3%)	1497 (100.0%)

Source: 1995 SSM Survey data

facilitate analysis of mobility at different ages. Now we need to determine whether there is a similar trend for women.

Table 7.1 is a table of women's inter-generational class mobility. As we did with men in chapter 5, we will consider the boldfaced numbers, i.e., the number of people whose class of origin and present class locations are identical. There are thirty such people in the capitalist class, which comprises 23.6% of those originating from the capitalist class. Looking at the bottom row of the total, only 6.9% of the female sample currently belongs to the capitalist class. People who have entered the capitalist class from other classes of origin account for about 5% of each class. Therefore, we can say that women who originated from the capitalist class are more likely to belong to that class than to have emerged from another class. Likewise, if we look at the boldfaced numbers referring to other classes, 58 new middle class women originated from the new middle class (19.0%); 250 working class women were born into the working class (70.2%); and 224 old middle class women originated from the old middle class (31.6%). In each case, the percentage of women who have come from the same class is larger than the percentages of women who have moved from other classes. Therefore, we can state that, like men, women generally tend to belong to the same class as their class of origin.

When, however, we compare the above table with the men's interclass mobility table (Table 5.1 (a)), we notice several differences. First, 38.6% of men from the capitalist class and 52.8% of men from the new middle class have remained in their original class, whereas the percentages of women who have remained in these two classes are only 23.6% and 19.0% respectively. The percentages of women who have moved from

Table 7.2 A comparison of male & female odds ratios of intergenerational mobility (father × respondent)

	Female	Male
Capitalist class	5.495	7.021
New Middle class	2.444	2.914
Working class	1.893	2.399
Old Middle class	2.458	4.148

Source: 1995 SSM Survey data

the capitalist and new middle classes to the working class are large, namely 48.0% and 60.8% respectively. As a consequence of this large movement to the working class, women's gross mobility rate is 0.625, which is higher than the men's rate of 0.594. The major reason for this discrepancy lies in the difference between men's and women's class composition. First, the proportion of men in the capitalist and new middle classes is a significantly larger proportion of the male population than the corresponding proportion of women. In other words, while the working class is the largest class for both men and women, the distribution of men across the four classes is more even than it is for women. This sexual difference in class composition is quite apparent in the differences between a father's and daughter's class position, which suggests that a huge number of women must move from the capitalist and new middle classes to the working class.

These differences in the sexual composition of the classes are not the only reason for higher class mobility amongst women, however. Table 7.2 shows differences in the odds ratios for men and women and indicates that the classes are more exclusive for men than women. As discussed in chapter 5, the odds ratio is an index of the degree of exclusivity of the classes based on the different classes of the respondents and their fathers, and independent of the class composition. Women's odds ratios are smaller than men's for all classes, which means that the classes are less exclusive for women than for men. In other words, compared to men, women move more freely from their class of origin.

But how, we might ask, can women be more free than men to move from their class of origin? The answer can be found by comparing the odds ratios of the four classes. The odds ratios are smaller for women than for men in all four classes, with the greatest differences in the capitalist and old middle classes. Both of these classes, as discussed, are primarily defined by their ownership of the means of production. Since, in most cases, sons inherit the means of production owned by their fathers (except in those instances where there are no male children), it is extremely difficult for daughters to succeed to their father's capitalist or old middle class locations. On the other hand, women from the new middle and working classes have a particular route for interclass mobility not generally open to men, that is, to marry a capitalist or old middle class man. Ironically, then, it is the patriarchal discrimination against women inheriting the means of production that allows them greater freedom to move from their class of origin.

Wife's and husband's class location

Does love surmount class?

People of all times and places have told stories of the tragic love between two people who cannot be united because of their different classes. Are such tales still pertinent in modern society? Are men and women still segregated by their class? Or do people today choose their marriage partner without any considerations of class?

Table 7.3 shows the class locations of people married between 1981 and 1995. The couples indicated in the boldfaced numerals in the diagonal line – those whose class locations are identical to their spouses – are slightly more numerous than the others,

Table 7.3 *Class location of married couples (couples married during 1981–1995)*

Wife's class	Husband's class				
	Capitalist	New Middle	Working	Old Middle	Total
Capitalist	**9** (75.0%)	2 (16.7%)	1 (8.3%)	0 (0.0%)	12 (100.0%)
New Middle	4 (5.3%)	**49** (64.5%)	20 (26.3%)	3 (3.9%)	76 (100.0%)
Working	9 (4.2%)	93 (43.1%)	**97** (44.9%)	17 (7.9%)	216 (100.0%)
Old Middle	0 (0.0%)	5 (18.5%)	11 (40.7%)	**11** (40.7%)	27 (100.0%)
Total	22 (6.6%)	149 (45.0%)	129 (39.0%)	31 (9.4%)	331 (100.0%)

Source: 1995 SSM Survey Data

comprising just over one-half of the total (50.2%). In other words, marriages between people who belong to the same class – class endogamy – remains a general pattern in Japanese society. This is even more pronounced when we consider that more than one-half of the couples that married across classes are unions between women of the working class and men of the new middle class. As these are primarily marriages between office ladies and salaried men who are relatively close in status and social standing, these too are effectively endogamous marriages. In contrast, almost two-thirds (64.5%) of new middle class women married new middle class men, while only slightly more than one-quarter (26.3%) of new middle class women married working class men. Evidently, romance, or at least marriage, is difficult between a new middle class woman and a working class man.

To determine whether this tendency towards class endogamy is strengthening or weakening we have divided the sample into three groups according to the year of marriage and examined the change by using the coefficient of openness, as we did in chapter 5. The results are shown in Figure 7.1. Trends of change in the coefficient of openness differ between classes. The coefficient of openness has consistently risen for the old middle class, showing that the old middle class is becoming more open about interclass marriage. In more concrete terms, before 1965, 71.9% of old middle class women married an old middle class man, in contrast to the 57.0% of women who married old middle class men between 1966 and 1980, and 40.7% for those married after 1981.

In contrast, the coefficient of openness has declined for capitalist and new middle class women for the period 1966–80 and 1981–95. In other words, these two classes have become more exclusive in terms of marriage. Of new middle class women who married between 1966 and 1980, 45.6% married a new middle class man, but 40.4% married a working class man. Thus, for that cohort, marriage between a new middle class woman and a working class man was relatively common. As we have seen before, however, after 1981 new middle class women apparently became biased towards choosing a new middle class man as their marriage partner. As a result, the number of marriages between new middle class women and men, which constituted only 5.5% of the total marriages that occurred between 1966 and 1980, had reached 14.8% after 1981. We may regard this as a strong barrier being formed between new middle class women and working class men.

Figure 7.1 Coefficient of openness of the couple at marriage by times of marriage

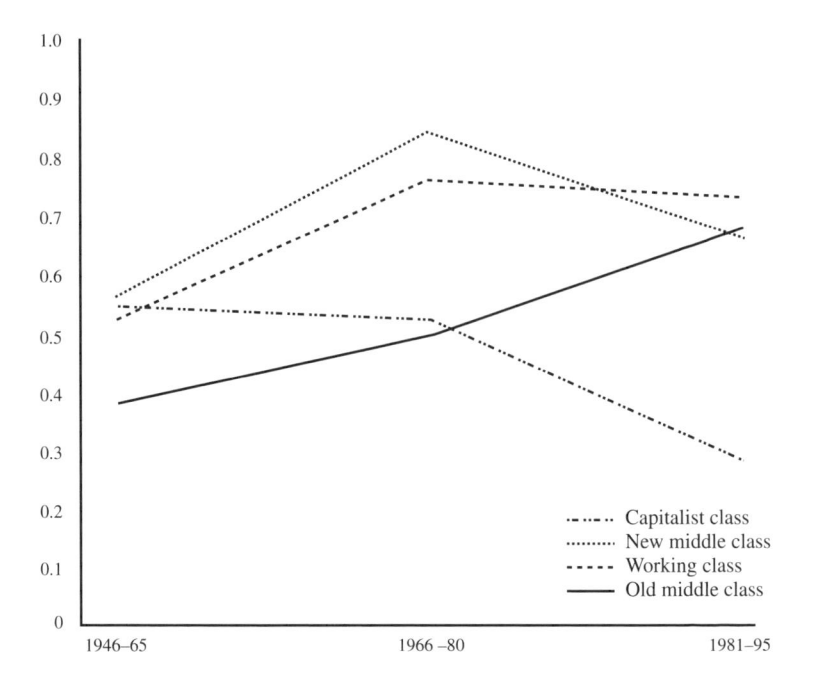

Source: 1995 SSM Survey data

Class locations of married couples

Although marriages between people of the same class are relatively common, there are many patterns of marriage and employment. Many women have no occupation, or have changed occupations upon marriage. The combinations of the class locations of married couples are diverse. Therefore, the entire female sample of the 1995 SSM Survey has been classified by: 1. their class location, 2. whether they have a spouse, and if so, by their spouse's class location. The results are shown in Table 7.4. Here, Japanese women are classified into 25 groups on the basis of the most basic economic and living conditions.

As shown in the boldfaced numbers in Figure Table 7.5, 733 women belong to the same class as their husbands. These women comprise 59.2% of the married women in couples in which both

Table 7.4 Husband's class location by wife's class location

Woman's class (present occupation)	Husband's class (present occupation) Capitalist	New Middle	Working	Old Middle	No spouse	Total
Capitalist	**88** (1) (3.3%)	6 (0.2%)	4 (0.2%)	5 (0.2%)	10 (0.4%)	113 (4.3%)
New Middle	7 (0.3%)	**72** (3) (2.7%)	36 (1.4%)	8 (0.3%)	60 (4) (2.3%)	183 (7.0%)
Working	37 (1.4%)	243 (6) (9.2%)	**330** (7) (12.5%)	75 (8) (2.8%)	274 (9) (10.4%)	959 (36.4%)
Old Middle	8 (0.3%)	26 (1.0%)	51 (1.9%)	**243** (11) (9.2%)	54 (2.1%)	382 (14.5%)
No Occupation	66 (2) (2.5%)	359 (5) (13.6%)	326 (10) (12.4%)	94 (12) (3.6%)	150 (13) (5.7%)	995 (37.8%)
Total	206 (7.8%)	706 (26.8%)	747 (28.4%)	425 (16.1%)	548 (20.8%)	2632 (100.0%)

Source: 1995 SSM Survey data

partners are employed. The degree of coincidence in the married couple's class locations is quite high, particularly in those cases where both partners in the couple belong to the working or old middle class. These numbers reach 330 and 243 respectively. The most prevalent class location of the husbands whose wives are not employed is in the new middle class, who number 359 people, accounting for 50.8% of the 706 women who have new middle class husbands. Half of the women without a spouse belong to the working class, and a large number of the rest do not have occupations.

Now, let us focus on 13 out of these 25 groups of women, each of which contains more than 60 women and comprises at least 2.3% of the total sample. Added together, the women in these groups total 2,380 and constitute 90.4% of the entire female sample. This is a sufficient number with which to create a general picture of contemporary Japanese women. Let us examine these women in detail, in the order of the capitalist class, new middle class, working class and the old middle class. Each woman's class location is identified principally on her own employment status. In cases where they are without employment, we use the husband's class location. Finally, we will look at single non-employed women. Identifying numbers in brackets are added to Table 7.4. The basic data of each group is summarized in Table 7.5.

Class Structure in Contemporary Japan

Table 7.5 *Profiles of women of the 13 groups*

	(1) Wives of S & MS enterprises enterprises	(2) Wives of enterprise managers	(3) Women with a double income	(4) Well-off un-attached	(5) Full-time house-wives	(6) Working house-wives I	(7) Working house-wives II	(8) Women of surplus population	(9) Unstable female workers	(10) Wives of working class	(11) Women living for family business	(12) Wives of crafts-men	(13) Women facing aging
Average age	48.6	48.0	42.0	31.9	44.2	42.9	45.2	48.1	35.4	46.3	52.3	49.3	55.0
Woman's income (10,000 yen)	285	64	319	290	23	163	148	148	237	23	152	23	125
Husband's income (10,000 yen)	892	903	620	-	663	644	461	415	-	456	577	448	-
Household income (10,000 yen)	1373	1090	1045	622	771	876	667	606	568	562	883	598	370
Employment status													
Employers & executives	45.0	-	0.0	0.0	-	0.0	0.0	0.0	0.0	-	2.9	-	-
Regular employees	0.0	-	65.3	81.7	-	35.0	37.9	38.7	72.3	-	0.0	-	-
Casual & part-time workers	0.0	-	34.7	18.3	-	59.7	55.8	54.7	25.2	-	0.0	-	-
Self-employed & liberal professions	5.7	-	0.0	0.0	-	0.0	0.0	0.0	0.0	-	12.3	-	-
Family workers	48.9	-	0.0	0.0	-	0.0	0.0	0.0	0.0	-	84.8	-	-
Occupations													
Professional	2.3	-	98.6	100.0	-	0.0	0.0	0.0	0.0	-	2.5	-	-
Managerial	8.1	-	1.4	0.0	-	0.0	0.0	0.0	0.0	-	0.0	-	-
Clerical	57.0	-	0.0	0.0	-	49.2	24.8	20.0	56.9	-	26.7	-	-
Sales	18.6	-	0.0	0.0	-	16.5	20.0	21.3	18.6	-	22.2	-	-
Skilled	8.1	-	0.0	0.0	-	10.3	15.8	18.7	10.6	-	9.9	-	-
Semi-skilled	2.3	-	0.0	0.0	-	16.9	27.0	28.0	9.5	-	7.8	-	-
Unskilled	0.0	-	0.0	0.0	-	6.2	11.2	10.7	4.0	-	3.7	-	-
Agriculture & Forestry	3.5	-	0.0	0.0	-	0.8	1.2	1.3	0.4	-	27.2	-	-

Women in Class Structure

Table 7.5 Profiles of women of the 13 groups (cont.)

	(1) Wives of S & MS enterprises enterprise	(2) Wives of managers	(3) Women with a double income	(4) Well-off un-attached	(5) Full-time house-wives	(6) Working house-wives I	(7) Working house-wives II	(8) Women of surplus population	(9) Unstable female workers	(10) Wives of working class	(11) Women living for family business	(12) Wives of crafts-men	(13) Women facing aging
Husband's occupations													
Professional	13.6	6.2	43.1	–	25.3	14.8	0.0	6.7	–	0.0	9.1	14.9	–
Managerial	25.0	36.9	12.5	55.0	14.8	14.4	0.0	0.0	–	0.0	0.4	0.0	–
Clerical	6.8	7.7	44.4	–	59.9	70.8	0.6	0.0	–	2.1	3.3	3.2	–
Sales	21.6	10.8	0.0	60.0	0.0	0.0	13.0	13.3	–	16.6	25.6	14.9	–
Skilled	26.1	26.2	0.0	43.9	0.9	0.0	38.2	37.3	–	33.4	22.7	29.8	–
Semi-skilled	2.3	9.2	0.0	24.6	0.9	0.0	32.1	9.3	–	32.8	12.4	8.5	–
Unskilled	3.4	0.0	0.0	68.3	0.0	0.0	13.0	6.7	–	12.3	0.8	4.3	–
Agriculture & Forestry	1.1	3.1	0.0	–	0.0	0.0	3.0	26.7	–	2.8	25.6	24.5	–
Receiving higher education (%)	25.3	31.8	63.9	55.0	29.5	25.1	6.1	13.3	27.8	9.8	11.1	20.4	12.7
Husbands receiving higher education (%)	42.0	48.5	69.4	–	57.4	37.2	6.7	12.1	–	13.6	18.6	19.4	–
Living with parent(s)	13.6	3.0	8.3	60.0	2.8	7.4	5.2	4.0	62.4	5.5	7.4	2.1	30.9
Status identification 'upper' or 'upper-middle'	62.2	56.9	45.1	43.9	36.9	34.2	22.0	23.0	24.8	25.7	36.5	33.7	20.0
Present society as 'fair', 'more or less fair'	32.5	31.7	36.6	24.6	36.4	28.0	23.1	23.9	26.4	28.4	29.6	21.1	25.9
'Satisfied' or 'more or less satisfied' with life	79.5	83.3	74.6	68.3	79.1	70.4	63.6	56.8	56.6	73.5	72.4	67.7	63.1
Want to let children have highest possible education	69.0	67.2	60.6	50.0	60.3	62.5	54.8	60.6	47.0	49.5	67.1	64.1	57.1
Children have tutors and/or cram schooling	48.8	50.0	23.6	17.5	35.1	34.3	32.4	37.5	25.1	31.5	35.0	43.5	35.4

167

Class Structure in Contemporary Japan

Table 7.5 Profiles of women of the 13 groups (cont.)

	(1) Wives of S & MS enterprises	(2) Wives of enterprise managers	(3) Women with a double income	(4) Well-off un-attached	(5) Full-time house-wives	(6) Working house-wives I	(7) Working house-wives II	(8) Women of surplus population	(9) Unstable female workers	(10) Wives of working class	(11) Women living for family business	(12) Wives of crafts-men	(13) Women facing aging
Gender Roles													
Men working; women family & home	38.6	50.8	16.7	16.7	48.2	30.0	31.2	30.7	33.9	49.2	48.1	54.3	41.5
Boys & girls with different upbringings	48.3	41.9	19.4	25.4	41.5	34.6	31.4	32.9	33.0	41.8	44.8	37.6	48.6
Women are suited for domestic work & child rearing	78.6	78.1	45.8	45.6	67.8	60.6	62.7	69.9	62.5	67.8	74.2	70.8	74.5
Work of housewife is socially significant	60.7	71.4	59.2	66.1	68.2	49.8	52.6	50.7	62.3	68.2	63.4	69.7	62.2
Women also stress a life with occupation	75.6	76.3	76.1	84.7	75.4	78.6	76.7	74.3	78.9	69.3	81.5	79.1	77.8
Housewife is fortunate	50.0	43.3	28.2	8.9	36.2	24.2	32.1	44.3	28.9	29.3	35.9	36.4	43.8
Husband's participation in domestic work													
Preparing meals & tidying up afterwards	23.3	26.9	37.1	-	46.8	46.2	48.0	43.2	-	39.9	37.1	34.0	-
Cleaning & laundry	27.9	19.2	40.0	-	37.0	40.3	41.5	37.8	-	37.0	30.1	30.0	-
Child rearing & minding	45.5	56.5	80.6	-	80.2	71.4	64.3	54.8	-	71.7	59.7	65.0	-
Inequity between genders (very much)	33.3	23.1	45.7	40.6	38.3	33.3	32.6	22.2	42.0	32.1	23.9	16.0	24.1

Source: 1995 SSM Survey data

Women of the capitalist class

There are two groups of women in the capitalist class: (1) capitalist class women married to capitalist class men: 'women of small or medium-sized enterprises'; and (2) women without occupations who are married to capitalist class men: 'wives of enterprise managers'.

(1) Capitalist class women married to capitalist class men: 'women of small or medium-sized enterprises'

Many women operate enterprises in conjunction with their husbands. In terms of occupations, 45.5% of them are employers and executives; the rest are primarily family workers. Their average age is 48.6 years, and although on average their personal income is not high, i.e., 2.85 million yen, their average household income amounts to 13.73 million yen, by far the highest of all groups.

How did they become members of the capitalist class? Primarily by marrying men already of the capitalist class. Almost sixty percent (59.1%) of the total fit this category. In addition, 39.4% of their husbands' fathers also belong to the capitalist class. In other words, their husbands were the owners or potential inheritors of small and medium-sized enterprises. The women now assist their husbands in running their enterprises. Furthermore, of these women, 30.8% were born into the capitalist class. We can therefore say that their present class locations were determined first by their parents' position and secondly by their husband's. It is, however, also worth noting that 22.7% of the husbands were members of the working class when they married. Perhaps, the husband set up a business independently, and the husband and wife have established their present position by cooperating together.

Even though these women are in the capitalist class, the scale of their business is extremely small. Up to 88.6% of them have less than 30 employees, 10.2% have 30 to 299 employees, and only 1.1% has more than 300 employees. It is also noteworthy that in their daily work, by far the largest proportion of the women (57.0%) are engaged in clerical work, 18.6% in sales work, and only 8.1% perform managerial duties. An expression that depicts these women's real role is 'women of small or medium-sized enterprises'.

While these women engage in paid work, they also single-handedly undertake the domestic labor in their households. Their husbands' participation in domestic affairs is one of the lowest of all the groups. Reflecting this situation, the proportion of women in this group who ascribe to traditional gender roles as expressed in the statement, 'men working; women tending family and home' is the second highest of the eight groups of employed women. Similarly, the proportions of women who support statements like 'boys and girls should be brought up differently' and 'women are more suited to domestic work and child rearing' are nearly the highest of all groups. Adhering to specific gender roles, these women live in traditional conjugal and family relationships, yet are employed and maintain a high standard of living.

(2) **Women without occupations who are married to capitalist class men: 'wives of enterprise managers'**

These women are full-time housewives whose husbands are generally managers of enterprises. Their average age is 48. Although they are without occupations, they have an average income of 0.64 million yen; a not insignificant amount. Approximately 15% of these women receive an income ranging from 2–10 million yen, most likely from assets. The average household income is 10.9 million yen, the second highest.

Like 'women of small or medium-sized enterprises (1)', many of their husbands (63.9%) were already members of the capitalist class at the time of their marriage. They are, however, slightly different from the 'women of small or medium-sized enterprises' in the scale of enterprise that their husbands manage. Just over one-half (54.5%) of these are enterprises with less than 30 employees, those with 30 to 299 employees make up 33.3%, and those with more than 300 employees comprise 12.1%. Thus the wives of managers of relatively large enterprises are much more common in this category. In addition, the percentage of the husbands who were in the new middle class at the time of marriage is 27.8% (compared to 13.6% for (1)). In other words, although many women in this group married the heir to a small or medium-sized enterprise, this group also includes many women whose husbands were salaried employees in clerical or managerial positions at the time of marriage and were later promoted.

These women assume sole responsibility for domestic labor, which they see as their rightful duty. The degree of their husbands' participation in domestic affairs is among the lowest of all the groups. More than one-half (50.8%) of these women endorse the sexual division of labor described in the saying, 'men working; women tending family and home'. Almost three-quarters (71.4%) of these women regard the 'work of the full-time housewife as socially significant' and 43.3% think of 'the full-time housewife as being fortunate'. As such, they approach their domestic duties with pride. They are extremely concerned with their children's educational advancement. Two-thirds (67.2%) consider it important to provide 'their children with the highest possible education' and 50.0% of them consider it important to supply 'their children with a personal tutor and/or a cramming school'. These responses are the highest for all groups. While these women are deeply involved in their families' enterprises, they embody an ideal of the modern housewife, with a clear-cut division of labor based on gender roles and a strong focus on the interests of their children.

Women of the new middle class

New middle class women can be divided into three groups: (3) new middle class women married to new middle class men: 'women with a double income'; (4) single new middle class women: 'well-off unattached women'; and (5) non-employed women married to new middle class men: 'the core group of full-time housewives'.

(3) **New middle class women married to new middle class men: 'women with a double income'**

These women are professionals, largely working for an enterprise, local government, a school, or the like, and whose husbands have white-collar jobs. Nearly half (46.5%) of them work for a government or municipal office. Almost two-thirds (65.3%) are regular employees and the remainder (34.7%) are casual and part-time workers. Their average age is 42 years, and their average income is 3.19 million yen, the highest of all the groups. The average income for full-time employees is 4.38 million yen. The average household income is 10.45 million yen; the highest after the capitalist class. More than-half (51.1%) of all households in this group have a housing loan, the largest of all groups; but this should be seen as evidence of their ability to repay the loan and interest. Around two-thirds of these people have received a higher education (63.9% of women and 69.4% of their husbands), the highest of all groups for both sexes.

These women can be characterized by their rejection of the traditional sexual division of labor. On the one hand, only 16.7% of these women support the sexual division of labor articulated in the statement: 'men working; women tending family and home'. And only 19.4% of them agree with the statement, 'boys and girls should be brought up differently'. Both of these responses are the lowest amongst all groups. On the other hand, 45.7% of women responded 'yes, very much so' to a statement that there is inequity between genders; this time the highest of all groups. Thus, we can presume that these women are greatly concerned with issues of gender discrimination. The extent of their husband's participation in domestic affairs is comparatively high, and their gender roles are not apparent. This suggests that they are aiming at an equal conjugal relationship.

Nonetheless, over one-third (36.6%) of these women regard the present society as 'fair' or 'more or less fair', highest of all the groups. The degree of satisfaction with their life is also relatively high. We can say that their anger at discrimination against women does not translate as anger and dissatisfaction with society at large. This is perhaps due to their relatively high social status.

(4) Single new middle class women: 'well-off unattached women'

These women are professionals mainly employed by an enterprise, local government, school or the like. They have no spouse. More than eighty percent (81.7%) are full-time employees and the rest are casual or part-time workers. Their average income is 2.9 million yen, which is not particularly high, but is relatively high amongst Japanese women. Their educational background is high, with more than one-half (55.0%) having received a higher education.

As one might expect, many of the women in this group do not accept the traditional sexual division of labor; only 16.7% support the statement 'men working; women tending family and home' – equal to the 'women with a double income (3)' as the lowest of all groups. Similarly, only 8.9% of these women agree that 'the full-time housewife is fortunate'. Hence, the vast majority of them are strongly disinclined towards becoming a housewife.

These women are sub-divided into two groups depending on whether or not they live with their parents. The average age of the women who live with their parents is 28, and their average income is only 2.51 million yen. However, their average household income is 9.42 million, and 58.8% of them identify their social status as 'upper' or 'upper-middle'. This is as high a response as the women of the capitalist class. While they strongly challenge traditional gender roles, 57.6% affirm the notion that 'women are suited for domestic work and child rearing'. In contrast, the average age of the women who do not live with their parents is 37.8 years, and their average income is 3.47 million yen. Only 21.7% identify their status as 'upper' or 'upper-middle'. Even though they engage in professional work, the life of a single woman is still not easy. Their living standard is quite high, however, compared with single working class women who do not live with their parents. In contrast to those still living with their parents, not many of these new middle class women (29.2%) consider 'women to be suited for domestic work and child rearing'. Perhaps, then, many of them have consciously chosen to live the single life.

Under the present circumstances, where women's wages are low, it may not be literally accurate to label this group, 'well-off unattached women'. Nonetheless, these women not only earn relatively high incomes, but they have stable, professional employment. We can also say that these women embody freedoms hard fought for in the face of Japan's continuing systemic discrimination against women. Some of these women will in time get married and move to another group. But with women increasingly receiving higher levels of education, this category of women will continue to grow and exert an influence disproportionate to its size.

(5) **Non-employed women married to new middle class men: the core group of 'full-time housewives'**

These women are full-time housewives whose husbands are generally white-collar workers. They are the largest group within the women's sample, constituting 13.6% of the total. As such, they are the core group representing the traditional image of the 'full-time housewife'. Their average age is 44.2 years, and their average household income is 7.71 million yen. The household income is not very high, but the husband's income is 6.63 million yen, the highest except for the capitalist class. Relatively few of these women have received a higher education (29.5%), yet more than one-half (57.4%) of their husbands have. Thus we see that many women in this group have achieved 'hypergamy' in terms of education. This is the big difference between them and the 'women with a double income (3)', who generally have a similar educational background to their husbands. Their satisfaction with life is as high as the capitalist class women, with 79.1% answering 'satisfied' or 'more or less satisfied' to questions concerning their quality of life.

In general, they have a strong tendency to support traditional gender roles, with 48.2% of them agreeing with the statement, 'men working; women tending family and home'. Even so, they tend to find that their husbands cooperate in assisting with domestic duties. Up to 80.2% appreciate that their husbands 'always' or 'sometimes' participate in 'child rearing and child minding'.[1] More than 85% of these women reported that they had 'no occupation' after 30 years of age. In other words, the majority have consistently been full-time housewives. Representing something of a departure from the prevailing stereotype, they are not overly concerned with their children's educational advancement. 'Providing their children with the highest possible education' is important for 60.3% of these women and providing 'a personal tutor and/or a cramming school' rates highly for 35.1% of them. These responses are a little higher than the average for all groups. Even though they do not live in luxury, they maintain a standard of living slightly higher than average, are slightly more interested in their children's education, and support their husbands, who are generally more highly educated and who devote their energies to Japanese companies. Thus, it is in this category that we find the 'typical full-time housewife' of contemporary Japan.

Women of the working class

Working class women can be divided into five groups: (6) working class women married to new middle class men: 'working housewives I'; (7) working class women married to working class men: 'working housewives II'; (8) working class women married to old middle class men: 'women of "surplus population"'; (9) single working class women: 'unstable female workers'; and (10) non-employed women married to working class men: 'wives of the working class'.

(6) Working class women married to new middle class men: 'working housewives I'

Typically married to white-collar workers and averaging 42.9 years of age, almost sixty percent (59.7%) of these women are employed part-time, with an additional 4.5% being engaged in home-based piecework. Only 35.0% are full-time employees. Approximately half (49.2%) work in clerical jobs, 16.9% are engaged in semi-skilled jobs, and 16.5% work in sales. Their average income is low at 1.63 million yen.

Compared to other women with white-collar husbands ('the core group of full-time housewives (5)'), we note several differences. Their husband's incomes average 6.44 million yen. Although this is only 0.2 million yen less than the average for husbands in the 'core' group, only 37.2% of the husbands have received a higher education, about 20% fewer than the husbands in the 'core' group. In addition, 37.9% of these women's husbands work for an enterprise with less than 300 employees, higher than the husbands of the 'core' group (31.4%). Looking at their living arrangements, 19.9% of the 'core' group live in company-owned housing, suggesting that they benefit substantially from company fringe benefit schemes, while only 5.7% of the 'working housewives I' live in company-owned housing. At the same time, the percentage of homeowners in this group is relatively high at 72.4% (compared to 62.8% for the 'core' group). But 39.3% have a home loan (compared to only 28.7% for the 'core' group), the second highest of all the groups. The need to make mortgage payments is, we might assume, the reason why many of these women work part-time. Almost 10% fewer of these women answered 'satisfied' or 'more or less satisfied' to questions about their quality of life than the 'core' group. This group, then, is situated in a slightly lower stratum than 'the core group of the full-time housewives (5)'.

Of these women, 30.0% agree with the notion of 'men working; women tending family and home'. This is lower than the capitalist class women and full-time housewives, but considerably higher than the working women of the new middle class. Similar tendencies are found in other attitudes. In general, they display a middle level of consciousness about gender roles. In summary, we can say that these are housewives who supplement their household income through part-time work, while also maintaining traditional gender roles within the home. Their part-time work ensures that they enjoy a standard of living that is slightly higher than average.

(7) **Working class women married to working class men: 'working housewives II'**

Comprising 12.5% of the sample, second only to 'the core group of full-time housewives (5)' and more than one quarter of all of the working women surveyed, these women do mainly part-time work and have working class husbands. Averaging 45.2 years of age, 55.8% are part-time workers, and an additional 6.1% are engaged in piecework at home. Only 37.9% are full-time employees. Their occupational classification breaks down as follows: 27.0% are semi-skilled workers, 24.8% clerical workers and 20.0% work in sales. The majority of these women work for small or medium-sized enterprises, with 44.8% of them working for an enterprise with less than 30 employees and 29.2% working for an enterprise with 30 to 299 employees. Only 6.1% have received a higher education; the lowest of all the groups. Their average income is 1.48 million yen, the lowest average income for women in employment.

The prevalent characteristics of this group will become more apparent when we look at their husbands' occupations. Only 6.7% of their husbands have received a higher education; again, the lowest of all groups. Most of their husbands (38.2%) are skilled laborers, 32.1% are semi-skilled laborers, while sales workers and unskilled laborers account for 13.0% each. Their average income is a low 4.61 million yen, and most of them work for small or medium-sized enterprises, with 35.2% working for enterprises with less than 30 employees and 31.3% for enterprises with 30 to 299 employees. In other words, this group includes quite a few people positioned at the lower stratum of the working class.

Only 22.0% of the women in this group identify their status as 'upper' or 'upper middle'; the second lowest of all the groups. The proportion of this group that considers society to be unjust and is dissatisfied with life is high. These women are typically married to a man in the lower stratum of the working class, usually a manual worker in a small or medium-sized enterprise. They can be typified as 'stoically striving women', shouldering the domestic and childcare load as well as supplementing their household income with earnings from part-time work.

(8) Working class women married to old middle class men: 'women of "surplus population"'

Apart from the husband's family business or profession, these women work outside the home to earn an income. They account for about one-sixth of the women who are married to old middle class men. With an average age of 48.1 years, the proportion of part-time workers is high (54.7%). Sixty percent of them are manual workers. Nearly one-half (46.7%) work for enterprises with less than 30 employees, and 31.1% work for enterprises with 30 to 299 employees. Combined, these factors strongly suggest that they occupy the lower stratum of the working class. Their average income is 1.48 million yen, the lowest (with 'working housewives II (7)') of all groups of working women. Their status identification is low, with only 23.0% identifying themselves as 'upper' or 'upper middle'. High proportions of these women consider society to be unjust and voice dissatisfactions about their life.

Again, the characteristics of this group become clearer when we look at their husbands' occupations. Over one-half of their husbands (54.7%) work in enterprises with only one employee, and their average income is 4.15 million yen; the lowest of all the groups. More than one-third (34.7%) of these women's husbands are employed in the construction industry, and a relatively large proportion (9.3%) in the transportation industry. These compare to 14.0% and 2.1% respectively for cases where both the husband and the wife belong to the old middle class. Agriculture, forestry and fisheries employ over one-quarter (26.7%) of the group, and the average income of the husbands engaged in these industries is only 2.13 million yen (in cases where both the husbands and wives are of the old middle class it is 4.33 million yen). In other words, since these husbands are self-employed in businesses that are too small to employ their wives, these women are forced to find work elsewhere.

'Surplus population' is crude economic terminology, that, in an inhumane way, indicates people who are unemployed or engaged in extremely low paid occupations because of the scarcity of employment opportunities. Most of the people in this group – both women and men – are part of a 'surplus population' generated in the simple commodity production sector. The women, though, have become employees in the working class of the capitalist mode of production, leaving their husbands in the simple commodity production sector. They thus belong to the lower stratum of the old middle class as well as the lower stratum of the working class. In this dual sense, we can say that these women strongly exhibit characteristics of the lower stratum.

(9) Single working class women: 'unstable female workers'

These single women are generally employed by non-family owned enterprises. They are young, averaging 35.4 years of age. Although a clear majority (72.3%) are full-time employees, approximately one-quarter of the group (25.2%) are part-time workers. Over one-half (56.9%) are engaged in clerical work, with a further 18.6% working in sales. There are not many manual workers in this group. More than one-quarter (27.8%) of the women in this group have received a higher education, the highest rate amongst working class women. Their average income is 2.37 million yen, at the middle of the range of incomes for working women.

Comparison to the other group of single women (the 'well-off unattached women (4)') highlights quite a few differences. Many women in this group have a low status identification and express dissatisfaction with their lives. The most conspicuous difference, however, is the strong tendency for these women to accept traditional gender roles. One-third (33.9%) of the women in this group agree with the statement 'men working; women tending family and home', the highest of all the female employees. More noteworthy, though, 62.5% of them consider 'women to be suited for domestic work and child rearing'.

As with the 'well-off unattached women', this group of single women can also be sub-divided according to whether or not they live with their parents. The average income of the two subgroups is approximately the same, and no difference is found in their gender role consciousness, but their social characteristics differ starkly. Almost two-thirds (62%) of these women live with their parents. Their average age is 28.6 years, and their average income is 2.34 million yen. Given that their household income includes their parents' income, it averages 7.91 million yen, indicating that their living standard is not low. About one-third (32.5%) of this group identifies their status as 'upper' or 'upper middle', a similar response to the married new middle class women.

In contrast, the average age of the women who do not live with their parents is much higher at 46.7 years. Their average income, however, is virtually identical, at 2.41 million yen. The most striking characteristic of this subgroup is the percentages of widows (30.1%) and divorcees (35.9%). These are much higher than for 'well-off unattached women', where the rates are only 8.3% and 12.5% respectively. Furthermore, 40.8% of this group lives with unmarried children, compared to only 16.7% for the 'well-off unattached women'. Unlike the 'well-off unattached women', the single status of these women has not been consciously chosen, but has instead been thrust upon them by circumstances beyond their control. Roughly 40% of them were unemployed at the ages of 25 and 30. Many had quit work upon marrying, but were then forced to return to work in order to support themselves after their divorce or the death of their husbands. Finding employment and financially supporting their children while single-handedly raising them cannot have been easy. Whether or not this is the reason cannot be determined, but only 12.9% of them identify their status as 'upper' or 'upper middle'.

Many of the younger women living with their parents will marry in due course, and a large proportion of them will become full-time housewives. Inevitably, some of them will eventually return to this group after having separated from their husbands. For those who do not marry, there is a high probability that some time in the future they will have to care for elderly parents while living on a meager income. In this sense, these women exemplify the risks that underlie the comfortable lives that women 'appear' to enjoy under the protection of parents or husbands.

(10) **Non-employed women married to working class men: 'wives of the working class'**

This category comprises full-time housewives whose husbands are employed as blue-collar workers or in the sales and services sector. These women account for 12.4% of the entire female sample, making it the third largest group. Their average age is 46.3 years and their husband's average income is 4.56 million yen, approximately the same level as the 'working housewives II (7)'. A large proportion (40.9%) of these husbands, however, work for large enterprises (with more than 300 employees) or a governmental or municipal office. This indicates that most members of this group belong to the upper stratum of the working class. Reflecting this fact, almost three-quarters (73.5%) of these women responded 'satisfied' or 'more or less satisfied' to questions about their quality of life, about 10% higher than the 'working housewives II'. Approximately one-quarter of these women had their own working class occupations between the ages of 35 and 40, which means that they partially overlap with the 'working housewives II'.

About one-half (49.2%) of these women affirm the statement, 'men working; women tending family and home', which suggests that they generally uphold traditional gender roles. Nonetheless, only 29.3% believe that 'full-time housewives are fortunate'; the lowest of the non-employed women. This reveals that they are not necessarily satisfied with their role as full-time housewives. Perhaps this is because they have a hard time managing family life on a small income. In comparison with the 'core group of full-time housewives (5)', their household income is at least 2 million yen less. Both these women and their husband's have very low levels of higher education, with a participation rate of only 9.8% for women and 13.6% for their husbands. Status identification and reported satisfaction with life are also low. It is thus clear that the lives and consciousnesses of full-time housewives differ greatly depending on their husband's class location.

Despite accounting for a large proportion of the female population, full-time housewives of working class men, unlike the 'core group of full-time housewives (5)', are rarely portrayed as protagonists in TV dramas or have any kind of profile in the mass media. Nonetheless, these women support Japan's manufacturing industries by taking responsibility for domestic work and childcare, thereby enabling their husbands to devote themselves to their work as blue-collar employees of large enterprises.

Women of the old middle class

Women of the old middle class can be divided into two categories: (11) Old middle class women married to old middle class men: 'women living for the family business'; and (12) non-employed women married to old middle class men: 'wives of craftsmen'.

(11) Old middle class women married to old middle class men: 'women living for the family business'

This group is characterized by the fact that these women work for the family business with their husbands. They account for 9.2% of the entire female sample. Their average age is 52.3 years, the second highest of all groups of women. Fully 84.8% are family workers, and while their average income is quite low at 1.52 million yen, their household income is reasonably high at 8.83 million yen. We might say that these women are the mainstay of the old middle class, since their household income is nearly 3 million yen higher than the other women married to old middle class men ('women of "surplus population" (8)' and 'wives of craftsmen (12)').

Breaking the group down according to industry of employment we find that most of these women work in sales and the restaurant industry (30.6%), with agriculture, forestry and fisheries a close second (26.0%), followed by the personal services industries (e.g., cleaning, hairdressing, operating public bathhouses, inns, etc. (16.5%)) and manufacturing industries (12.4%). Looking at both partner's occupations we find that 62.8% of these couples are engaged in the same occupation, with agriculture, forestry and fisheries the most common (25.2%), followed by sales (17.8%) as the second most common industry to employ both members of the couple. Other combinations include cases where the husband has a professional position and the wife does clerical work (5.4%), and those where the husband is employed in skilled work and the wife in clerical work (9.1%). Thus, there appears to be a division of labor in many instances, with the wife assisting or supporting the husband. This suggests that the work of these women is often essential to the 'family business'.

Despite both the wife and the husband working, these women generally support traditional gender roles, with 48.1% agreeing with the statement 'men working; women tending family and home' and 74.2% agreeing that 'women are more suited to domestic work and child rearing'. At the same time, 81.5% of these women also believe that 'women should have an occupation'; as high a response as the 'well-off unattached women (4)'. This signifies the dual roles these women perform: as a 'wife keeping the house' and a 'worker maintaining the family business'. The attitude of these women towards a gendered division of labor is less strict and more ambiguous than their affirmation of the above traditional proposition suggests. Until several decades ago the majority of Japanese women belonged to this classification. Even though the number of these women has decreased, they still make up nearly 10% of the total. This indicates that the modern family model – which presupposes modern industry – has neither uniformly nor universally permeated through contemporary Japanese families.

(12) **Non-employed women married to old middle class men: 'wives of craftsmen'**

These women are full-time housewives of men who operate a family business or are self-employed trades-people. Their average age is 49.3 years, and their average household income is rather low at 5.98 million yen. The husband's income is 4.48 million yen, the second lowest of all the groups. Their husbands' occupations include: carpenters, plasterers or steeplejacks (10.6%), fisherman and drivers (4.3% each), tailors or fitters, joiners or furniture makers, painters or sign writers (3.2% each), etc. These occupations are typically sole-operators or self-employed and are based on the individual's skills and experiences. These women generally provide support for their husbands behind the scenes. Considering the husbands' occupations and their low incomes, these women share several characteristics with 'women of surplus population (8)'. However, more than 70% of these women reported 'no occupation' after the age of 30, which suggests very little movement between the two groups.

This group has a strong tendency to support traditional gender roles, with 54.3% affirming the statement 'men working; women tending family and home' and 79.8% agreeing that 'women are more suited to domestic work and child rearing'. Both of these percentages are the highest across all groups. Only 16.0% of these women consider that 'much' inequity exists between genders, the lowest of all the groups. These attitudes are in keeping with the conservatism of the old middle class combined with characteristics of the full-time housewife. On the other hand, only 21.2% of these women consider the present society 'fair' or 'more or less fair', the lowest of all the groups and revealing a strong sense of injustice. While they affirm the traditional gender roles and live accordingly, the standard of living of these women is generally low and the feeling of unfairness is strong. With some exceptions, we can say that these women exhibit strong characteristics of the lower stratum of the old middle class.

Women facing aging

(13) **Single non-employed women: 'women facing aging'**

Single non-employed women average 55 years of age, the highest of all the groups. Women in their sixties comprise 60.7% of the group and 5.7% of the entire female sample. But we must note that approximately 20% of this group are women in their twenties and thirties who live with their parents. This latter sub-group are so-called 'domestic helpers' who may marry in the future, and are therefore not considered central members of the group. For this reason, the following discussion will focus only on the women in their forties or older. Even then, they constitute 4.6% of the entire female sample. Their average age is 62, and more than three-quarters are either widowed (67.8%) or divorced (9.1%) while the remaining 23.1% are unmarried.

Their average income is 1.33 million yen, with 54.7% of them concentrated in a bracket between 0.7–2.5 million yen. They are mainly pensioners. Although we must be careful in making generalizations since the sample is fairly small, there is a considerable difference between their average incomes according to marital status. The unmarried women have an average income of 1.06 million yen, the widows 1.52 million yen, and the divorcees only 0.51 million yen. In addition, roughly 40% of the unmarried and divorced women and 10% of the widows have no income. Old age for unmarried or divorced women is economically very severe. The household income is extremely low at 3.55 million yen. One-third (33.9%) of these women live by themselves, and 24.0% live with someone else; usually either an unmarried child (comprising more than one-half of such cases) or an elderly parent (about one-quarter of such cases), and 22.5% live with a married child. In other words, these women are confronting their own aging while either living alone, or caring for an elderly parent, or they are increasingly dependent on their own children.

Only 14.2% of these women identify their status as 'upper' or 'upper middle', and only 26.1% of them consider the present society to be 'fair' or 'more or less fair'. Yet 61.7% of them are 'satisfied' or 'more or less satisfied' with life. This ratio is about the same for the women who live alone. Confronted with aging and great anxieties about life, we can say that, at least for the time being, these women lead lives with composure.

Women's class society

Having examined women in terms of their class location, marital status, and their husbands' class location, we can see that the wide variety of everyday lives and life courses of Japanese women more or less conform to only 13 different patterns. The factors determining women's lives are more complex than is the case for men. Nevertheless, many of their lives have been determined by only a few factors, such as their own class location, marital status, and their husband's class location.

We can characterize the interrelationships between these various groupings of women in the following way.

Initially, many of the women go out into the world as young, single working class women (9). Depending on their educational background and occupations, many of them find a life partner and advance to the next stage of life as one of 'the core group of full-time housewives (5)', 'the working housewives I (6)', 'the working housewives II (7)', or the 'wives of working class men' (10). Some women live fulfilling lives as typical full-time housewives, enjoying their husbands' large income (5). Some women work part-time in order to supplement the household income or to repay a home loan, and maintain a standard of living somewhat better than average (6). Looking after the children and the husband who works for a small or medium-sized enterprise, some women combine this with working as a laborer to maintain family life (7). Some women, who have typical working class husbands, single-handedly undertake domestic work and child rearing, and struggle on with a meager household budget (10). Although these women's husbands are alike, in that they work for an enterprise or a government or municipal office, there are many differences and discrepancies in the lives of the women themselves. Having acquired professional qualifications at university, a small group of women go out into the world as 'well-off unattached women (4)'. Most of their marriage partners belong to the new middle class, and thus they become 'women with a double income (3)' or 'the core group of full-time housewives (5)'. Most of the women who have not been married, or who have been divorced or widowed, live as single female workers in their middle to old age (9); they have low wages and unstable employment conditions, and sometimes children to look after.

Many women with old middle class parents, or an old middle class husband come to take one of the following paths. Namely, the 'women of surplus population (8)', 'women living for the family business (11)', or 'wives of craftsmen (12)', depending on the nature and the scale of the family business. Women who have capitalist class parents, or who have married a capitalist class man generally take either the path of the 'women of a small and medium-sized enterprise (1)' or the 'wives of enterprise managers (2)'.

Before long old age approaches. Within several years of the death of their husbands, many women become one of the 'women facing aging (13)'. While they only represent a small percentage of the entire female population at any given time, it appears that a majority of women reach this stage towards the end of their lives.

Male-centered, patriarchal structures have imposed the role of the housewife upon women, and in the workplace this structure has portrayed women's work as a secondary form of labor. When we combine the patriarchal structure and class structure, we can see the given, inescapable stage settings for women's lives. Therefore we must conclude that, although in many different ways to men, women certainly experience the class structures of society.

8 Closed-up Political Space

Class and political party support

Is class politics waning?

A discussion of class cannot avoid the problem of politics, for politics is the very realm in which the concept of class must demonstrate its validity. As discussed in chapter 2, some class researchers have attempted to forecast future political trends according to changes in the Japanese class structure. In contrast, those who argue against class theory argue that people's party political allegiances often do not correspond to their class locations and that political parties have lost their class related characteristics. Hence, they argue that the concepts and lived experiences of class have declining relevance. Pakulski and Waters, in *The Death of Class* (1996), for example, base their argument that class politics is waning on three points: 'a decline of class voting and class-based allegiance to political parties; a decline of class-based organizations; a decline in the use of class imagery and consciousness in politics' (Pakulski and Waters 1996: 133).

Pakulski and Waters assert that because class is so closely associated with politics, the weakening of the relationship between politics and class spells the death of the concept of class. Their conclusion, however, turns on a false premise of class theory that can be traced to *The Communist Manifesto* (Marx and Engels 1848) and which sees classes as the primary political actors. Abandoning this premise, we can see that the relationship between class and politics is still an important one, as politics continues to determine how a society's resources are distributed and how various interests are negotiated. In this sense, the phenomenon of class or strata remains inextricably entwined with the practice of politics.

That the relationship between class and political parties has weakened is undeniable. The phenomena of increasing 'conservatism', which began in the 1980s, the restructuring of the political parties in the mid-1990s, and the surge in the numbers who claim to support 'no party' that shook Japan at the end of the twentieth century, all served to weaken the bond between class and politics. The Socialist Party of Japan (SPJ) had once boasted many parliamentarians among its members, most of whom were the representatives of Kokurō (National Railway Workers' Union), Jichirō (All Japan Prefectural and Municipal Workers' Union), and Nikkyōso (Japan Teachers Union) and other nationwide labor unions; it was even called the 'Political Department of Sōhyō' (General Council of Trade Unions of Japan)'. But the SPJ has since dissolved, with its remnants dispersed to minority parties such as the Social Democrat Party, or to factions of the Democratic Party of Japan.

Takatoshi Imada sees these changes in postwar Japanese politics in terms of a continuum from 'class politics to status politics to life politics'. According to Imada, class politics dominated Japan while two major political powers, one conservative and the other progressive, were in opposition to each other until the society became more affluent through advanced economic development. On the one hand, there was a labor movement based on class ideology supporting progressive political parties, and, on the other, there was the conservative Liberal Democratic Party (LDP). With increased economic development, though, people have become primarily concerned with the promotion and stability of their status. Responding to these needs, political parties stopped addressing class politics and shifted their focus to 'status politics'. Amidst this process of change the LDP succeeded in transforming itself into a party designed to protect and promote the rights and interests of various interest groups. This heralded the so-called 'conservatism' of the 1980s. In the post-modern era of today, however, people are pursuing individual goals such as self-realization and confirmation of identity over and above materialistic achievements. As a result, there is a shift from status politics to 'life politics'. Thus far, political parties have failed to respond to this change; hence the increasing numbers supporting 'no party' (Imada 1989, 2000).

Ichirō Miyake, a leading researcher of political party support and voting behavior, however, contests this assertion, claiming that the most influential factor determining political party support is occupation. He asserts that many people are in fact highly conscious of political parties that represent their occupation

(Miyake 1985, 1989). Analyzing the 1995 SSM Survey data, Masaru Miyano also claims that the relationship between occupation and political party support did not change much between 1955 and 1991 when political parties were restructured. He concludes that 'as far as occupation is concerned, class politics has not declined' (Miyano 1998). What, though, is the reality?

Structure of political party support

The 1995 SSM Survey asked two questions about political party support. One asks which political party the respondent supported at the time of the study. The other asks which political party the respondent supported in 1991, before the new political parties were formed. For the time being we will concentrate on political party support in 1991, because the new system was not yet stabilized in 1995; the two parties named New Frontier Party and New Party Sakigake having gathered a certain amount of support by then. Table 8.1 summarizes the relationship between the three class and strata classifications (classes, four occupational classifications, and income strata) and political party support.

Using any of these classifications, a person's location indicates a statistically significant influence on their political party support. In terms of income strata, however, there is almost no difference between the four categories [strata] in the level of support for progressive political parties. The difference between the four categories in the ratios of support of the LDP also remains at about 10%. Therefore, the influence of income strata is small. In contrast, class and occupational categories have a profound impact on people's political party support. Especially in terms of the class categories, the level of capitalist and old middle class support for the LDP is almost twice as high as the new middle and working classes', while the new middle and working classes' support for the progressive political parties is almost three times the level of the capitalist class. Cramer's V Coefficient (of association) is exceptionally high at 0.149. This indicates that class location is a significant factor in determining political party support. I have attempted to examine the relationship between political party support and many other variables in my analysis. These variables include strata categories and responses to questions regarding social consciousness, such as, status identification and degree of life

Table 8.1 Relationship between class/strata location and political party support (in 1991)

(a) Class

	LDP	Middle-of-the road	Progressive	No party to support
Capitalist	62.0	4.3	6.4	27.2
New Middle	31.1	5.1	18.5	45.3
Working	30.0	7.8	17.1	45.1
Old Middle	54.5	5.4	11.4	28.8

Cramer's Coefficient V = 0.149   significance level < 0.001

(b) Four categories of occupation

	LDP	Middle-of-the road	Progressive	No party to support
Upper non-manual	35.9	4.6	15.7	43.8
Lower non-manual	37.1	5.6	13.4	43.9
Manual	37.5	8.8	17.3	36.4
Agriculture	58.5	3.2	12.9	25.4

Cramer's Coefficient V = 0.085   significance level < 0.001

(c) Income strata (million yen)

	LDP	Middle-of-the road	Progressive	No party to support
< 3.5	36.6	6.0	17.2	40.2
3.5–6.5	37.6	7.1	15.8	39.4
6.5–12	38.6	7.1	16.5	37.8
> 12	47.7	4.9	14.6	32.8

Cramer's coefficient V = 0.044   significance level < 0.01

Note: 'Middle-of-the Road' = Kōmei, Minsha, Shin Jiyū Kurabu Shamin-ren
'Progressive' = Socialist and Communist

Source: 1995 SSM Survey data.

satisfaction. I was, however, unable to find a more influential variable on political party support than that of class location.[1] It is evident that political party support is formed on the basis of class location, and in this sense it is true to say that 'class politics' is still alive.

Another way of thinking is possible, however. While there is no doubt that political party support varies greatly depending on a person's class location, the political party that garners the largest support across all four classes is the LDP. Added to this, 45% of the new middle and working classes express support for 'no party'. Given these facts, we can say that while class location is an important basis for determining political party support, its influence is not decisive. Occupation, income, strata identification and the degree of life satisfaction, etc. exert much less influence. Therefore, we can also say that political party support can no longer be entirely explained in terms of class and strata location or factors related to them.

Collapse of 'class based parties'

Is class politics in fact waning? In order to ascertain this it is necessary to examine how the relationship between class location and political party support has changed historically. Table 8.2 tabulates this relationship.

In 1965, 66.7% of the capitalist class supported the LDP but only 25.7% of the working class. In contrast, only 14.7% in the capitalist class supported progressive political parties, compared to 48.4% of the working class. The old middle class showed a similar tendency to the capitalist class. The tendency in the new middle class is closer to the working class' preferences, although with moderately higher support for the LDP, and slightly less support for progressive parties. Thus, in 1965 support for the LDP and the progressive political parties was strongly class based, with the capitalist and old middle classes supporting the former, and the working and new middle classes tending to support the latter. This, then, was truly the age of 'class politics'.

Between 1965 and 1991, support for the LDP had barely changed in any of the classes, with the exception of a slight increase in working class support in 1985. In contrast, support for the progressive parties altered a great deal over the same period. New middle class support dropped from 40.9% to 18.4%, while working class support dropped even more dramatically, from 48.4% to 18.7%. Restructuring of political parties during the 1990s did nothing to reverse this trend. While LDP support experienced a small reduction between 1991 and 1995, the support for progressive parties almost halved in the same period. This coincided with a large increase in the number of respondents expressing their support for

Table 8.2 *Changes in the relationship between class affiliation and political party support (male) (%)*

		LDP	Middle-of-the road	Progressive	No political party	Difference between LDP & progressive
Capitalist	1955	49.5	14.6	8.7	27.2	40.8
	1965	66.7	5.1	14.7	13.5	52.0
	1975	64.1	4.6	7.8	23.5	56.3
	1985	61.0	5.9	8.8	24.3	52.2
	1991	64.2	3.4	6.0	26.3	58.2
	1995	47.8	1.7	3.5	47.0	44.3
New Middle	1955	24.8	25.4	27.3	17.6	−2.5
	1965	35.2	8.3	40.9	15.6	−5.7
	1975	33.9	8.9	26.2	31.0	7.7
	1985	36.7	10.3	18.4	34.5	18.3
	1991	33.2	5.8	18.4	42.6	14.8
	1995	28.6	2.5	9.3	59.7	19.3
Working	1955	31.7	22.3	29.1	16.9	2.6
	1965	25.7	8.7	48.4	17.2	−22.7
	1975	28.2	9.1	29.5	33.2	−1.3
	1985	34.4	11.0	19.9	34.7	14.5
	1991	33.3	8.8	18.7	39.3	14.6
	1995	29.8	2.6	12.3	55.2	17.5
Old Middle	1955	50.5	12.2	13.4	23.8	37.1
	1965	58.0	3.9	19.3	18.8	38.7
	1975	58.1	4.0	12.2	25.7	45.9
	1985	56.2	4.0	7.2	32.6	49.0
	1991	50.5	6.3	13.4	29.9	37.1
	1995	41.6	1.4	7.2	49.8	34.4
Total	1955	42.3	16.6	18.6	22.4	23.7
	1965	42.4	6.6	33.9	17.1	8.5
	1975	41.4	7.1	21.8	29.6	19.6
	1985	42.1	8.8	15.6	33.5	26.5
	1991	40.1	6.7	16.1	37.1	24.0
	1995	33.7	2.2	9.4	54.6	24.3

Source: SSM Survey data of respective years.

'no political party', which amounted to nearly 60% of the total of the new middle and working classes in 1995.

What happened to the working class to so dramatically erode its support for the progressive parties? Figure 8.1 outlines changes in working class support for both the LDP and the progressive parties according to the scale of the enterprise the respondent is employed

Class Structure in Contemporary Japan

Figure 8.1 Changes in political party support of working class by the scale of enterprise (male)

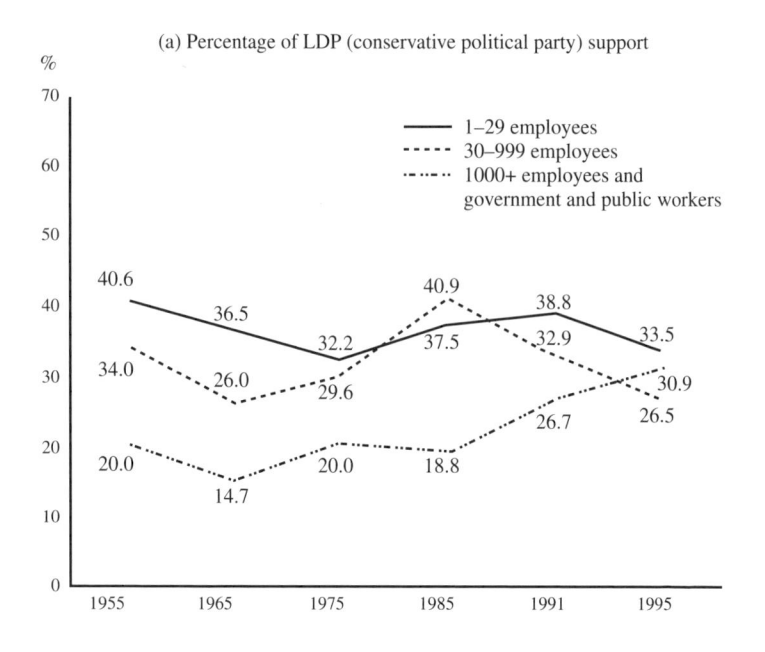

(a) Percentage of LDP (conservative political party) support

— 1–29 employees
---- 30–999 employees
—·—·— 1000+ employees and government and public workers

Year	1–29	30–999	1000+
1955	40.6	34.0	20.0
1965	36.5	26.0	14.7
1975	32.2	29.6	20.0
1985	37.5	40.9	18.8
1991	38.8	32.9	26.7
1995	33.5	30.9	26.5

(b) Percentage of progressive political party support

Year	1–29	30–999	1000+
1955	25.8	27.7	33.9
1965	37.9	49.4	59.2
1975	23.5	30.4	37.6
1985	11.6	16.6	37.7
1991	15.2	16.9	26.1
1995	10.3	11.3	17.7

Source: SSM Survey data of each study year

by. Changes in working class political party support can be summarized as follows.
1 The period from 1955 to 1965 can be called, 'the establishment of class politics'. No matter what the scale of the enterprise, support for the progressive parties rose rapidly, while support for the conservative party declined. Support for the progressive parties reached 60% amongst workers in large-scale enterprises and with government and public workers, all of whom had powerful labor unions. Thus, the progressive parties had a powerful working class base.
2 From 1965 to 1975, however, progressive party support declined greatly across all enterprises, although LDP support changed only slightly, resulting in the support levels for the LDP and the progressive parties becoming almost equal. Most strikingly, in that period the percentage of LDP support in enterprises with up to 29 employees easily surpassed the progressive parties. Thus the era when progressive parties represented the majority of the working class did not last long. Nevertheless, the ratio of progressive party support was still close to 40% for workers in large enterprises, government and public offices, indicating that the large labor unions remained active.
3 In 1985, the conservatism of workers in small and medium-small enterprises rapidly increased. Support for progressive political parties was halved, and support for the LDP rose to around 40%. The LDP won the 1986 general election by a landslide, securing 300 out of 511 seats. This was interpreted as an increased atmosphere of conservatism. At this time though, no change was observed in either the LDP or progressive party support in large enterprises or amongst government and public sector workers. This data seems to suggest that large enterprises and government and public sector workers had retained progressive influences. However, when this data is analyzed in more detail, such conclusions become questionable. In 1985, working class support for the progressive parties varied depending on whether the respondents were labor union members or not. To be precise, 32.5% of all union members, and, more particularly, 41.3% of union members employed by a large enterprise, government or public office supported progressive parties, compared to only 12.5% of non-union members (including workers whose workplaces have no labor unions). Overall, 58.0% of the people

who supported progressive parties were members of a labor union, and 42.0% were union members employed in large enterprises, government or public offices. In sum, by 1985 the massed support base of the progressive political parties had been reduced to the labor unions of large enterprises, government or public offices.
4 By 1991, support for the progressive parties had drastically declined, even amongst workers employed by large enterprises and government and public offices, falling short even of support for the LDP. By 1995, when political parties were restructured, this support had declined further, to about one-half of the rate of support for the LDP. Thus, by 1991 the progressive political parties had effectively lost their support base. Many of the people who had formerly supported them now supported no party at all. For workers in small and medium-small enterprises very little had changed, as their increasing conservatism had already registered in 1985. Thus, a majority of the working class now supports no party, followed by those who support the LDP (conservative political parties), with the supporters of the progressive political parties having become a small minority. This pattern is more or less constant, regardless of the scale of the enterprise for which they work.

Who is the principal agent of change?

As mentioned earlier, the relationship between class and politics has been regarded as one of the most important problems in Marxist social theory.

Traditional Marxist theory considered the working class to be the principal agent of social change. Not only is it the largest class, but it is also the most exploited. The theory held that members of the working class would realize their class interest, develop solidarity through political organizations, overthrow their class oppressors and thus abolish the private ownership of the means of production. Orthodox Japanese Marxism maintained that the new middle class and the old middle class, with some exceptions, would follow the working class and participate in social transformation as described in Lenin's doctrines of labor-peasant collaboration and the Commintern's United Front.

Often noted, however, is the fact that most socialist revolutions did not take place in advanced capitalist nations with strong working classes, but rather in largely developing nations. In the Russian Revolution, for example, the driving force lay as much with the peasants as with the working class and the revolution was lead by intellectuals such as Lenin. Most instances of social upheaval in advanced capitalist countries have been initiated by anti-establishment students and intellectuals, rather than by members of the working class. This was especially true in the late 1960s when student uprisings occurred simultaneously in various parts of the world. This underlined the importance of the role of intellectuals in social transformation. Since then some theoreticians have argued that the principal transformational agent is not the working class but the new middle class.

One theorist, Serge Mallet, a French Marxist who was also a leader of a socialist political party, called this new transformational agent the 'new working class'. According to Mallet, the skills of workers were being replaced by machinery through technological development, and laborers were thus losing their job autonomy. In contemporary industry, however, while the contribution of direct productive labor has become less important due to the spread of automation, the importance of a department involving research, development and monitoring has increased, and the workers in such departments are regaining their occupational autonomy. In addition, since these workers earn relatively high wages and their basic needs have already been met, they are not concerned solely with profit distribution, but raise demands of a higher order. These higher demands include the elimination of the economic rulers' bureaucratic control and the realization of overall autonomy in management. While the 'new working class' is not revolutionary in the sense of violently seizing political power, it truly is revolutionary in the sense that it tries to fundamentally change the structure of capitalist production (Mallet 1963, 1971).

Alain Touraine suggests that the role of this intellectual class will spread beyond the organizations of production. Technological and scientific developments have increased the systematic management of people, not only in their roles as producers, but also as consumers. In this sense, Touraine argues that we have come out of a society of exploitation, and into a society of alienation. Contemporary social conflict is therefore not between capitalists and workers but between the political and economic decision making organizations and the people who are forced to submit to them. Therefore, struggles to resist this control do not manifest in economic activities, but rather in political and cultural ones. The targets of the struggle become self-management within an enterprise, decentralization of power, and the more general desire for the 'replacement of private life over productivity'. Touraine claims that at the forefront of these movements is the 'counter-elite', which is largely comprised of professionals (Touraine 1969).

Both Mallet's and Touraine's theories are too weak to explain why the 'new working class' or 'professionals' will stand up to the prevailing order. If economic exploitation is not sufficient to motivate people to struggle against the system, why would a growing sense of alienation inspire them to take action? Alvin Gouldner tries to overcome these weaknesses, explaining the new middle class's motivation for change in terms of its economic interests and cultural characteristics. According to Gouldner, a 'new class' is acquiring power in contemporary society by profiting from a different kind of capital: cultural or human capital. This new class is competing with the traditional capitalist class for control and management of the economic and political system. This is a struggle between the class that legally owns the means of production and the class that actually controls the production process through knowledge and mastery of its technological aspects. The new class is itself elitist and self-centered, its members intending to use their professional knowledge in order to expand their own profits and power. And yet, the new class is interested in overthrowing capitalism because by so doing they can destroy the old capitalist class's power-base, thereby expanding their own interests. The new class, however, possesses a unique culture that Gouldner calls a 'culture of critical discourse', which endows them with the characteristics of the 'universal class', exposes the injustice of the existing authority and power, abolishes discrimination, and liberates people from conventional hierarchies. Thus, the new class can form an alliance with the popular working class to oppose the old capitalist class and its social order. Hence, 'the new class is the most progressive force in modern society, and is a center of whatever human emancipation is possible in the foreseeable future' (Gouldner 1979: 83). Gouldner thus explains the new middle class's motivation for social change via an insight into its economic self-interest based on the ownership of knowledge.

In present day Japan, however, the new middle class does not support progressive political parties. Therefore, it may be hard to maintain that it is the principal agent of change while we continue to measure this in terms of political party support. We do not, however, need to view political party support as absolute. The following may explain why the new middle class is not supporting the progressive political parties; why the majority of them are saying that they do not support any party. The reason might simply be that contemporary Japanese political parties are not responding to the demands or expectations of the new middle class, or that political parties are failing to mobilize their potential power as the primary agents for social change. The same can be said about the working class. It is important to understand what sort of society these classes desire and whether or not they have the will and the conditions needed to realize such a society.

Class location and economic ideology

What kind of society do people in each of these classes desire? In this section, we will focus our attention on the economic aspects of society.

There were several questions in the 1995 SSM Survey regarding what people desire in terms of the economic system. Of these questions, we will focus on two that relate to major changes in contemporary Japan. The first concerns the deregulation of the economy; the second, the growing preeminence of meritocracy.

Table 8.3 summarizes the responses to these two questions by class. The capitalist class reports the greatest level of agreement with the deregulation of the economy, followed by the old middle class. In contrast, many new middle class people disagreed with this statement. In response to the question about the distribution of wealth and status, most people in each class answered 'effort (b)', but the responses to 'achievement (a)' differ greatly between classes. The 'achievement' answer was much higher for the capitalist and new middle class respondents than for the working and old middle classes. Thus, we can say that those who agree with economic deregulation are predominantly from the capitalist class, and those who agree that the distribution of wealth and status should be determined entirely by achievement are also from the capitalist and new middle classes.

As both questions seek the respondent's views on free market economic principles, the answers can be regarded as indicators of

Table 8.3 Views about relaxation of economic restrictions and distribution principles (%)

(a) It is better to have fewer governmental regulations concerning the economy

	Agree	More or less agree	Cannot decide	More or less disagree	Disagree	Total
Capitalist	39.4	21.3	26.9	7.5	5.0	100.00
New Middle	27.0	25.8	26.5	9.8	11.0	100.00
Working	25.5	23.4	35.9	8.7	6.5	100.00
Old Middle	30.4	22.8	30.7	9.5	6.5	100.00
Total	28.1	23.7	31.8	9.0	7.4	100.00

Cramer's V coefficient = 0.077   significance level < 0.005

(b) What kinds of people deserve positions of high status and/or economic affluence?

	Achievement[a]	Effort[b]	Need[c]	Equality[d]	Don't know[e]	Total
Capitalist	31.9	54.8	8.4	3.6	1.2	100.00
New Middle	33.7	49.8	10.6	4.4	1.6	100.00
Working	21.5	57.1	10.0	7.0	4.4	100.00
Old Middle	18.3	61.7	8.9	5.9	5.2	100.00
Total	24.4	56.3	9.8	5.9	3.7	100.00

Cramer's V coefficient = 0.094   significance level < 0.001

Notes:
a The more a person achieves, the more he/she gets
b The more effort a person makes, the more he/she gets
c A needy person gets as much as he/she needs
d Everyone gets about the same
e I don't know

Source: 1995 SSM Survey data

people's economic ideology.[2] Although one deals with the macro level and the other the micro, the two questions are equally concerned with an evaluation of the capitalist economy. When we combine the answers to the two questions – 'A' economic deregulation and 'B' meritocratic distribution – we can discern four types of economic ideology in the responses. The position that agrees with both questions seeks pure free market principles in both

Figure 8.2 Class affiliation, occupation and ideology

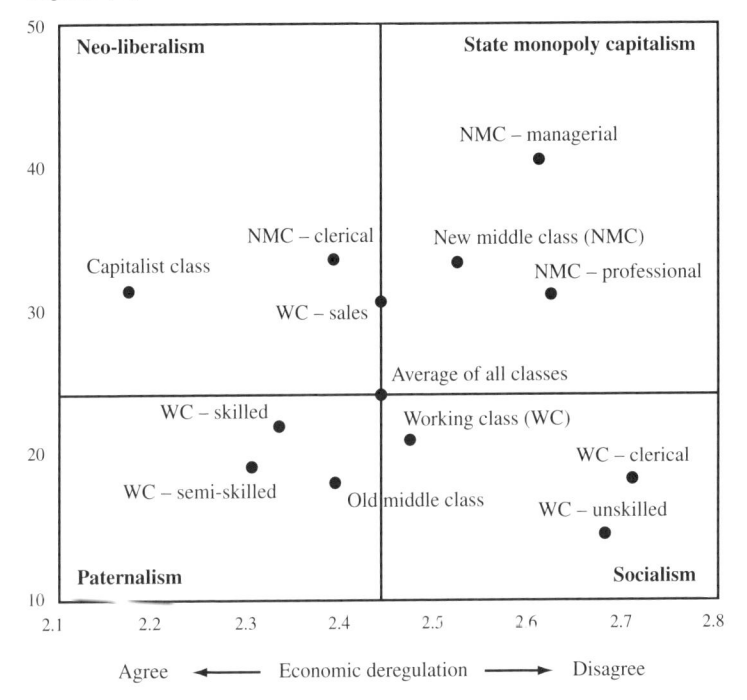

[Figure: Scatter plot with x-axis "Economic deregulation" ranging from 2.1 (Agree) to 2.8 (Disagree), and y-axis "Achievement emphasis (%)" ranging from 10 to 50. Four quadrants labeled: Neo-liberalism (top-left), State monopoly capitalism (top-right), Paternalism (bottom-left), Socialism (bottom-right). Data points plotted:
- NMC – managerial (~2.6, 42)
- NMC – clerical (~2.4, 35)
- Capitalist class (~2.2, 32)
- New middle class (NMC) (~2.55, 33)
- NMC – professional (~2.65, 31)
- WC – sales (~2.4, 30)
- Average of all classes (~2.5, 29)
- WC – skilled (~2.3, 23)
- Working class (WC) (~2.5, 23)
- WC – clerical (~2.7, 22)
- WC – semi-skilled (~2.25, 20)
- Old middle class (~2.4, 20)
- WC – unskilled (~2.65, 18)]

Note: Achievement [axis] shows the percentage of answers of 'achievement' to the question of desirable distribution principle.

Relaxation of restrictions [points] are derived from giving one point to 'agree', two points to 'more or less agree', three points to 'cannot decide', four points to 'more or less disagree', and five points to 'disagree', and averaging the results.

Source: SSM Survey data

the macro and micro spheres of the economy; we call this view 'neo-liberalism'. The position that disagrees with 'A' but agrees with 'B' seeks to maintain macro-control over the economy while distributing social resources competitively and can be called 'state monopoly capitalism'. The position that disagrees with both 'A' and 'B' opposes free market principles and can be called 'socialism'. The position that agrees with 'A' but disagrees with

'B' desires to leave the macro economy to market mechanisms, but wishes to distribute social resources equally; we tentatively call this 'paternalism'.

The answers to the above two questions are totaled by class location and plotted in Figure 8.2. For the new middle class and the working class, occupational status has also been shown. Whereas the capitalist class tends to support neo-liberalism, the working class, despite internal differences, is inclined to support socialism. The tendencies of the two middle classes are contrasting, with the new middle class strongly supporting state monopoly capitalism, and the old middle class supporting paternalism. In other words, neo-liberalism is supported mostly by the capitalist class, and not supported by the working class; the new middle class supports the micro aspect, i.e., meritocracy, and the old middle class affirms the macro aspect of economic liberalism, i.e., economic deregulation. Therefore, the capitalist class and the working class are poles apart in terms of economic ideology, and the two middle classes occupy different centralist positions.

This constellation of economic ideology is extremely interesting considering the characteristics of each class. It is unsurprising, given its large economic interests, that the capitalist class affirms the idea of a free-market economy that promotes competition and rewards high achievement. In contrast, the working class wants a governmentally managed, stable economy in which every effort is rewarded and income equality is high. This accords with this class's interests, its low income and economic weakness. The old middle class desires a liberal economy and thinks income should correspond to effort, even though they are uncompetitive compared with members of the capitalist class. In keeping with their interests, the new middle class wants a managed, stable economy, but for income to be distributed according to merit. Studying these different class attitudes and interests, it is the working class which is most critical of the established economic order of neo-liberalism.

The working class cannot become the principal agent of change

Despite its critical attitude to the prevailing economic system, it remains hard to imagine the working class becoming the principal agent of change. This is because the working class is largely alienated from the political process and is politically inactive. As seen in chapter 4, generally speaking, the working class displays little knowledge of or desire to be involved in politics. This can be confirmed with typological analyses of the different classes' political consciousness. Unless this changes, it is hard to foresee how the working class could play a leading role in instigating political and economic change. The typology of political consciousness used here is derived from the following two studies.

Ichirō Katase and Michio Umino have divided political party support into four types according to responses to the statement, 'Politics is too difficult for me to understand', combined with party support. The four types are as follows: 1. People who are highly cognitive of politics and support a political party are called 'cognitively mobilized partisans'; 2. People who are highly cognitive of politics but do not support a political party are called, 'cognitively mobilized nonpartisans'; 3. People who are not very cognitive of politics but support a political party are called 'formal partisans'; 4. People who are not very cognitive of politics and do not support a political party are called 'non-cognitive, non-partisans'. An analysis of these types has revealed that many professionals and large enterprise white-collar employees qualify as cognitively mobilized nonpartisans. Katase and Umino conclude that the increasing influence of this type will extend the scope of future politics beyond the framework of the existing party political system. Because this type tends not to be bound by the constraints of social relationships and are free to make autonomous judgments, they assume the characteristics of the counter-elite (Katase and Umino 2000).

Hisataka Kobayashi (2000) has divided respondents into four strata by combining their political party support and their responses to two statements: 'It is better to leave politics to those who enjoy it', and, 'The best way to know what to do in this complex world is to rely on leaders and experts'. The four strata are defined as: 1. 'Active supporters' have a strong orientation to participate in politics and support a political party; 2. 'Opportunistic supporters' demonstrate a weak orientation to participate in politics but support a political party; 3. 'Participants with dilemmas' display a strong orientation to participate in politics but do not support any political party; 4. The 'politically alienated' have a weak orientation to participate in politics and do not support a political party. Kobayashi reveals that many professionals and white-collar workers fit into the third category – participants with dilemmas –

Table 8.4 Political consciousness and class affiliation

(a) Types of political party support

	Cognitively mobilized partisans	Cognitively mobilized nonpartisans	Formal partisans	Non-cognitive nonpartisans	Total
Capitalist	**36.6**	27.4	22.6	13.4	100.00
New Middle	27.6	**47.6**	10.6	14.2	100.00
Working	21.0	28.6	19.5	**30.8**	100.00
Old Middle	26.1	23.4	**25.8**	24.6	100.00
Total	24.9	31.6	19.2	24.3	100.00

Cramer's V coefficient = 0.151   significance level < 0.001

(b) Types of support and participation

	Active supporters	Opportunistic supporters	Participants with dilemmas	Politically alienated	Total
Capitalist	**35.9**	24.4	26.3	13.5	100.00
New Middle	24.8	13.4	**46.3**	15.5	100.00
Working	20.3	21.0	31.0	**27.7**	100.00
Old Middle	23.0	**27.8**	26.3	23.0	100.00
Total	23.2	21.0	33.1	22.7	100.00

Cramer's V coefficient = 0.129   significance level < 0.001

Source: 1995 SSM Survey data

and that many low wage earners and blue-collar workers in medium-small enterprises fit into the fourth category – the politically alienated. Kobayashi concludes that since there is no political party representing the interests of the participants with dilemmas, their need to participate in politics remains unfulfilled in the existing political system.

Table 8.4 shows the relationship between the above two typologies of political consciousness and class location. In each consciousness type the one that shows the highest percentage of the four classes is indicated in bold numerals. From this analysis the following pictures have emerged regarding the four classes. Many of the capitalist class are 'cognitively mobilized partisans' and 'active supporters'. They generally have a good knowledge of politics and consciously support the LDP's policies and political ideology. Many of the old middle class are 'formal partisans' and 'opportunistic supporters'. Their political knowledge is scant, and they support the LDP out of habit, with no desire to directly participate in politics. Many of the new middle class are 'cognitively mobilized non-partisans' and 'participants with dilemmas'. Although many of them have a good knowledge of politics and wish to be more politically active, they do not support a specific political party because no political party represents their interests or articulates their political ideology. Many in the working class are 'non-cognitive, non-partisans' and 'politically alienated'. Their knowledge of politics is minimal and they generally do not wish to be more involved in the political process. Hence, they do not exert much influence on any political party nor on politics in general. Summing up the political consciousness of these four classes we can see the political climate in contemporary Japan; although the LDP does not have the support of the majority of Japanese citizens, it commands a clear majority of the people who support a particular political party and vote for it.

As seen in chapter 4, the working class has the lowest income and the highest rate of dissatisfaction with life. For some reason, though, these facts have not resulted in the working class becoming more politically active as a way of furthering its interests. The new middle class, however, has a good understanding of politics as well as a desire to be more directly involved in politics. Hence, if a future political party can harness this potential, the new middle class will play a leading role in political change. What sort of society, however, does the new middle class desire? A society where their abilities and achievements are more highly valued and where they, rather than the capitalist class, have the initiative. In such a society, the division between the new middle class and the working class is probably clearly demarcated. This is one possible model of a future society, but the desire for such a society never gains widespread support and so does not represent an issue that unites the new middle class with the other classes.

What, then, can be concluded from this analysis? Firstly, the reality is that the working class cannot be the principal agent of political change. Secondly, the society as a whole does not trust the new middle class to realize the dreams of the majority. Given this, we need to design a new society, one not constrained by the framework of class; one that does not look to a particular class to generate a blueprint for the future society or to act as the main transformational agent. How can we conceptualize a society that is equitable and just in an adequate sense, and that a majority of people will agree with? We will address this crucial problem in the next chapter.

9 Towards a New Egalitarian Society

Inescapable expansion of disparities

Social and economic disparities between the classes in Japan will continue to expand for some time into the twenty-first century. There are at least three reasons for this: economic globalization; the intensification of information technology (IT); and the reinforcement of meritocracy and the increasing diversification of employment.

Globalization and IT revolution

Economic globalization entails a restructuring of the international division of labor. Under the international division of labor that developed during colonialism and endured through most of the twentieth century, developed nations produced industrial goods and developing nations produced primary goods. Thus, the majority of people in developed nations were economically and materially better off than the majority of people in developing nations. As long as there were employment opportunities in manufacturing, the working class in developed nations had a reasonable – and reasonably secure – level of income, one which they could expect to improve with increased productivity. However, as many developing nations have industrialized, they have increased their share of the international manufacturing industry; and this to a significant extent through the relocation of industry from the developed to the developing nations, which has resulted in the de-industrialization of developed nations.

The developed nations are now characterized by knowledge intensive industries that require advanced technology. They also house the headquarters for multi-national corporations. Both draw most of their employees from the educated, new middle class. Another, less skilled field that has not shifted offshore is the tertiary sector: sales, services and transportation. These industries directly provide goods and services, and must therefore remain located close to the consumer. They are labor intensive, and are generally staffed by members of the working class. The reduced demand for unskilled labor caused by de-industrialization puts a strong downward pressure on the wages of workers in these tertiary industries. Growing income and social inequities between the new middle class, employed in vital, knowledge intensive industries and multi-national enterprises, and the working class, employed in insecure tertiary industries, thus appear unavoidable.

The IT revolution has played a major role in the expansion of social disparities. It has long been acknowledged that there is a 'digital divide' between people who use and benefit from information technology and those who do not.

Various data substantiate the existence of a digital divide. Figure 9.1 shows changing trends in the rate of personal computer ownership by income bracket using the 1999 edition of the Japanese *National Survey on Consumption Behavior* (Management and Coordination Agency, administered September to November, 1999). This survey asked respondents if they owned a personal computer and, if so, when he/she first acquired one. Five years before the survey, the ownership rate was less than 20% across all income strata. At that stage, ownership of a personal computer remained a remote possibility regardless of a person's income.

Since then, however, the ownership rate has risen rapidly for those in the middle to high-income strata. At the time of the survey, approximately 50% of those with an annual income of 6–8 million yen, and more than 80% of those with an annual income in excess of 12.5 million yen owned a personal computer. In contrast, the ownership rate is still around 20% for people in the low-income bracket, i.e., those earning less than 4 million yen per annum. Thus, we can see a very large gap between the lower and the middle to high-income brackets.

There is a similar disparity in Internet usage between the classes. According to the 1999 *Communication Usage Trend Survey* (Ministry of Posts and Telecommunications, administered in October 1999), there is a large disparity in the Internet usage rate at different incomes. Only 5.5% of the people earning less than 4 million yen and 13.4% of those in the 4–6 million yen bracket used the Internet. This contrasts with a usage rate of 30.6% for those earning 10–15 million yen and 36.0% for those earning more than

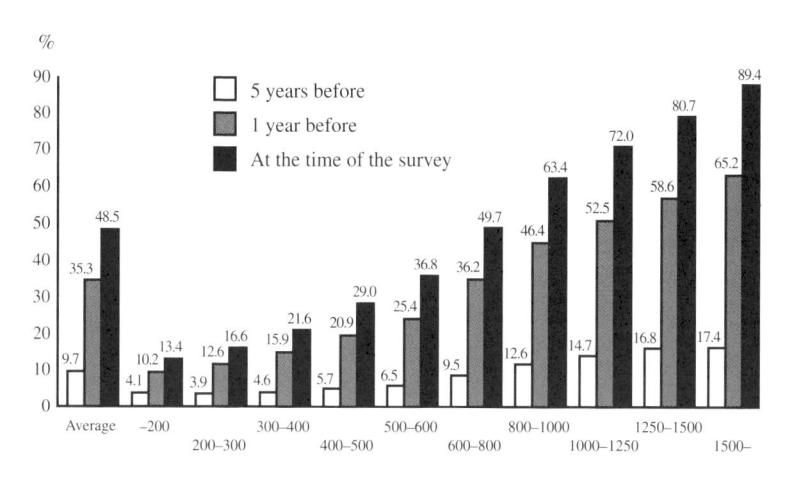

Figure 9.1 Rate of personal computer consumption ownership (%)

Income (Thousand yen)	5 years before	1 year before	At the time of the survey
Average	9.7	35.3	48.5
–200	4.1	10.2	13.4
200–300	3.9	12.6	16.6
300–400	4.6	15.9	21.6
400–500	5.7	20.9	29.0
500–600	6.5	25.4	36.8
600–800	9.5	36.2	49.7
800–1000	12.6	46.4	63.4
1000–1250	14.7	52.5	72.0
1250–1500	16.8	58.6	80.7
1500–	17.4	65.2	89.4

Source: 1999 edition of National Survey on Consumption Behaviour

15 million yen. Furthermore, only 16.6% in the income bracket of more than 10 million yen said that the Internet 'will not be necessary in the future, either', compared with 34.2% in the 4–6 million yen bracket and 61.0% in the less than 4 million yen bracket who gave that response. There seems little prospect of this large gap closing. Furthermore, according to *A Survey on the Internet Diffusion Rate*, conducted by Nikkei BP Co. (administered in August 2000), the rate of Internet diffusion was 49.4% for the 10 million yen income stratum, a 9.0% increase on the year before. However, the rate was 11.0% for people earning less than 3.5 million yen, an increase of only 0.5%. Based on these survey results, the report has concluded that it is evident that there is a stratum of people who cannot use the Internet and that they are being 'left behind'.

The gap in Internet usage corresponds to differences in many other information related behaviors. *A Survey on the Japanese Usage of Information* by the Dentsō Institute for Human Sciences has measured information literacy, using the formula: 'information literacy = skill factors + mental factors'. The survey asks eight questions to measure the skills required for personal computers and

Table 9.1 Information media usage rates by literacy group

	HH	MH	MM	ML	LL
Internet usage	88%	67%	19%	5%	3%
Book usage (specialist, etc.)	74%	68%	42%	17%	12%
Magazines other than comics	79%	65%	56%	52%	32%
Cinema and theatre	55%	43%	36%	21%	26%

Internet usage, and fourteen questions regarding social interests, self-realization needs, information dissemination needs, etc., to assess the mental factors. From their answers to these questions each respondent's literacy point was calculated and the respondents were classified into five groups:
- 'HH' (highest information literacy),
- 'MH' (upper middle literacy),
- 'MM' (middle literacy),
- 'ML' (lower middle literary), and
- 'LL' (lowest literacy).

Analyses of these groups by occupation and income reveals that people in managerial and professional/technical occupations (7.1% and 11.7% respectively of all respondents) make up 21.4% and 19.0% respectively of the HH group. The 14.5% of respondents in the more than 10 million yen income stratum constitute 26.1% of the HH group. Regarding use of the internet, 88% of the HH group use it, compared with 67% of the MH group, 19% of the MM group, 5% of the ML group, and only 3% of the LL group. While the extreme differences between these groups is significant, even more noteworthy is the fact that the difference in information literacy closely corresponds to the disparities in the usage of more traditional media as can be seen in Table 9.1.

In sum, it becomes apparent that the gaps in information literacy and the digital divide are closely connected to the gaps in the familiarity to legitimate media and culture, and embedded in the class characteristics of Japanese culture discussed in chapter 4. The development of information technology, then, has perpetuated and perhaps deepened the disparities that already existed between the classes.[1]

However, we must note that while the figures presented in Table 9.1 and the discussion above are particular to the Japanese context, the IT revolution is a global phenomenon and many societies in many nations are experiencing a similar expansion in the disparities in information literacy between classes. As Esping-Andersen has pointed out, 'the old pluralist hope that we shall all blend into one satisfied middle class has been replaced with fears of polarization and closure' (1999: 150). Despite this, the effects of the IT revolution will, in time, be widespread in Japan. It has often been pointed out that one of Japan's great strengths is its broad-based literacy; the fact that nearly everyone in the country possesses the basic intellectual skills of reading, writing and arithmetic. This has been one of the reasons why social inequality has not become too extreme in Japan. As the importance of information literacy increases, however, this situation is changing. For the first time since WWII, Japanese society will experience increasing disparities in the basic intellectual skills of its citizens.

Collapse of Japanese employment practices

In the face of globalization the Japanese practices of lifetime employment and the seniority system are collapsing. This will continue to expand the disparities between the classes and the differences within them.

Postwar Japanese employment practices were far from egalitarian, but the hierarchy was organized around seniority, so that the greatest inequalities existed between young, middle-aged and older workers. The family-based wage system, often called 'living wages', also institutionalized an income disparity between male and female workers, with men being paid higher wages on the assumption that they were the primary source of family income. This system presupposed that the male employees work long hours in order to provide for their families. There was also a disparity between employees of large enterprises, where lifetime employment and the seniority system applied, and employees of small and medium-sized enterprises and non-regular employees, none of whom benefited from these practices. Furthermore, the seniority system did not guarantee across-the-board pay rises for workers in the same enterprise. Rather, after competing over a long period of time, there was often a considerable disparity in the outcome for different employees. Still, for male workers in large-scale enterprises, life-long employment and the seniority system kept the differences in incomes relatively small.

However, since the Plaza Agreement of 1985, these employment practices have been gradually breaking down; a process that has accelerated during the long depression that began in the mid-1990s. According to the Ministry of Labor's *A Survey on Employment Management*, the proportion of enterprises that 'emphasize lifetime employment' dropped from 27.1% in 1990 to only 9.9% in 1999. In 1993, 11.0% of enterprises stressed the 'seniority system' and 37.8% emphasized the 'ability system' (meritocracy), but by 1999 the percentages were 2.3% and 49.5% respectively. If we include the responses, 'compromise of the two' and 'cannot say either', it becomes evident that almost all enterprises have adopted a meritocratic system.

As the numbers of part-time, casual and dispatched workers have been increasing, so too has the diversification of employment. In 1970, part-time workers (those who work less than 35 hours a week) comprised only 6.7% of the total workforce, but by 1999 had reached 21.9%. Non-regular workers, including dispatched and temporary workers, accounted for 25.6% of the total workforce, and 45.1% of working women. Long-term economic depression has accelerated this tendency. There were 600,000 fewer full-time employees in the year 1998–99, while the number of part-time workers increased by 250,000 during the same period (Labor Force Survey).

In the future, these forms of employment diversification will be consciously promoted by many enterprises. For example, in 1995, Nikkeiren (The Japan Federation of Employers' Associations) proposed that the structure of employment should be divided into three tiers:

- 'workers with long-term, accumulated ability' – similar to the seniority system where the managerial and comprehensive positions take a leading role;
- 'workers with highly professional ability' – a core of which consists of specialist white-collar workers. These people are employed on relatively long but fixed term employment contracts, with their annual income being performance based; and
- 'workers under flexible employment' – which centers on clerical, technical and sales positions. These employees are on relatively short-term contracts and paid at fixed hourly rates or according to on-going job evaluation.

Until now, the new middle class and the working class were, for the most part, employed on the same basis, which maintained a sense of unity between them. Under this new proposal, however, they will be clearly demarcated in terms of the conditions of their employment.

Many Japanese people appear to be cognizant of the expansion of these disparities. In the 1999 Japanese *National Survey on Life Preferences*, only 4.8% of respondents agreed that the social goal of maintaining 'little inequality in income and assets' is currently being met (this category includes 'fully met' and 'more or less met'). In contrast, 50.2% of people said that the goal is 'not met' (= 'not much met' + 'almost not at all met'). In 1978, these ratios were 10.2% and 40.7% respectively. Hence, more people now experience Japanese society as unequal.

As Kazuo Seiyama has pointed out, assertions regarding the expansion of the disparities between classes and strata have often been made in the past. Reflecting on the history of such assertions, Seiyama argues that this most recent claim is merely a reiteration of an old story, an illusion produced by a sense of anxiety (Seiyama 2000). As the above data demonstrates, however, the current growth in the disparities between classes is far from an illusion and is attributable to indisputable macro socio-economic causes, such as, globalization, the IT revolution and a restructuring of Japan's employment practices.

Why the expansion of disparities is unjustifiable

There are numerous reasons to argue that the expanding disparities between the classes are undesirable. Increasing inter-class disparities cause greater hardships for those most disadvantaged, accelerating the erosion of social cohesion, and contributing to various social problems. The intensification of both intra- and inter-class competition creates a society of 'winners' and 'losers'. But since some people are not persuaded by these reasons, we must briefly explore philosophical arguments about justice to clearly elucidate why these class disparities cannot be ethically justified.

Disparities between classes cannot be deemed unethical in-themselves – in principle and without qualification – for the counterfactual conception of a totally equal society, one where resources were distributed perfectly evenly, is highly problematic. People's incentive to work and socially contribute would most likely be weakened. If everyone were treated totally equally, individual needs would be ignored and, for example, those with disabilities – people who require greater resources in order to maintain an average quality of life – would suffer. In such a society, then, an increased disparity in the distribution of wealth might in fact be a good thing. What, then, would represent an unjustifiable disparity in wealth distribution?

Justice as fairness

John Rawls (1971) provides a starting point for discussing this problem. In *A Theory of Justice* Rawls tries to establish the principle of 'justice as fairness' beginning from an 'original position' in which people's social status, class location, inherited assets, innate abilities and physical strength etc. were covered by a 'veil of ignorance'. People in this original position cannot think or act according to prejudice formed by their circumstances or interest. At this point people will, as a matter of course, agree with the principle that 'no one should be advantaged or disadvantaged by natural fortune or social circumstance' (Rawls 1971:18). Rawls sees this as foundational to a notion of 'justice as fairness', and conducive to his famous 'difference principle' wherein, social and economic inequalities are allowed only when they are 'arranged to the greatest benefit of the least advantaged'.

The difference principle means 'an agreement to regard the distribution of natural talents as a common asset and to share in the benefit of this distribution whatever it turns out to be' (Rawls 1971:101). People do not create their ability entirely through their own effort, rather they inherit it from parents or develop it through their social circumstances. In this sense, people's abilities are common social resources, and it is not justifiable for an individual to monopolize the profit derived from them. Therefore, disparities which are derived from talent and ability as well as ascribed status, race and social circumstances are not unconditionally acceptable. Thus Rawls has overcome the limitations of conventional liberal theories that advocate equality of opportunity even whilst accepting inequities arising from differences in talents and abilities, and establishes new foundations for contemporary liberalism.

Rawl's theory has since been scrutinized and advanced by theorists of analytical Marxism, such as Dworkin, Arneson, Cohen and Roemer, all of whom seem to arrive at a principle of 'responsibility and compensation' which contends that 'equality of opportunity requires that people be compensated for handicaps induced by factors over which they have no control' (Roemer 1994; cf. Arneson 1989, Dworkin 1981). It goes without saying that the 'factors over which they have no control' include the circumstances of their upbringing and their innate abilities.

Sources of unjustifiable gaps

From this perspective we can say that there are four main sources of unjustifiable social disparities in contemporary Japan: inheritance; private ownership of the means of production; innate abilities and skills acquired through the circumstances of one's upbringing; and market mechanisms.

Inheritance

According to Tachibanaki (1998: 145), 44.5% of the total assets in Japan are acquired through inheritance. Yet, only 24.6% of households have received an inheritance, with the average of these amounting to 105.3 million yen.

Inherited capital can be invested, while an inherited house or land can free up other money for investment purposes. This applies also to assets and educational expenses which are gifted *inter vivo*. Thus, inheritances provide an advantage in the accumulation of capital and assets, producing other, indirect forms of economic inequality. Inheritance is one of the main contributors to the economic disparities in Japanese society and, being produced independently of a person's ability and effort, these disparities cannot be ethically justified.

Private ownership of the means of production

Owners of the means of production can gain profits by employing the means of production they own. The same is true of financial assets; in contemporary capitalism, capital produces capital and thus the owners of financial assets are owners of the means of production. When the means of production have been plundered or inherited from others, profits derived from them cannot be ethically justified. What, then, when one has accumulated the fruits of one's own labor, invested them and thereby gained a profit? The English philosopher, John Locke, justified this kind of profit as 'private ownership based on one's labor', an idea that remains widely accepted today. However, even in this case, the accumulation of profits and the accompanying economic disparities are unjustifiable.

Although the initial investment in the means of production may have originally been the result of one's own labor, the means of production are depleted and consumed in the production of goods and the provision of services. So, continuing operations requires that profits be continuously reinvested to replenish the means of production. Thus, even though the original investment in the means of production was the product of an individual's own labor, it is gradually but wholly replaced by the profits derived from income not of one's own labor. Marx made this point in *Groundwork for the Critique of Political Economy* (1857–58) where he concluded that even if the capital was originally the product of one's own labor, this only serves to establish the complete separation of ownership from labor,[2] and eventually it is the exploitation of other people's labor that creates the profits for investors. Hence, there is no clear basis for justifying the disparities resulting from the ownership of the means of production. In this connection, Rawls does not regard the liberty to own the means of production as a basic liberty to be guaranteed to all (Rawls 1971).

Private ownership of the means of production produces profits. It also demonstrably produces distinct social losses. In societies where deriving non-labor income from the profits of one's investments in the means of production is valorized, energies and abilities are predominantly mobilized to generate and accumulate more and more wealth through the exploitation of other peoples' labor. Social welfare and other non-profit enterprises become devalued. Abilities and skills not connected to the making of profits and the acquisition of the means of production are less highly valued and it becomes difficult for individuals to nurture a diverse array of talents. Therefore, we need either to abolish the private ownership of the means of production, or design a distributive mechanism that does not allow the exclusive acquisition of profit to the private owners of the means of production.

Ability

As Rawls pointed out, we cannot unconditionally affirm the social and economic disparities created by innate abilities or those acquired through the circumstances of one's upbringing. These abilities are common assets of the society, and therefore the profits produced by them should flow back to the society. But if the disparities created by differences in ability are allowed to stand, the effort to redistribute profit becomes enormous and invariably leads to social friction. At the same time, it is not a desirable situation when people with lesser abilities become resigned to receiving compensations given to them by those with greater abilities. Hence, in the long run, it is better to invest in measures that work towards equalizing people's abilities.

Many people accept that disparities generated by innate abilities are justifiable. According to the *National Survey on Life Preferences* conducted in 1999, 50.7% of respondents 'agreed' (= 'agree' + 'more or less agree') with a statement that 'it is natural to have inequities in income, etc. because of differences in innate abilities'. Only 15.1% 'disagreed' (= 'disagree' + 'more or less disagree') with this statement. It is notable, however, that 25.1% of people in their late teens expressed their 'disagreement', but by their early twenties only 21.8% reported their 'disagreement'; which is still considerably higher than the average of all ages. This suggests that an acceptance of the social and economic disparities generated from differences in innate ability increases with age; i.e., acceptance is formed through years of exposure to a society characterized by various structural inequities.

The expansion of disparities due to market mechanisms

Market mechanisms are inclined to over-value differences in the quality of commodities and in the abilities of people. They expand the economic disparities by rewarding particular abilities with incomes much larger than those accorded other abilities.

For instance, at present the Windows operating system has an overwhelming share of the personal computer software market, and Microsoft, the company which developed this software, has gained an enormous profit. This, however, does not mean that Windows is overwhelmingly superior to competing operation systems. On the contrary, its many defects have long been acknowledged. How, then, did Windows obtain such a massive market share? As Takamitsu Sawa has pointed out, various chance factors worked to Windows' advantage. Furthermore, contrary to economic textbook explanations, once Windows had acquired a reasonably large share of the market, it benefited from a mechanism called an 'increase in marginal profit', i.e., once investment has doubled, the return on investment more than doubles (Sawa 2000: 118). In stock investment and exchange transactions, fortune or misfortune often produces enormous wealth or loss. The operations of the market are truly 'uncontrollable factors', and we cannot justify the extreme economic disparities that they produce.

In addition, disparities produced by market mechanisms breed moral decay and generate social losses. Guided by the market, people direct their abilities and efforts towards the acquisition of profit, and neglect activities which would improve social welfare. In Japan during the period of the so-called bubble economy, this moral decay rapidly progressed. Sawa has argued that the bubble economy was a 'period of moral vacuum', because 'people came to despise work ethics such as hard work, effort, trustworthiness, cooperation, responsibility, etc. as old fashioned, and instead came to respect the disposition of a gambler' (Sawa 2000: 92). This, too, reduces the diversity of the abilities and propensities that a particular society nurtures in its people.

Remaining problems

Many other problems remain unresolved.

Resolving the inequities generated through inheritance is relatively straightforward. We could decrease inequities by increasing the inheritance tax rate, with the exception of certain assets and possessions such as graves and objects with ritualistic significance that are an essential part of the continuation of the traditional culture. Special provisions might need to be made with regards to the succession of enterprises from one generation to the next, e.g., agricultural land and equipment or the means of production owned by self-employed people. Nevertheless, the structures perpetuating disparities caused by inheritance must be fundamentally changed.

The other three areas, though, are more problematic and represent greater challenges for effective change.

Is it possible to abolish the private ownership of the means of production, or reorient the economy away from the acquisition of profit, without repeating the past failures of 'socialism'? What sort of alternative economy is conceivable? Similarly, it is not a simple matter to equalize people's abilities. If it is neither possible nor desirable to make people's abilities identical, how, then, do we define 'equality of abilities'? Again, even though market mechanisms are incredibly problematic, we cannot simply abolish them, because prices formed through 'free-market' mechanisms provide important feedback about the levels of demand and supply for both manufactured and simple commodities and provide important incentives to investors. If we accept that the market is an inevitable and essential part of a modern economy, in what form shall we retain it?

In order to prevent the expansion of the disparities and to design a widely affirmed egalitarian society, we must confront these rather daunting problems. In doing this, we must tackle problems that socialism – which claimed to realize an egalitarian society – did not properly address.[3] What follows is a brief discussion of various responses to the questions: 1. What is an egalitarian society? and 2. How can we design an egalitarian society?

What is an egalitarian society?

The Utilitarian theory of equality and its problems

What constitutes social 'equality'? A long-standing representative view on this matter is utilitarianism. Utilitarian philosophy produced many influential meditations on the questions surrounding social equality, but perhaps the most typical is the 'equality of marginal utility'. This asserts that if a society has one additional unit of goods to distribute and it awards this to wealthy members of the society, to people who already own a lot of goods, then it does not greatly increase the degree of happiness ('happiness' is the measure of utility for utilitarians). If, however, the unit of goods is distributed amongst poorer members of society then the degree of happiness increases more dramatically. Therefore, when one unit of goods is distributed to people who have high marginal utility, the utility of the whole society is increased and at the same time social equality is attained. If this pattern is continued, the marginal utility of everyone eventually becomes equal and the total utility of the society is maximized.

Amartya Sen, though, finds a fundamental flaw in this argument, illustrating it with the following example. Imagine that there is a disabled person, A, and an optimistic 'pleasure-wizard', B, who is expert in enjoying life. Suppose that, with the same income, A can obtain half the utility that B can. Since B therefore has a higher marginal utility, if we were to uphold the theory of the equality of marginal utility, we would then distribute more income to B. 'Utilitarianism must lead to this thanks to its single-minded concern with maximizing the utility sum. The pleasure-wizard's superior efficiency in producing utility would pull income away from the less efficient cripple' (Sen 1982: 357). This problem arises because the equality of marginal utility presupposes that utility functions the same for all people.

Another utilitarian theory of equality focuses on the 'equality of total utility'. This assumes differences in the utility function between people, and attempts to equalize the degrees of happiness. This position is commonly called 'utility equality' or 'welfarism'.

This position has problems too. How does a society deal with someone who needs high quality wine and caviar in order to feel an average level of welfare,[4] or a person who is physically unfit, yet still believes that his/her life will be worthless unless he/she climbs to the top of Mt. Everest on foot?[5] In order for these people to feel average welfare, society must lavish an enormous amount of resources upon them. Then there is the opposite case. According to Sen

> Our mental reactions to what we actually get and what we can sensibly expect to get may frequently involve compromises with harsh reality. The destitute thrown into beggary, the vulnerable landless laborer precariously surviving at the edge of subsistence, the overworked domestic servant working around the clock, the subdued and subjugated housewife reconciled to her role and her fate, all tend to come to terms with their respective predicaments. (Sen 1991: 15)

Thus some may feel quite happy with relatively few goods. This situation is called 'adaptive preference formation'. Welfarism is not concerned with this predicament, since the source and quality of the satisfaction are not questioned, the satisfaction derived from discriminating against each other or restricting each others' freedom also comes to be treated as a 'utility', similar to other sorts of satisfaction (Rawls 1971: 30).

Sen summarizes the problems inherent to utilitarianism in the following phrases: 'physical condition neglect' and 'valuation neglect'. Rejection of utility-based approaches 'requires consideration of the actual conditions of living of a person (physical and mental) and also the need to consider the person's valuation activity (under actual or counterfactual circumstances), going beyond what he or she actually desires'. When speaking of 'valuation activity', Sen is referring to 'mental activity of valuing one kind of life rather than another'. He argues that judgments of welfare should be made on the basis of deliberative valuation of an achievement of a person; what he or she manages to do or to be' (Sen 1999: 7, 14–15).

Equality of capability

An influential alternative to welfarism is Rawls' theory of the 'equality of primary social goods'. Rawls specifically defines 'liberty and opportunity, income and wealth, and the bases of self-respect' as 'things that every rational man is presumed to want' (Rawls 1971: 62). If we define equality in terms of distribution of objective and fundamental goods, instead of the subjective feelings of utility, we can avoid problems caused by the above examples of expensive tastes or the formation of adaptive preferences. Once the primary goods have been offered equally, goal setting and the means of attainment can be left to the discretion of the individual.

Although appreciative of Rawls' theory, Sen points out that it 'seems to take little note of the diversity of human beings'. If we were to adopt Rawls' 'equality of primary social goods', exactly the same amount of primary goods would be distributed to a disabled person as to anyone else. Thus, it fails to take into consideration differences in 'health, longevity, climatic conditions, location, working conditions, temperament and even body size'. Because people's needs differ according to their various differences, a society which equally distributed primary goods would not necessarily treat people equally. The advantage gained from goods is not determined by the amount of goods an individual owns, but the relationship between the individual and the goods (Sen 1982: 366).

What Sen proposes, then, is an 'equality of capability'. What people can achieve with a given set of goods he calls 'functionings', and the set of functionings that people can achieve with the goods that they can choose he calls 'capability'. Functionings are what people achieve with goods under various conditions and are, therefore, distinguishable from goods themselves and from utility. Capability is a set of functionings that people can choose from and, as such, represent their 'degree of freedom to achieve welfare'. Thus Sen's concept of the equality of capability overcomes the drawbacks of both welfarism, which focuses on utility, and of Rawls' theory, which centers on goods (Sen 1985: 6–11).

Given that capability is only a set of possibilities, there is no inevitability in the choices that people make. Guaranteed an equal capability, people then choose functionings according to their own preferences. Although, as a consequence, differences emerge in the welfare of individuals, these can be justified because they are the result of individual choice. In other words, 'equality of capability' provides for an equality of opportunities to achieve functionings; it does not enforce a specific function or set a standard for welfare. In this sense, Sen's approach can be said to have overcome the limitations of previous conceptions of the 'equality of opportunities' and the 'equality of results'. We cannot satisfy ourselves with 'equality of opportunities', which means that there is no institutional barrier, but neither can we accept the 'equality of results', which guarantees an identical result for all people. What is needed is an equality that ensures that people can choose a life of equal value regardless of the differences in the circumstances of their upbringing or their natural abilities. Equality of capability guarantees a wide range of options in life for all people and, as such, is the true condition for a free society.

Of course, many problems remain. To begin with, what sorts of things are actually included in 'capability', and how do we measure inequality? How do we deal with areas where differences in innate ability or physical conditions cannot be overcome? We do not need to be pessimistic about these or fall into agnosticism because most of the inequality in contemporary Japan is of the kind that can be easily assessed, easily estimated, and is not directly related to innate abilities or physical conditions.[6]

A design for an egalitarian society

Conditions of an egalitarian society

As argued above, two actions are required to remove unjustifiable inequality: 1. the abolition of the private ownership of the means of production, or the development of a scheme where the acquisition of profit is not exclusively reserved for the private owner of the means of production, and 2. the control of market forces. Socialism tried to 'solve' these two problems by nationalizing the means of production and totally regulating the economy through government control. History, though, has taught us that this is not a viable solution.

Nonetheless, a kind of socialism is required for a society to address these two problems. Socialism is not reducible to Marxism. Various forms of socialist thought existed before Marx's ideas became prominent and some of these continue today. The Marx of *The Communist Manifesto* and his followers, the Communist Party of the Soviet Union, and the various socialist parties that followed them did not recognize these alternative forms of socialism. Unfortunately, with the collapse of the Soviet Union and the Eastern Bloc, all forms of socialism have been discredited and the very notion of socialism has become something of a taboo. If, however, people consider an 'egalitarian society' to be desirable, then it will be necessary to change the economic system – including ownership rights – and socialism, in some guise, must be reconsidered. Human beings have a right to choose the economic system of the society in which they live. Locke advocated private ownership based on one's own labor, and claimed that people had a right to choose a new political structure by refusing any political structure that did not realize this. Similarly, people have a right to change the economic system in order to realize freedom and equality, in the sense that a wide array of life options are guaranteed to all.

New 'socialism'

Roemer has summarized three alternative visions for an egalitarian society, i.e., a 'new socialism': 1. labor-managed firms, 2. managerial enterprises with alterations in ownership, and 3. associative democracy (Roemer 1994).

The labor-managed firms model advocates a fundamental change in the relationship between labor and capital, with workers themselves owning and managing capital investments. This vision has existed since the early twentieth century. It enables a democratic administration of an enterprise and overcomes the traditional alienation of labor. On the negative side, there is the difficulty of procuring capital, the danger of great wage fluctuations caused by changes in the performance of a firm, and the possibility that technological innovation would decline because the goals of employment and reasonable wages would take precedence over profit making.

As to the managerial enterprise with alterations in ownership, Roemer has himself proposed a unique idea of coupon socialism. In this proposed economic system a coupon currency would run in parallel with the existing money currency. These coupons would be the sole means by which stocks could be purchased. All citizens would be issued with the same quantity of coupons, and it would be illegal to exchange coupons for normal currency or transfer coupons to another person. Hence, unspent coupons would be returned to the national treasury at the time of death. This prevents individuals from accumulating vast amounts of stock and ensures that all citizens have equal access to the capital of any given enterprise, receive dividends, and have voting rights regarding the enterprise's operation. In other words, under this system, citizens acquire a second voting right, which we might call an economic vote. Roemer has further discussed the method of capital procurement and the role of the state in this, and has explained by way of mathematical simulation that the system functions sufficiently and that disparities between the wealthy and the poor scale down as a result. This system maintains the current situation in which enterprises compete against each other for market share and where a small group of managers decide upon the company's direction. As such, it has been criticized by leftist commentators as 'a weak advance at best over capitalism' (Roemer 1994).

The third proposal, 'associative democracy', does not change the ownership of the enterprise in the legal sense, but regulates the behavior of the enterprise by reinforcing the influence of labor unions, environmental groups, consumer groups, etc. The obvious question arising from this proposal is: who will organize these various groups and ensure that their influence alters company policies?

All of these proposals more or less involve a change in the ownership of the means of production. If adopted they would bring about a reduction of economic disparities and would correct the failures caused by market mechanisms by socially controlling the enterprise's behavior.

Towards a 'non-class society'

Let us consider these proposals in terms of class structure.

The labor-managed firm model totally changes the form of ownership of the means of production in the legal sense as well as the effective sense of control, and intends to change the whole ownership and labor process at a single stroke. Under this system there would be no capitalist class and no distinction between the new middle class and the working class. If the system were implemented on a large scale, though, internal strata differentiation would inevitably result. Besides, since the boundary between the inside and the outside of the firm is maintained in this plan, and the extent of participation is limited to the workers, this cannot escape a sort of 'production-centered principle'. Thus, even with labor-managed firms, it would still be necessary to have broader social control over the firms' activities.

Coupon socialism alters the ownership of the means of production in a legal sense, but does not fundamentally change the way enterprises are structured. Although the owner capitalist would disappear, the managers would continue to exist, and the distinction between the new middle class and the working class would remain.

The associative democracy model intends to actually change the ownership of the means of production through the influence of various community groups. It is an attractive plan which is tied to an idea of the 'subordinate integration of the market economy to civil society' (Hashimoto 1990), and a 'new welfare nation which has embedded the market in the society' (Gotō 1997). Unless, however, it is accompanied by effective institutions that substantially change the ownership relations in the broader society, the changes under this system would most likely remain local and be dependent upon the strength of individual groups. Hence, most of the present class structure would be preserved.

Partial characteristics of these three plans reflect aspects of the egalitarian society, which have their origin as plural aspects of the class society. Therefore, the three plans are not considered in opposition to one another, but as complementary. By combining various elements of each plan, we could realize the goal of an egalitarian society.

Some practical steps in this direction would include: 1. making the hierarchical structure of enterprises less severe, and promoting worker participation; 2. ensuring the citizen's democratic participation in the market economy as an inherent right; and 3. placing the activities of enterprises under the control of various civic groups. In the 'egalitarian society' that would emerge if these measures were adopted, class itself would not necessarily disappear, but the disparities and differences between the classes would become much smaller. Also, once people are guaranteed the 'equality of capability' they will be able to choose their class location according to their own preferences and aptitudes. This is not a 'classless society', but rather a 'non-class society'; a vision of society to which the vast majority of citizens would consent.

Notes

Chapter 1

1 Tumin (1964) for example, traces the history of class theory to Plato and regards Aristotle, Augustine and Machiavelli as its pioneers.
2 See Uchida (1970) regarding Smith's views on class.
3 According to Shūichi Katō, Jean-Paul Sartre thought that 'dialectics' could be helpful as a guiding tool to develop thinking but unnecessary once thinking moves into the phase of describing the world (Katō 2000, p. 171).
4 Some Marxian scholars argue that strata represent internal divisions of a given class. This interpretation differs from the kinds of strata concepts that are widely in circulation today.

Chapter 2

1 This point still applies today. For instance, after the controversy over the theory of the new middle stratum in the late 1970s (which I will introduce later), the claim that 'the majority of Japanese employees have become white-collar' emerged. However, since technicians and manufacturing employees (including mining and construction workers), who form the core of blue-collar work, assumed the top position from agriculture, forestry and fisheries workers in the early 1960s, they have continued to be the largest occupation until the present. In 1999 they were more than 1.5 times the number of clerical workers, totaling 19.42 million. If we add together all white-collar workers, including professional-technical workers and managers, they finally surpassed the number of technicians and manufacturing employees in 1988. However the whole category of white-collar workers makes up only 36.1% of the total workforce in 1999.

2 A discussion of the link between the controversy surrounding the signing of the 1960 Security Treaty and the theory of mass society appeared in a feature article by Matsushita, Ueda and Shimizu in the October 1960 edition of *Shisō* entitled 'A Re-examination of the Theory of Mass Society'.
3 This discussion of Ōhashi's life and published works draws on Sakayori, Tokita, Nomura and Nozawa (1984).
4 In this context, 'middle class consciousness' is not the distinct consciousness of the middle class, but an ambiguous feeling that one is located in the 'middle' strata of society. In Japan, this is called 'chūryū-ishiki', which means midstream feelings.
5 For problems in the Sawyer report, see Ishikawa (1994) and Tachibanaki (1998). The important points are: 1. the statistics used in this report are from the end of the 1960s to the early 1970s. Japan's period of high economic growth was in its final stages and it was also a time when income disparities were at their smallest; 2. the Japanese statistics used here do not include farms or singles, giving the appearance that disparities in income distribution are insignificant. The conclusions of this report have been refuted by several studies (e.g., Tachibanaki 1998).
6 However, in an article entitled 'The Illusion of the "Middle Class"', published a year after the dispute, Kishimoto (1978), after claiming the concept of class was a tradition of economics from Quesnay to Keynes, explained that class existed in contemporary Japan and class rather than status is the fundamental classification in society.
7 *Asahi Shimbun*, 1 January 1990.

Chapter 3

1 There have been numerous studies of this type. See Robinson and Kelly (1979) and Koo and Hong (1980) for early examples.
2 On this point, see Wright (1989) and Hashimoto (1999).
3 Women who execute simple goods production at home are also classified as members of the working class.
4 The SSM Survey is discussed in some detail in chapter 4.
5 For details, see Hashimoto (1995).
6 As discussed in chapter 4, the SSM only surveyed men in its first three studies (1955, 1965 and 1975).

7 The increase in the proportion of the capitalist class is attributable in part to changing measurements in the SSM Survey from 1985 to 1995. Like many other surveys, the SSM Surveys of 1985 and earlier did not specify whether or not family workers should be included in the number of employees at the enterprise where the respondent works. The 1995 SSM Survey specifically instructed that family workers should be included in this calculation. Accordingly, some proportion of self-employed proprietors who had previously been treated as belonging to the 'less than five' category in the pre-1995 surveys were now classified as belonging to the 'five or more' category.

Interestingly, we also observe a significant increase in the proportion of company executives in the Population Census, a pattern suggesting some further augmentation of the capitalist class. However, before and during the period of high economic growth (1960s), many farm households had five or more family workers. Thus, the 1995 SSM survey data tends to overestimate the size of capitalists amongst respondents' fathers. To rectify this, we have classified the respondents' fathers as belonging to the old middle class if they were non-white collar employees in establishments employing ten workers or less.

Promenade: transgressions of class borders

1 The following is a selective reconstruction of the narrative combining elements of the original text and the film versions of the story.
2 Based on information provided by Karimoku Group, headquartered in Aichi Prefecture; possibly the real-life model for Tsurumoku Furniture, Inc.
3 Andrea Branzi is an Italian interior designer. In the 1960s he belonged to a school of radicalism and experimental design. He is now seen as a key representative of Italian design, practicing architecture and town planning, and has published numerous books.
4 A couple is legally married upon establishing their family register. For details of the family registration system in Japan, see Sugimoto 2003, pp. 146–53.

5 I am indebted to Mr Hisada (http://plaza3.mbn.or.jp/~hisada/index.html) for various facts regarding 'Tsurumoku Bachelor Dormitory'.
6 According to the 1995 SSM Survey, among husbands of women whose fathers' main occupations were professional, 70.1% of the husbands were professionals, administrators and clerical workers, and 61.2% of them had a higher education. In contrast, only 19.4% of these men were employed in manual labor.

Chapter 4

1 Numerous books and articles on Japan's class and stratification structure have been published on the basis of the SSM Survey. The major English-language publications include: Ishida (1993), Kosaka (1994) and *International Journal of Sociology*, vol.30, no.1–2, 2000 (Special Issues: The Composition of Stratification and Class in Contemporary Japan) containing the following articles:
   - Kanomata, Nobuo and Kikkawa, Tōru, 'Guest Editor's Introduction'.
   - Seiyama, Kazuo, 'The Modern Stratification System and Its Transformation'.
   - Hashimoto, Kenji, 'Class Structure in Contemporary Japan'.
   - Kondō, Hiroyuki, 'The Meritocracy Hypothesis and Trends in Educational Opportunity'.
   - Watanabe, Tsutomu and Satō, Yoshimochi, 'Analysis of Labor Markets in Postwar Japan'.
   - Kikkawa, Tōru, 'Changes in the Determinants of Class Identification in Japan'.
   - Yamaguchi, Kazuo, 'Married Women's Gender-Role Attitudes and Social Stratification'.

   I would like to thank the 1995 SSM research committee for their kind permission for me to use the SSM Survey data in the present study.
2 Six years in primary school plus three years of middle school education is compulsory for Japanese children. Upon finishing these nine years of compulsory education, more than 97% of pupils advance to high school according to the 2000 Basic School Survey of the Ministry of Education and Science.

3 The SSM Survey inquired about income by providing multiple-choice answers. Respondents were asked to choose one out of the 17 income ranges, and when the income exceeded the available range they were asked to provide an actual amount. The accuracy of this income register is therefore quite high. It must be remembered, though, that when surveyed people tend to indicate a lower amount than their actual income, a general problem of wealth and income surveys, arising perhaps because 'it is in the best interest of most people to underestimate their wealth and income in order to pay less tax and/or receive more benefits' (Edgell 1993).
4 In the 1995 SSM Survey, multiple choices were provided for answering questions about assets. The highest choice stipulated an amount 'over one hundred million yen', for which one hundred and fifty million yen was used to calculate the average.
5 The 'progressive parties' referred to are the Socialist Party of Japan and the Japan Communist Party. When the survey was conducted in 1995, neither the Social Democratic Party nor the Democratic Party was yet formed. In post-World War II Japan, the names and affiliations of the opposition political parties have been in almost continual flux. Nevertheless, there remains a discernible 'left-right' distinction in Japanese politics and we use the term 'progressive parties' as an umbrella for those left-leaning parties in opposition to the conservative (and dominant) Liberal Democratic Party.
6 The total of women's working hours almost invariably exceeds men's when hours of unpaid, domestic work are combined with hours of paid work. Hence, the fact that women's paid working hours are shorter disguises the broader issue of their exploitation.
7 The response, 'there is no subordinate' was offered for the statement, 'I decide almost all of the work content of my subordinates'. This response is included in the 'not applicable' category.
8 As discussed in Chapter 3, it is necessary to categorize clerical workers in different classes in accordance with their gender, which determines the potential for access to promotion and power in the workplace. However, most SSM researchers bundle these workers all together in the 'middle stratum'.
9 Considerable class differences appear when responses to this question are analyzed according to gender and age. For

example, only two-fifths of new middle class women report any type of acquaintance with 'factory workers' and less than half have acquaintances with 'agriculture and fisheries' workers.
10 Satō (1981, 1987) clarified the kinship ties between politicians and businessmen.
11 See Poulantzas (1969, 1978) and Wright (1978) for representative examples of efforts to counter such critiques.

Chapter 5

1 Satō does not directly write about this second point in his book *Japan as an Unequal Society*, but on page 45 he concludes that 'we cannot extract specific mobility factors from the table alone', and refers us to an article (Satō 1994) in which he discusses the matter in greater detail. Here we have simply summarized the relevant points from this article.
2 In fact, 'pure mobility rate' and 'unrealized mobility rate' can be calculated for each class, but this is not a common practice, and we have not done so here.
3 Satō later explained the reason for focusing on people's occupation at age 40, based on knowledge gained from previous studies dealing with careers of white-collar employees. Since it has been known that people who have taken a managerial position by the age of 40 become the core group of managers, he says that he can 'extract most managerial occupations' by looking at people aged 40 (Satō 2000c). Although such studies have been conducted, these only deal with male white-collar employees working for large corporations. It is misleading to apply these findings to UWE, a majority of whom are employees or executives working for small to medium-sized corporations.
4 Shima's (2001) analysis of the 'student life survey' conducted by the Ministry of Education has shed light on the fact that differences in the rate of advancement to universities have expanded rapidly between income strata in the 1990s.

Chapter 6

1 'Agricultural workers' in this chapter refer to household members who are fifteen years old and over and are engaged in any work in farming. The 'farm household population' refers

to the total population of farm households, regardless of whether or not they are employed in the agricultural sector.
2. We are aware that the phrase, 'differentiation of the peasantry,' is often used in Marxist literature to describe the process that we are examining in this chapter. Bearing in mind that an overwhelming majority of the postwar Japanese farming population are not landless peasants, however, we deliberately employ the term 'the farming class' to represent one of the two subcategories in our four-class model (cf. chapter 4) while avoiding cumbersome expressions about the farming 'subclass'.
3. These figures are based on the Survey on Employment of Farm Household Populations conducted by the Ministry of Agriculture, Forestry and Fisheries.
4. These calculations include the non-employed because they constitute a significant proportion of women. Calculations which are based only on the employed tend to produce misleadingly low outflow rates.
5. Tsuburai (1995) has confirmed this point using the SSM survey data.
6. Differences are significant at 0.05 level.
7. According to the appendix statistical table of the *Agricultural White Paper* in 1996. The original data is from the Census of Agriculture and Forestry.
8. Farm Household Survey Report of the 1995 Census of Agriculture and Forestry.

Chapter 7

1. This is, however, due to the fact that the wives highly appreciate their husbands' little help, accepting that 'domestic work and child rearing are women's work', rather than because the husbands actually cooperate in domestic work and child rearing. Several surveys investigating the assessment of the husband's participation in domestic work indicate that the wife's assessment is higher than her husband's (Rengo Josei-kyoku 1995, Iwai and Inaba 2000).

Chapter 8

1. The only exception is the consciousness that 'I am progressive' (i.e., agreement or disagreement with a statement, 'if asked

whether conservative or progressive, my stance is progressive'). Compared with class location, this has a relatively high correlation with political party support. However, since this question is closely related to political party support, it is almost tautological to say that the consciousness 'I am progressive' determines political party support.
2 According to Hisataka Kobayashi, political ideology indicates 'general consciousness that people have about the desirable circumstances regarding what the society as a whole should be' (Kobayashi 2000). Here, however, we have used the term economic ideology, since we are focusing on problems related to the economic domain, i.e., deregulation and meritocracy.

Chapter 9

1 The digital divide involves both gaps between strata in each society and even large differences between nations. Although there is no room to detail the latter, let us note that 20% of the wealthiest nations make up 93.3% of Internet users (based on United Nations Development Program, *Report on Human Development*).
2 This claim is generally called the *Umschlag des Aneignungsgesetzes* (inversion of the law of appropriation).
3 As Shōji Yoshizaki indicates: 'Various thoughts of socialism including Marxism have not necessarily offered vivid theoretical proposals concerning the problem of equality which is supposed to be its proper function. Reflecting now, I think that the inertness of the equality discussion must have been the theoretical root that invited the failure of 'socialism', and can not help regretting it' (Yoshizaki 1998: 217).
4 This is a frequently cited example, but I personally do not know whether fine wine and caviar go well together.
5 This example is based on Roemer (1994).
6 Satō (2000a, 2000c) denies any attempt to measure the relative equality of opportunity at present. This, however, makes the existence of apparent inequality of opportunities ambiguous, and effectively condones inequality as a result. Inequality exists and is presently measurable in many different ways: in opportunities for educational advancement due to disparities in wealth, for promotion by gender, for employment by ethnicity, and between people of advanced nations and developing nations.

Since Satō only looks at intergenerational mobility where the final results – although they can be predicted to a considerable degree, and many studies have been carried out to this end – are only known a few decades later, he seems to have failed to grasp the broader picture of the problem of inequality.

References

Arneson, R., 1989, 'Equality and Equal Opportunity for Welfare', *Philosophical Studies* No.1.
Bourdieu, Pierre, 1970, *La Reproduction,* Edition de Minuit.
Bourdieu, Pierre et Passerton, Jean-Claude, 1964, *Les héritiers*, Edition de Minuit.
Bungei Shūnjū Henshūbu, 2000, 'Shin kaikyū shakai Nippon (Japan as new class society),' *Bungei Shūnjū*, March.
Braverman, Harry, 1974, *Labor and Monopoly Capital*, Monthly Review Press.
Crompton, Rosemary, 1993, *Class and Stratification*, Polity Press.
Delphy, Christine, 1984, *Class to Home*, University of California Press.
Dworkin, R., 1981, 'What is Equality?', *Philosophy and Public Affairs* vol.10, no.3–4.
Edgell, Stephen 1993, *Class*, Routledge.
Eguchi, Eiichi, 1978, 'Nōson ni okeru kajō jinkō pūru no atarashii keisei (New formation of the pool of the excessive population in agricultural villages),' *Nōgyō no kōzō henka to rōdō shijō* (Structural changes in agriculture and the labor market), edited by Chūō Daigaku Keizai Kenkyūsho (Institute of Economic Research at Chuo University), Chūō Daigaku Shuppanbu.
Endō, Kōshi, 1999, *Nihon no jinji satei* (Japan's system of personnel assessment), Mineruba Shobō.
.... 2000, 'Chingin (Wages),' Ōhara Shakai Mondai Kenkyūsho zasshi (Journal of the Ohara Research Institute of Social Issues), issue 501.
Esping-Andersen, Gøosta, 1999, *Social Foundations of Post-industrial Economies*, Oxford University Press.
Fujita, Shōzō, 1957, 'Genzai kakumei shisō ni okeru jakkan no mondai (Some issues in contemporary revolutionary thought),' *Chūō Kōron*, February.
Giddens, Anthony, 1973, *The Class Structure of the Advanced Societies*, Hutchinson.

.... 1989 *Sociology*, Polity Press.
Gotō, Michio, 1997, 'Shin fukushi kokkaron josetsu (An introduction to a theory of the new welfare state),' *Nihon shakai no taikō to kōsō [Kōza: Gendai Nihon 4]*(Alternative and conception in Japanese society [Series: Contemporary Japan, vol. 4]), edited by Osamu Watanabe and Michio Gotō, Ōtsuki Shoten.
Gouldner, Alvin Ward, 1979, *The Future of Intellectuals and the Rise of the New Class*, The Seabury Press.
Hamashima, Akira, 1957, 'Kaikyū kōzō, kaikyū kankei oyobi kaikyū kōdō (Class structure, class relations and class action),' *Kaikyū to kumiai [Kōza shakaigaku dai 6-kan]* (Classes and unions [Series: Sociology, vol. 6]), edited by Tadashi Fukutake et al., Tokyo Daigaku Shuppankai.
Hara, Akira, 1979, 'Kaikyū kōsei no shin suikei (New estimates of the class composition),' *Ryō taisen-kan no Nihon shihon shugi* (Japanese capitalism between World War I and II), edited by Yoshio Andō, Tokyo Daigaku Shuppankai.
Hara, Junsuke, 1994, 'Political attidues and social strata,' *Social Stratification in Contemporary Japan*, edited by Kenji Kosaka, Kegan Paul International.
.... 1998, 'Ryūdōsei to kaihōsei – Sedaikan shakai idō no sūsei [Shōwa shoki – 1995] (Fluidity and openness: trends in intergenerational mobility [From the early Shōwa period to 1995]), *Shakai kaiso idō no kiso bunseki to kokusai hikaku [1995-nen SSM chōsa shiriizu 1]* (Basic analysis and international comparisons of social mobility [1995 Social Stratification and Mobility study series, vol. 1]), edited by Hiroshi Ishida.
Hara, Junsuke and Seiyama, Kazuo, 1999, *Shakai kaisō: Yutakasa no naka no fubyōdō* (Social stratification: Inequalities amid affluence), Tokyo Daigaku Shuppankai.
Hashimoto, Kenji, 1985, 'Kyōiku ni yoru kaikyū kettei to kaikyū kōzō no saiseisan (Class determination by education and the reproduction of class structure),' *Tokyo Daigaku Kyōiku Gakubu kiyō* (Journal of the Faculty of Education at the University of Tokyo), vol. 25.
.... 1986, 'Gendai Nihon no kaikyū bunseki (Class analysis of contemporary Japan),' *Shakaigaku hyōron* (Journal of the Japan Sociological Association), vol. 37, no. 2.
.... 1990a, 'Kaikyū shakai to shite no Nihon shakai (Japan as a class society),' *Shakai kaisō no kōzō to katei [Gendai Nihon no kaisō kōzō]* (Structures and processes of social stratification

[Stratification structures of contemporary Japan]), edited by Atsushi Naoi and Kazuo Seiyama, Tokyo Daigaku Shuppankai.

.... 1990b, 'Gendai shihon shugi kokka no kiki to kōkyōiku seido (The crisis of the modern capitalist societies and the system of public education), *Gendai kyōiku kagaku-ron no furontia* (The frontiers of contemporary educational science theories), edited by Haruyoshi Ebihara, Nobuaki Kurosawa, Masaya Minei and Eideru Kenkyūsho.

.... 1995, '"Kigyō shakai" Nihon no kaikyū kaisō kōzō to josei rōdōsha (Class and stratification structure of Japan as a 'corporate-centered society and female workers'),' *'Kigyō shakai' Nihon no naka no josei rōdōsha* (Female workers in Japan as a 'corporate-centered society'), edited by Nihon Rōdō Shakai Gakkai (The Japanese Association of Labor Sociology), Tōshindō.

.... 1997, '"Dō kyū sei" no kiseki – Shokugyō to shakai kaisō (The trajectory of 'classmates,': Occupation and social strata),' *Atarashii sangyō shakaigaku* (New industrial sociology), edited by Susumu Inuzuka, Yūhikaku.

.... 1998, 'Sengo Nihon no kaikyū kōzō: Kihon kōzō to hendō katei (Class structure in postwar Japan),' *Shakai kaisō idō no kiso bunseki to kokusai hikaku [1995-nen SSM chōsa shiriizu 1]* (Basic analysis and international comparisons of social mobility [1995 Social Stratification and Mobility study series, vol. 1]), edited by Hiroshi Ishida.

.... 1999, *Gendai Nihon no kaikyū kōzō: Riron, hohō, keiryō bunseki* (Class structure in Contemporary Japan: Theory, methods and quantitative analysis), Tōshindō.

Hayashi, Chikio, 1995, *Sūji kara mita Nihonjin no kokoro* (The minds of the Japanese statistically examined), Tokuma Shoten.

Honda, Tatsuo, 1950, 'Nihon jinkō mondai no shiteki kaiseki (Historical analysis of the population problems in Japan),' *Kikan jinkō mondai kenkyū* (Quarterly journal of the studies of population problems), vol. 6, no. 2.

Imada, Takatoshi and Hara, Junsuke, 1979, 'Shakaiteki chii no ikkansei to hi-ikkansei (Status consistency and inconsistency),' *Nihon no kaisō kōzō* (Stratification structure in Japan), edited by Ken'ichi Tominaga, Tokyo Daigaku Shuppankai.

Imada, Takatoshi, 1989, *Shakai kaisō to seiji* (Social strata and politics). Tokyo Daigaku Shuppankai.

.... 2000, 'Posuto modan jidai no shakai kaisō (Social stratification in the postmodern age),' *Shakai kaisō no posto modan*

References

[Nihon no kaisō shisutemu 5] (The postmodern of social stratification [Japanese social stratification system, vol. 5]), edited by Takatoshi Imada, Tokyo Daigaku Shuppankai.

Ishida, Hiroshi, 1993 *Social Mobility in Contemporary Japan*, Stanford University Press.

Ishida, Kazuo, 1984, 'Howaito kraraa rōdōsha to shin-chūkansō no keisei (White-collar workers and the formation of the new middle strata,' *Rōdōsha no kōsei to jōtai [Nihon no rōdō kumiai undō 2]* (The composition and the conditions of workers [The labor union movements in Japan, vol. 2]), edited by Nihon no rōdō kumiai undō henshū iinkai (Editorial committee of the labor union movements in Japan), Ōtsuki Shoten.

Ishikawa, Tsuneo (ed.), 1994, *Nihon no tomi to shotku no bunpai* (The distribution of wealth and income in Japan), Tokyo Daigaku Shuppankai.

Ishiwata, Tadao, 1958, 'Ji- san-nan mondai no seikaku (The characteristics of the problems of second and third sons),' *Sekai*, August.

Iwai, Noriko and Inaba, Akihide 2000, 'Kaji ni sanka suru otto, shinai otto (Those husbands who engage in household chores and those who do not), *'Jendaa, shijō, kazoku [Nihon no kaisō shisutemu 4]* (Gender, market and family [Social stratification system in Japan, vol. 4]), Tokyo Daigaku Shuppankai.

Kanomata, Nobuo and Kikkawa, Tōru 2000 (spec.eds) *International Journal of Sociology*, 'Special Issues: The Composition of Stratification and Class in Contemporary Japan' vol.30, nos.1–2.

Katase, Kazuo and Umino, Michio 2000, 'Mutōhasō wa seiji ni dō kakawaru no ka: Mutōhasō no henbō to seiji sanka no yukue (How do nonpartisans participate in politics? The changes of nonpartisans and the direction of political participation), *Kōheikan to seiji ishiki [Nihon no kaisō shisutemu 2]* (The sense of justice and political participation [Social stratification system in Japan, vol. 2]), edited by Michio Umino, Tokyo Daigaku Shuppankai.

Kawashima, Takeyoshi, 1957, *Ideorogii to shite no kazoku seido* (The family system as ideology), Iwanami Shoten.

Kinoshita, Ritsuko, 1988, *Tsuma-tachi no kigyō sensō* [Wives' enterprise warfare], Shakai Shisōsha.

Kishimoto, Shigenobu, 1978, *'Chūryū' no gensō* (Illusion of belonging to the 'middle class'), Kōdansha.

Kobayashi, Hisataka, 2000, 'Seiji ideorogii ha seiji sanka ni dō eikyō suruno ka – Gendai Nihon ni okeru sanka to byōdo no ideorogii (How does political ideology influence political participation? Participation and the ideology of equality),' *Kōhei-kan to seiji ishiki [Nihon no kaisō shisutemu 2]* (The sense of justice and political participation [Social stratification system in Japan, vol. 2]), edited by Michio Umino, Tokyo Daigaku Shuppankai.

Koike, Kazuo, 1981, *Nihon no jukuren* (Skill formation in Japan), Yūhikaku.

────── 1991, *Shigoto no keizaigaku* (Economics of work), Tōyō Keizi Shimpōsha.

Koo, H. and Hong, D-S., 1980, 'Class and income inequality in Korea,' *American Sociological Review*, vol. 45, 610–26.

Kosaka, Kenji (ed.), 1994, *Social Stratification in Contemporary Japan*. Kegan Paul International.

Kumazawa, Makoto, 1981, *Nihon no rōdōsha-zō* (The portraits of Japanese workers), Chikuma Shobō.

────── 1993, *Shinpen: Nihon no rōdōsha-zō* (New edition: The portraits of Japanese workers), Chikuma Shobō.

──────, Gordon, Andrew and Hane, Mikiso (trs.), 1996, *Portraits of the Japanese Workplace*, Westview Press.

Lenin, Vadimir Il'ich, 1917, *State and Revolution*.

Mallet, Serge, 1963, *La Nouvelle Classe Ourvrière*, Seuil.

────── 1971, *Le Pourvoir ouvrière*, Editions Anthropolos.

Marx, Karl, 1847, *Misère de la Philosophie*.

────── 1852, *Der archtzehnte Brumaire des Lois Bonaparte*.

────── 1852, A Letter to Joseph Weydemeyer.

────── 1857, *Grundrisse der Kritik der politischen Ōkonomie*.

────── 1861–63, *Theorien über den Mehrwert*.

────── 1867, *Das Kapital*, Bd. I.

────── 1894, *Das Kapital*, Bd. III.

Marx, Karl and Engels, Friedrichi, 1844, *Die heilige Familie oder Kritik der kritischen Kritik*.

────── 1848, *Manifest der Kommunistischen Partei*.

Matsushita, Keiichi, 1956, 'Taishū kokka no seiritsu to sono mondai-sei (The estabishment of mass nationhood and its problematique),' *Shisō*, November.

────── 1960, 'Taishū shakairon no konnichi-teki ichi (The current position of the mass society theory),' *Shisō*, October.

Milliband, Ralph, 1969, *The State in Capitalist Society*, Weidenfeld and Nicolson.

References

Mills, Charles Wright, 1951, *White Collar*, Oxford University Press.

Minobe, Ryōkichi and Matsushita, Keiichi, 1960, 'Chūkan kaikyū wa sodatsu ka? (Will the middle class grow?),' *Asahi Journal*, 24 January.

Mitsumata, Nobukuni, 1966, 'Tōkei kenkyū (2) – Kaikyū kōseihyō no sakusei (Statistical studies (2) – The construction of class composition tables), *Yuibutsu shikan* (Historical materialism), edited by Hyōe Ōuchi and Sakisaka Itsurō, vol. 2, Kawade Shobō.

Miyake, Ichirō, 1985, *Seitō shiji no bunseki* (Analysis of patterns of support for political parties), Sōbunsha.

────── 1989 *Tōhyō kōdō* (Voting behavior), Tokyo Daigaku Shuppankai.

Miyano, Masaru, 1998, 'Shokugyō to seitō shiji (Occupation and political party support),' *Seiji ishiki no genzai [1995-nen SSM chōsa shiriizu 7]* (The present state of political consciousness [1995 Social Stratification and Mobility study series, vol. 7]), 1995-nen SSM Chōsa Kenkyūkai (1995 SSM Study Group).

Murakami, Yasusuke, 1977, 'Shakai hendō o toraeru aratana shiten o motomete – Shin chūkan kaisōron (In search of a new perspective for the analysis of social change: New middle strata theory), *Asahi kōkoku geppō* (Asahi advertising monthly), September.

────── 1984, *Shin chūkan taishu no Jidai* (The age of the new middle mass), Chūō Kōronsha.

Nakayama, Shigeru, 2001 'Introduction: Occupation period 1945–'52' in Nakayama, Shigeru, Kunio Gotō and Hitoshi Yoshioka (eds) *A Social History of Science and Technology in Contemporary Japan, Vol.1 The Occupation Period 1945–1952*, Trans Pacific Press, Melbourne, pp.23–56.

Nakayasu, Sadako, 1995, *Rōdōryoku ryūshutsu to nōgyō kōzō [Nakayasu Sadako ronbunshū I]* (Outflow of the labor force and the structure of agriculture [Collection of papers by Sadako Nakayasu, vol. 1]), Nōrin Tōkei Kyōkai.

Namiki, Shōkichi, 1955, 'Nōka jinkō no sengo 10-nen (The farm population in the ten year period after the end of World War II),' *Nōgyō sōgō kenkyū* (Comprehensive studies of agriculture), vol. 9, no. 4, pp. 1–46.

────── 1956, 'Nōka jinnkō no idō keitai to shūgyō kōzō (The movement of the farm population and the employment structure),' *Nōgyō ni okeru senzai shitsugyō* (Latent unemployment in agriculture), edited by Seiichi Tōbata, pp. 195–214, Nihon Hyōronsha.

.... 1960, *Nōson wa kawaru* (Agricultural villages change). Iwanami Shoten.

Naoi, Atsushi and Seiyama, Kazuo (eds), *Shakai kaisō no kōzō to katei [Gendai Nihon no kaisō kōzō 1]* (The structure and process of social stratification [Stratification structure in contemporary Japan, vol. 1], Tokyo Daigaku Shuppankai.

Nihon Kyōsantō Chūō Iinkai Keizai Chōsa-bu (Japan Communist Party, Central Committee, Economic Survey Group), 1965, 'Nihon kaikyū kōsei no genjō (The present situation of class composition in Japan),' *Zen'ei* (The vanguard), February.

Nihon Tōkei Kenkyūsho (Japan Institute of Statistical Research), 1958, *Nihon Keizai Tōkeishū* (A collection of statistics on the Japanese economy), Nihon Hyōronsha.

Nojiri, Shigeo, 1942, *Nōmin rison no jisshō-teki kenkyū* (An empirical study of cityward migration of agricultural villagers), Iwanami Shoten.

Nikkeiren (The Japan Federation of Employers' Association), 1995, *'Japanese Management' in the New Age*.

Nomura, Masami, 2000, 'Chiteki jukuren-ron no jisshō-teki konkyo (Empirical basis of the intellectual skill formation theory),' *Ōhara Shakai Mondai Kenkyūsho zasshi* (Journal of the Ōhara Research Institute of Social Problems), no. 503.

Nosaka, Sanzō, 1961, 'Nihon Kyōsantō Dai 8-kai Taikai Chūō Iinkai no seiji hōkoku (The political report of the Central Committee of the Eight Congress of the Japan Communist Party), *Zen'ei* (The vanguard), September special issue.

Oguma, Eiji, 2002, *A Genealogy of 'Japanese' Self-images*, Trans Pacific Press.

Ōhashi, Ryūken, 1959, 'Shakai kaikyū Koseihyō no igi to genkai (The significance and limitations of the social class composition table),' *Kyoto Daigaku Keizai Gakubu sōritsu 40-shūnen kinen keizaigaku ronshū* (Economics papers prepared for the 40th anniversary of the foundation of the Faculty of Economics at Kyoto University), Yūhikaku.

.... 1968, 'Sengo Nihon no kaikyū kosei to saikō keieishasō chūkakubu (Class composition and the core of the top business executive class in postwar Japan), *'Gendai no keizai to tōkei – Ninagawa Torazō sensei koki kinen* (The economy and statistics today: In celebration of the seventieth birthday of Professor Torazō Ninagawa), Yūhikaku.

.... (ed.), 1971, *Nihon no kaikyū kōsei* (Class composition in Japan), Iwanami Shoten.

Oka, Kazumasa (ed.), 1986, *Seisen: Fukuri kōsei kitei to tsukurikata* (Careful selection: Rules of welfare facilities and methods of their establishment), Keiei Shoin.

Ōkōchi, Kazuo, 1950, 'Chin rōdō ni okeru hōken-teki naru mono (Feudal elements in wage labor),' *Keizaigaku ronshū* (Papers on economics), vol. 19, no. 4.

Ōuchi, Tsutomu, 1969, *Nihon ni okeru nōminsō no bunkai* (Class differentiation of the peasantry in Japan), Tokyo Daigaku Shuppankai.

Ozawa, Masako, 1985, *Shin 'kaisō shōhi' no jidai* (The age of new 'class-based consumption patterns'), Nihon Keizai Shimbunsha.

Pakulski, Jan and Waters, Malcolm, 1996, *The Death of Class*, Sage.

Parkin, Frank, 1978, 'Social stratification,' *History of Sociological Analysis*, edited by Tom Bottomore and Robert Nisbet, Basic Books.

Poulantzas, Nicos, 1969, 'The problem of the capitalist state,' *New Left Review*, no. 58.

.... 1973, 'On social classes,' *New Left Review*, no. 78.

.... 1975, *Classes in Contemporary Capitalism*, NLB.

.... 1978, *L'Estat, le Pouvoir, le Socialism*, Presses Universitaire de France.

Quesney, François, 1758, *Tableaus Économiques*.

Rawls, John, 1971, *A Theory of Justice*. Harvard University Press.

Rengō Josei-kyoku (Japanese Trade Union Confederation, Bureau for Women) (ed.), 1995, *Josei no rōdō, seikatsu jikan* (Women's work and daily schedule), Rōken Shuppan.

Robinson, R.V. and Kelly, J., 1979 'Class as conceived by Marx and Dahrendorf: Effects on income inequality and politics in the United States and Great Britain,' *American Sociological Review*, vol. 44, 38–58.

Roemer, John E. 1982, *A General Theory of Exploitation and Class*. Harvard University Press.

.... 1986, 'New directions in the Marxian theory of exploitation and class,' *Analytical Marxism*, edited by John E. Roemer, Cambridge University Press.

.... 1988, *Free to Lose*, Harvard University Press.
.... 1994, *A Future for Socialism*, Harvard University Press.
Sakayori, Toshio, Tokita, Yoshihisa, Nomura, Yoshiki and Nozawa, Masanori (eds), 1984, *Gendai Nihon no kaikyū kōsei to shotoku haibun* (Class composition and income distribution today), Yūhikaku.
Satō, Tomoyasu, 1981, *Keibatsu – Nihon no nyū esutaburisshumento* (Matrimonial nepotism: Japan's new establishment), Tachikaze Shobō.
.... 1987, *Monbatsu – Kyū kazaoku-sō no fukken* (Noble lineage: The reinstatement of the old nobility), Tachikaze Shobō.
Satō, Toshiki, 1994, 'Sedai-kan idō ni okeru kyōkyū-gawa yōin – Jinkō saisei to shūgyō senkō (Supply-side factors in inter-generational mobility: Population reproduction and employment preference), *Riron to hōhō* (Theories and methods), vol. 7, no. 2.
.... 2000a, '"Shin chūkan taishū" tanjō kara nijūnen (Twenty Years Since the Birth of "The New Middle Mass")', *Chūō Kōron*, May.
.... 2000b, *Fubyōdō shakai Nippon – Sayonara sō-chūryū* (Japan as an unequal society: Farewell to a totally middle-class society), Chūō Kōronsha.
.... 2000c, 'Soredomo susumu "fubyōdō shakaika" – senbatu to kikai to "kaikyū" (Nevertheless, a trend towards an unequal society continues: Selection, opportunities and 'class'), *Chūō Kōron*, November.
Sawa, Takamitsu, 2000, *Shijō shugi no shūen* (The end of marketism), Iwanami Shoten.
Sawyer, Malcolm, 1976, 'Income distribution in OECD countries,' *OECD Economic Outlook Occasional Studies*, July.
Sen, Amartya, 1982, *Choice, Welfare and Measurement*, Basil Blackwell.
.... 1985, *Commodities and Capabilities*, Elsevier Publishers.
.... 1999 *Commodities and Capabilities*, Oxford University Press.
Scott, John and Watanabe, Masao, 1998 *Kaikyūron no genzai – Igirisu to Nihon* (The class discourse today: Britain and Japan), Aoki Shoten.
Seiyama, Kazuo, Naoi, Atsushi, Satō, Yoshimichi, Tsuzuki, Kazuharu, and Kojima, Hideo, 1990, 'Gendai Nihon no kaisō kōzō to sono sūsei (The stratification structure and its trend in contemporary Japan),' *Shakai kaisō no kōzō to katei [Gendai*

Nihon no kaisō kōzō 1] (The structure and process of social stratification [Stratification structure in contemporary Japan, vol. 1], edited by Atsushi Naoi and Kazuo Seiyama, Tokyo Daigaku Shuppankai.

Seiyama, Kazuo, 2000, 'Chūryū hōkai ha "monogatari" ni suginai (The dissolution of the middle class is nothing but a 'fictitious narative'),' *Chūō Kōron*, November.

Shibata, Shingo, 1957, '"Taishū shakai" riron e no gimon – Marukusu shugi gakuto no tachiba kara (Questions about the 'mass society' theory: From the view point of a Marxist scholar), *Chūō Kōron*, June.

Shima, Kazunori, 2001, 'Kōdo seichō-ki ikō no daigaku shingaku kōdō to kyōiku kikai ni kansuru jisshō-teki kenkyū (An empirical study of university entrance behavior and educational opportunities after the high growth period),' An unpublished PhD thesis submitted to the Graduate School of Decision Science and Technology, Tokyo Institute of Technology).

Shima, Yasuhiko, Udaka, Motosuke, Ōhashi Ryūken and Usami, Seijirō (eds), 1976, *Sengo Nihon no kaikyū kōsei [Shin Marukuru keizaigaku kōza 6]* (The class composition of postwar Japan [New Marxist economics series, vol. 6]), Yūhikaku.

Shimada, Toshihide, 1957, 'Nihon no kaikyū kōsei (Japan's class composition), *Zenei* (The vanguard), November.

Shimizu, Ikutarō, 1960, 'Taishū shakairon no shōri (The victory of the mass society theory),' *Shisō*, October.

Shinohara, Hajime, Takahashi, Akira, and Tamura, Hajime, 1960, 'Nihon ni okeru shin chūkansō no ishiki to kōdō (The consciousness and behavior of the new middle strata in Japan), *Keizai Hyōron*, May.

Shōji, Kōkichi, 1981 'Gendai shakai no kaikyū kōzō' (Class structure of modern societies), *Keizai hyōron* (Economics review), January.

Smith, Adam, 1776, *An Inquiry into the Nature and Causes of the Wealth of Nations*.

Sieyès, Emmanuel Joseph, 1789, *Qu'est-ce que le Tiers Éstat?*.

Sugimoto, Yoshio, 2003, *An Introduction to Japanese Society*, Cambridge University Press.

Tachibanaki, Toshiaki, 1998, *Nihon no keizai kakusa* (Economic disparities in Japan), Iwanami Shoten.

Takeda, Akira, 1974, 'Nihon ni okeru sōzoku keishō no kankō:

Sōsetu (Practice of inheritance and succession in Japan: A general introduction),' *Kōza: kazoku 5, Sōzoku to keishō* (Series: Family, vol. 5, Inheritance and succession), pp. 303–19, Kōbundō.
Tanaka, Seisuke, 1992, 'Kaikyū (Class),' *Keizaigaku jiten dai 3-han* (Dictionary of economics, third edition), Iwanami Shoten.
Tanaka, Yoshihisa, 1974, *Shiseikatsu shugi hihan – ningen-teki shizen no fukken o motomete* (A critique of privatism: In pursuit of the rehabilitation of human nature), Chikuma Shobō.
Tanuma, Hajime, 1957, 'Nihon ni okeru "chūkansō" mondai (The problematique of the 'middle strata' in Japan), *Chūō Kōron*, Decmber.
.... 1964, 'Shakai kaikyū kōsei no dōkō to kadai (The trend and problems in studies of social class composition), *Keizai*, November.
Tashiro, Yōichi, 1976, 'Nōka rōdōryoku ryūdōka no gendankai-teki seikaku (The characteristics of the present phase of the increased fluidity of the farm work force), '*Gendai Nihon shihonshugi ni okeru nōgyō mondai* (Agricultural problems in present-day Japanese capitalism), Ochanomizu Shobō.
Teruoku, Itsuko, 1989, *Yutakasa to wa nanika* (What is affluence?), Iwanami Shoten.
Tokita, Yoshihisa and Takagi, Tadao (eds), 1982, *Nihon shihon shugi to rōdōsha kaikyū [Kōza konnichi no Nihon no shihonshugi 7]* (Japanese capitalism and the working class [Series: Capitalism in Contemporary Japan, vol. 7], Ōtsuki Shoten.
Tominaga, Ken'ichi (ed.), 1979, *Nihon no kaisō kōzō* (Social stratification in Japan), Tokyo Daigaku Shuppankai.
.... 1986, *Shakaigaku genri* (Principles of sociology). Iwanami Shoten.
.... 1990, *Nihon no kindaika to shakai hendō* (Japan's modernization and social change), Tokyo Daigaku Shuppankai.
.... 1992, 'Sengo Nihon no shakai kaisō to sono hendō 1955-1985 (Social stratification and its changes in postwar Japan 1955-1985),' *Gendai Nihon shakai: 6 Mondai no shosō* (Contemporary Japanese society series: vol. 6, Various aspects of problems), edited by Tokyo Daigaku Shakai Kenkyūsho (Institute of Social Science at the University of Tokyo), Tokyo Daigaku Shuppankai.
.... 1995, *Shakaigaku kōgi* (Lectures on sociology). Chūō Kōronsha.

.... 1998, 'Kaisō (Social stratification),' *CD-ROM Sekai dai hyakka jiten dai 2-han* (CD-ROM World encyclopedia, second edition), Heibonsha.

Tominaga, Ken'ichi and Tomoeda, Toshio, 1986, 'Nihon shakai ni okeru chii hi-ikkansei no sūsei 1955-1975 to sono imi (Status inconsistency and its trend from 1955 to 1975: Its significance),' *Shakaigaku hyōron* (Japanese sociological review), vol. 37, no. 2.

Toshitani, Nobuyoshi, 1974, 'Nōka no keishō to sōzoku no jittai (The reality of succession and inheritance in farm househoulds),' *Kōza: Kazoku 5 Sōzoku to keishō* (Series: Family, vol. 5, Inheritance and succession), pp. 364–83, Kōbundō.

Touraine, Alain, 1969, *La Société Post-industrielle*, Gonthier.

Tsuburai, Kaoru, 1995, 'Kyōdai jun'i to shakai idō (Sibling order among sons and social mobility),' *Kaisō idō kenkyū no genzai [Heisei 6-nendo kagaku kenkyūhi hojokin kenkyū seika hōkokusho]* (Social stratification and mobility studies today [Report based on the findings of the research project funded by a 1994 science research grant]), pp. 69–77.

Tumin, Melvin, 1964, *Social Stratification*. Prentice-Hall.

Uchida, Yoshihiko, 1970, 'Hottan: shimin shakai no keizaigaku-teki sotei – Sumisu no uketometa mono to nagekakeru mono (The beginning: Economic Definition of civil society – What Smith received and threw at us), *Keizai gakushi [Keizaigaku zenshū 3]* (A history of economic theories [Corpus of economics, vol. 3]), edited by Yoshihiko Uchida, Eiji Ōno, Kazuhiko Sumiya, Mitsuharu Itō and Kiyoaki Hirata, Chikuma Shobō.

Ueda, Kōichirō, 1960, 'Taishū shakairon to kiki no mondai (The mass society theory and the problems of the crisis),' *Shisō*, October.

Umemura, Mataji, Akasaka, Keiko, Minami, Ryōshin, Takamatsu, Nobukiyo, Arai, Kurotake and Itō, Shigeru, 1988, *Chōki keizai tōkei 2 rōdōryoku* (Long-term economic statistics, vol. 2, Labor force), Tōyō Keizai Shimpōsha.

Watanabe, Kazuhiro and Koutari, Yūji, 1984, *Kinkonkan* (The new rich and the new poor), Shufunotomosha.

Watanabe, Masao, 1997, 'Weber ni okeru kaikyū no gainen (Weber's notion of class),' *Hitotsubashi Daigaku kenkyū nenpō shakaigaku kenkyū*, no. 36.

Weber, Max, 1921–22, *Wirtschaft und Gesellschaft*.

Weber, M., 1958, *From Max Weber*, Gerth, H. H. & Mills, C. W. (eds.), Oxford University Press.

Wolferen, Karel van, 1989, *The Enigma of Japanese Power*, Macmillan.
Wright, Erik Olin, 1978, *Class, Crisis and the State*. New Left Books.
……….. 1979, *Class Structure and Income Distribution*, Academic Press.
……….. 1985, *Classes*, Verso.
……….. 1989, *The Debate on Classes*. Verso.
Yoshida, Yoshiaki, 1995, *Nihon-gata teichingin no kiso kōzō* (Basic structure of Japanese-type low wages). Nihon Keizai Hyōronsha.
Yoshizaki, Shōji, 1998, *Riberarizumu – 'Ko no jiyū' no kiro* (Liberalism: The turning point of 'individual freedom'), Aoki Shoten.

Index

agriculture 8, 113, 136–141, 143, 146–156, 181
  agricultural household 98, 135–143, 149, 151–156, 159
  agricultural population 135–139
  agricultural worker 103, 135–139, 148–149, 154–156, 225, 230
alienation 72, 77, 195, 196, 221
Allied Occupation Forces 136
Althusser, L. 46
Aristotle 2, 225
Asahi Shimbun 27, 226
associative democracy 221–223

Basic Survey of Schools 64, 65
bubble burst 39
bubble economy 36, 216
blue-collar 29–32, 38, 65, 179–180, 202, 225
bourgeoisie 5–7, 52–55, 61
Braverman, H. 45, 47–49, 51–52, 54, 68, 99–100

capitalism 6, 17, 19, 41–44, 50, 53, 136, 196, 222
  American 12
  contemporary 26, 48, 213
  Japanese 24, 34
  modern 16, 23
  monopoly 16–17
  state monopoly 199–200

capability 219–220, 224
  equality of 219–220, 224
Capital 5, 43–44, 48
caste 14
Census of Agriculture and Forestry 138, 231
civil society 223
class
  capitalist x, 8–9, 22–24, 41–42, 44–47, 52, 56–61, 82, 88–111, 169–171
  death of xi, 186
  definition of 40
  gender and 158–159
  lower 4
  new middle x, 16–20, 44, 48, 56–61, 88–111, 171–174
  old middle x, 20, 56–61, 88–111, 180–182
  ruling 4, 18, 24, 85, 104
  significance of 40
  upper 107, 109, 113
  working x, 4, 7–9, 16–20, 22–26, 28, 33–34, 41–43, 46–48, 50–52, 56–61, 73–77, 88–111, 174–180, 200–203
  ...analysis 3, 13, 15, 40, 54–55
  ...categories 3, 10, 21–23, 25, 56–57, 59, 61, 108, 122, 188
  ...composition 17–19, 21–26, 33, 59–60, 114–118, 127, 161

247

...consciousness 226
...discourse 6, 8, 15
...for itself 8
...identification 87
...in itself 8
...interest 4, 194
...politics 186–193
...society 4, 6, 17, 37, 38, 111, 158, 183, 222–224
...structure xi, 3–8, 10, 16, 20, 27, 30, 41–61, 95, 113, 116, 120, 131, 135, 157, 185, 186, 222–223
...struggle 4–5, 15, 19, 34
...studies x, 1–2, 6, 10, 13, 14, 15, 20, 51, 59
...theory 1–12, 14–15, 19, 26, 33–35, 40–61, 85, 108, 186, 225
...voting 186
classless society 4, 12, 33, 224
non-class society 224
clerical work 24, 27, 29–30, 32, 43, 58–59, 169, 176, 178, 181, 225, 228, 229
communism 5, 7
communist society 85
consumer durable 87, 90–94, 110
contradictory class locations 52
Crompton, R. 9, 14
culture 14, 92, 105–110, 196, 208, 216
  cultural capital 107–109, 131–133, 208
  cultural resources 13
  cultural skill 107
  cultural stratification 14

differences between the sexes 96–98, 152–153
de-industrialization 205–206
Delphy, C. 158, 159
dialectic 6, 49, 225
digital divide 206–208, 232
discrimination 27, 42, 69, 157, 162, 172–173, 196, 218
disparity x–xi, 2, 35, 39–40, 50, 56, 131, 205–217, 222–223, 226, 232
  economic xi, 39
  income xi, 2, 27, 39
  widening of 37–38, 205–217
  ...among the working class 19
  ...expansion of 211–212
  ...in asset 36
  ...in education 131
  ...in information literacy 209
  ...in Internet usage 206
  ...in purchasing power 36

economic deregulation 197–198
economic ideology 197–200, 232
Edgell, S. 14, 229
education 11, 13, 27, 32, 37, 40, 64, 105, 107, 147, 213, 228, 232
  compulsory 90, 94, 147, 228
  higher 131–134, 147, 150–151, 228
  educational achievement 86, 133, 151
  educational background 13, 33, 36–37, 59, 86–87, 169–183
  educational opportunities 107–109, 131, 149–152
  Japanese education system 109

248

Eguchi Eiichi 153
emigrant 138–140, 146–147, 155
emigration 138, 139, 141, 154, 155
Endō Kōshi 32
Engels, F. 5–7, 186
Esping-Andersen, G. 209
estate 3, 14
ethnicity xi, 159, 232
exploitation 49–51, 53–56, 58, 95, 97–98, 153, 195–196, 214, 229
 capitalist 50
 feudal 50, 55, 98, 153
 socialist 50
 socially necessary 51
 status 50
 ...theory 49–51
 ...through unequal exchange 56
 Class Exploitation Correspondence Principle 49

family worker 55, 58, 90, 94, 98, 169, 181, 227
farm household 135–143, 150–156, 227, 230–231
 part-time farm household 138–140
farm household labor force 139–141
farming class 59, 135–156, 231
 differentiation of 8, 135–156
 Entbauerung 136
 feudalistic landlord–like ownership system 136
Fujita Shōzō 16–17

functioning capitalists 44–45, 47
functionings 219–220

gender 14, 85, 90, 91–92, 94, 97–98, 105, 158–159, 229, 232
 ...class 14
 ...role 170–182
General Council of Trade Unions of Japan 187
Giddens, A. 9–10, 14
globalization 205, 209, 211
Gotō Michio 223
Gouldner, A. 196

Hara Akira 25
Hara Junsuke 32, 34, 58, 113
Hashimoto Kenji 14, 57, 58, 113, 159, 223, 226, 228
high economic growth 27, 34, 226, 227
Hirota Teruyuki 150
historical materialism 50
Honda Tatsuo 138
housewife 59, 82, 157, 171–177, 179–180, 184–185, 218

IT revolution xi, 205, 206, 208, 209, 211
Imada Takatoshi 32, 113, 187
immigrant 139
immiseration 6–8, 34
 immiseration thesis 6–8
Inaba Akihide 231
income 3, 12, 13, 19, 32, 33, 36, 40–42, 44, 58, 87–99, 110–111, 152–153, 155, 157, 188, 190, 200, 203, 205, 211, 214–215, 217–219, 226, 229–230

disparity of xi, 2, 27, 39
distribution 37
differences between the sexes 96–98, 152–153
differences between the classes 95–99, 169–184
independent proprietor 7, 58, 60
industrialization hypothesis 112–114
industrialization 34, 136
information literacy 207–209
inheritance 108, 131, 150, 213, 216
Internet 206–208, 232
Ishida Hiroshi 228
Ishida Kazuo 34
Ishikawa Tsuneo 226
Ishiwata Sadao 150
Iwai Noriko 231

Japanese employment practices 209–211
joint-classification xii

Kanomata Nobuo 228
Katase Kazuo 201
Katō Shūichi 225
Kawashima Takeyoshi 150, 152
Kikkawa Tōru 228
Kinoshita Ritsuko 72
Kishimoto Shigenobu 27, 33, 226
Kobayashi Hisataka 201, 202, 232
Koike Kazuo 30, 31, 32
Kondō Hiroyuki 228
Koutari Yūji 2
Kumazawa Makoto 70, 72, 84

Labor-peasant collaboration 194
labor process 48–49, 68–70, 73, 99–102, 223
labor union 20, 26, 103, 187, 193, 194, 222
landlord 5, 8, 41, 42, 50, 136
Lenin, V.I. 4, 55, 105, 194, 195
lifestyle 10–12, 14, 32, 105
lifetime employment 209–210
Locke, J. 213, 221

Mallet, S. 195–196
managerial labor 8
managerial position 48, 86, 119–120, 170, 230
manager 23, 47–48, 52, 58, 103, 124, 169–170, 210, 225, 230
managerial enterprises 221–233
managerial worker 18, 28–30, 34, 43–45, 58, 122, 208, 210
manual worker 48–49, 65–66, 75–77, 82, 176–178
market situation 9–10
marriage 94, 143, 158, 162–164, 170, 184
Marx, K. 2, 4–14, 34–36, 38, 41–48, 54–55, 136, 214, 221
Marxian theory 55
Marxism x, 2, 12, 18, 34, 35, 47, 55, 194, 212, 221, 232
  analytical xi–xii, 49–54, 212
  structuralist xi–xii, 46–47
Marxist theory 5, 34–35, 46, 49, 194

Index

mass society 16–20, 23, 226
  controversy over 16–20
  ...society theory 16–20, 23, 226
Matsushita Keiichi 16, 18, 19, 23, 226
meritocracy 30, 73, 197–198, 200, 205, 210, 232
Meslier, J. 2
middle class consciousness x–xi, 29, 36, 38, 226
middle strata society 60
Mills, C.W. 18, 28
Ministry of Agriculture, Forestry and Fisheries 151, 231
Ministry of Education and Science 228
Ministry of Labor 17, 210
Ministry of Posts and Telecommunications 206
Mita Munesuke 27
Mitsumata Nobukuni 25
Miyano Masaru 188
mode of production xii, 5, 7, 46–47, 52–53, 95–96, 157–158, 177
  capitalist 42, 46, 52, 56, 95, 136, 157, 177
  feudal 46, 55
  simple commodity production 46, 52, 55, 56, 95–96, 136, 177
modern family 181
modernization 113
money capitalist 44–45
Murakami Yasusuke 27–36

Namiki Shōkichi 138, 153–154
neo-liberalism 199–200

New Middle Stratum Controversy 27–33
new middle mass 27–29, 32, 33
new middle stratum society 18
Nojiri Shigeo 149
Nomura Masami 32
Nomura Yoshiki 226
Nosaka Sanzō 24

Odaka Kunio 86
Oguma Eiji xi
Ōhashi Ryūken 20–26, 56, 226
Ōhashi method 20–26, 56
Ōkōchi Kazuo 153
Ōuchi Tsutomu 136
owner capitalist 223
Ozawa Masako 36

Pakulski, J. 186
Parkin, F. 11, 12
party 50, 186–197, 201–203, 232
  class based 190
  Weber on 12
  ...support 87, 91–94, 186–190, 193, 197, 201, 232
  Democratic Party of Japan 187
  Democratic Socialist Party 17
  Japan Communist Party 16, 21, 23–25, 35, 229
  Liberal Democratic Party 17, 20, 91–92, 94, 187–188, 190–191, 193–194, 202–203
  New Frontier Party 188
  New Party Sakigake 188

Social Democratic Party 187, 229
patriarchy 55, 98, 153, 155, 162, 185
peasant 2, 8, 3, 6–8, 23–24, 43–44, 56, 194–195, 231
  differentiation of the peasantry 231
  labor-peasant collaboration 194
  personal networks 103–105
petit bourgeoisie 11, 16, 24, 46–47
  new 47
  traditional 46–47
Plato 2, 225
polarization 6, 7, 8, 43, 45, 209
polarization thesis 6, 8
Population Census 227
Poulantzas, N. 45–47, 51, 52, 54, 230
profit 3, 34, 41, 50, 105, 195–196, 212–216, 220–221
proletariat 4–7, 33, 52–53, 159

QC activity 69, 72–73, 80–81
Quesnay, F. 3, 226

Rawls, J. 212, 214, 218–220
real estate 87, 90–91, 94, 131
reproduction 8, 143, 158
reproductive labor 158
revolution 2–3, 5, 7, 14–15, 24–26, 34, 50, 194–195, 205–206, 208–209, 211
  bourgeois 50
  democratic 24, 26

socialist 5–7, 14–15, 24, 34, 50, 194
Russian Revolution 195
Ricardo, D. 8
Roemer, J. 45, 49–51, 53–56, 153, 212–213, 221–222, 232

sales worker 65, 78, 169, 176
Sartre, J.P. 225
Satō Tomoyasu 230
Satō Toshiki 32, 37–39, 87, 113–114, 119–122, 124–125, 127, 230, 232
Satō Yoshimichi 228
Sawa Takamitsu 215–216
seasonal work 154
Seiyama Kazuo 34–35, 113, 211, 228
Self-Defense Force 15, 24
self–employed 7, 23, 29, 34, 38, 43, 55, 58, 75–76, 82, 94, 102, 111, 127, 136, 141, 152–154, 177, 182, 216, 227
self-management 20, 196
  labor-managed firms 221, 223
semi-autonomous wage earner 53
Sen, A. 217–220
seniority system 31, 209–210
sexual division of labor 87, 158, 171–172
Shibata Shingo 17
Shimada Toshihide 22–23, 25
Shimizu Ikutarō 226
Shinohara Hajime 19
sibling order 87, 150, 152, 155
Sieyès, E. 3

skill 10, 30–32, 48, 50, 51, 53, 55, 107, 182, 195, 205–206, 207, 209, 213–214
  cultural 107
  intellectual 30–32, 209
  semi-skilled worker 147, 175, 176
  skilled worker 22, 44, 48, 50, 55, 58, 176, 181–182
  unskilled worker 58, 147, 176, 206
small employer 53
Smith, A. 3–5, 38, 41, 44, 225
social mobility 10, 110, 112–134, 139–152
  cross-class 112–134, 139–152
  intergenerational 112–127, 141–144, 232
  intragenerational 75, 112, 127–131
social stratification x, 2, 10–15, 17, 25–29, 32–35, 37–38, 40–41, 86–87, 136, 228
social strata 38
  income strata 188, 206, 230
  lower strata 13, 155
  middle strata 23, 60
socialism 4–7, 26, 34, 50–51, 199–200, 216–217, 221–224, 232
SSM Survey xi, 32, 59, 61, 75, 77–78, 86–88, 98, 226–229
state 4, 17, 46, 50, 105, 199
  ...apparatus 46, 105
status x, 3, 9–13, 18–19, 28, 32, 50–51, 53, 84, 87–88, 90–91, 112–113, 116, 118, 129, 172, 176, 197, 212, 226
  employment 18, 25, 33, 56–57, 86, 165
  marital 87, 91, 183–184
  occupational 97, 120, 200
  ...identification 19, 28, 87–88, 94, 177–178, 188
  ...inconsistency 13, 19, 28, 32
  ...politics 187
Stinchcombe, A. 41
stratum 175–179, 182, 207–208, 225, 229
  middle 92, 225, 229
  new middle 225
  old middle 18, 23
Sugimoto Yoshio xii, 227
supervisory labor 18, 43
surplus population 42, 138, 153–154, 174, 177, 181–182, 184
surplus value 42–44

Tachibanaki Toshiaki 37, 213, 226
Takabatake Michitoshi 27–28
Takagi Norio 34
Takeda Akira 150
Tanaka Seisuke 2, 70
Tanuma Hajime 18–19, 23–24
Tashiro Yōichi 138
Teruoka Itsuko 36
The Communist Manifesto 2, 4–7, 15, 35, 39, 41, 43, 54, 186, 221
Tokita Yoshihisa 34, 226
Tominaga Ken'ichi 12–13, 27–28, 32–33, 35, 87, 113, 150
Tomoeda Toshio 13

Toshitani Nobuyoshi 150
Touraine, A. 195–196
Toyota-style of production
  management systems 79
Tsuburai Kaoru 87, 150, 231
Tumin, M. 225

Uchida Yoshihiko 225
Ueda Kōichirō 226
Umino Michio 201
united front 24, 26, 194
unpaid work 158
utilitarianism 217–218

Voltaire 2

Watanabe Kazuhiro 2, 36
Watanabe Masao 10, 12, 30
Watanabe Tsutomu 228
Waters, M. 186
Weber, M. 9–14
welfarism 218–220
white–collar 27–29, 31–33,
  38, 64, 113, 122, 125,
  171, 173, 175, 201, 210,
  225, 227, 230
Wolferen, K.v. 2, 35, 36
World War II 21, 86, 94, 135,
  136, 138, 144, 150–151,
  154, 209, 229
Wright, E.O. 9, 14, 41, 45,
  51–56, 98, 153, 226, 230

Yamaguchi Kazuo 228
Yoshida Yoshiaki 98
Yoshizaki Shōji 232